ADVANCE PRAISE

"The Luckiest Guy in the World provides a master class for what authentic public service should look like. Bob Abrams, and his vision of public service, is a tonic for our nation and a reminder of the importance of authentic leadership. His central legacy in a lifelong career in public service is the invention of the role of the modern State Attorney General. Under Abrams's leadership, the New York AG's Office became a force for change and a model for the nation. Abrams's leadership at the National Association of Attorneys General, and the power of his vision and character, spearheaded the impact of 'multi-state' actions. Leaders like Bob Abrams don't come along often."

~Phil Weiser, Attorney General of Colorado;
former Dean of the University of Colorado Law School

"Robert Abrams's absorbing memoir is a fascinating journey through the public life of a remarkable elected official. Abrams created an enduring public law office that has fought tirelessly for the rule of law for all Americans who now live better lives because of its unending pursuit of justice. The voice of Robert Abrams contained in this book should be read and understood by public leaders everywhere."

~James Tierney, Director of Attorney General Clinic
at Harvard Law School

"In his memoir, Bob Abrams beautifully describes his immigrant roots, his working class neighborhood, and we become totally engaged in the arc that leads him into public life. For those interested in the workings of government, it provides a front row seat to experience some of the most important political events in New York. This is a good read not just because it chronicles the fascinating life of one of New York's most accomplished public servants, but because it is the story of someone who never stopped trying to use government to make life better for ordinary people."

~Cesar Perales, former Secretary of State of New York

"Here is a story of American politics at its best, democracy in action, told through the real-life experience of Robert Abrams. In one compact, delightful read Abrams takes us from the city streets of the Bronx to the chambers of state government in Albany, to the great halls of Moscow and the storied city of Jerusalem. Here is how one talented, dedicated individual immersed

his life in American politics and the legal profession to positively impact all of our lives. READ THIS BOOK!"

~**Hubert H. Humphrey III, former Attorney General of Minnesota**

"At a time when people yearn for integrity, compassion, and good judgment in public office, longtime New York Attorney General Bob Abrams's story will inspire. His handling of controversies has made Bob Abrams a model of courage for public officials across the country. If Bob Abrams feels he's the 'luckiest guy the world,' I say, the world is truly lucky to have him in it! This book will have a treasured place in my library."

~**Janet T. Mills, Governor of Maine**

"Anyone affiliated with government or politics is fortunate that Bob Abrams has written *The Luckiest Guy in the World*. It is a blueprint on entering, surviving, and thriving in public service with class and dignity. It is authentic without arrogance, truthful, and revealing. Abrams's passion, compassion, and conviction emerge while portraying public service as an honorable profession."

~**Keith Wright, former member of the New York State Assembly (Harlem)**

"This book is a terrific read. Bob Abrams exemplified the best of his generation . . . Bob stood with the AIDS community and fought tirelessly against discrimination while taking an instructive role in overturning the state's and nation's sodomy laws . . . He was part of a group of elected officials who put their commitment to civil rights up front, risking the hateful backlash from our opponents . . . His unequivocal early support of gay rights will always be an important and indelible part of the LGBTQ movement's history . . . His book serves as a lesson and reminder of how progressives help shape the world for the better."

~**Allen Roskoff, Co-Author and Chief Lobbyist of the nation's first Gay Rights Bill**

"Your memoir is full of so much history. You've been a loyal, dedicated, hard-working public servant who served the people of the Bronx so well for many years. I am grateful and honored to have shared your journey and walked the walk with you. Your hard work, commitment, and fight for Justice made a difference and brought about change and renewal! Bravo! Excellent and inspiring—a must-read."

~**Father Louis Gigante, St. Athanasius Church, South Bronx**

"*The Luckiest Guy in the World* is an inspirational glimpse of a man who is dedicated to doing the right thing for causes and principles that he deeply cares about. I found each chapter fascinating. Among Bob Abrams's important contributions to the public good, he displayed extraordinary leadership in bringing the Jewish and the Latter-day Saints communities closer together, respecting each other's common humanity. A reflection of his upbringing and life of service, he has a gift for uniting people. He stands with courage and determination whether it is in the world of politics, justice for humanity, faith, or family."

~John R. Taylor, Director of Interfaith Relations, Retired,
The Church of Jesus Christ of Latter-day Saints

"This remarkable book is the story of how a man can co-mingle the joys and responsibilities of marriage and family life with the excitement and challenges of politics. It is also the story of how a political leader can hew unswervingly to an ethical standard yet also make a difference in the world, be a cosmopolitan man yet also affirm his particularist faith community. There are many practical lessons here: great organizational guidelines for administering a public office, how to help the downtrodden without abandoning the entire collective, and how to take the values of beloved parents and carry them through life. Add to all of this Abrams's masterful storytelling abilities and sense of humor, including the ability to laugh at himself— and you have a great read."

~Blu Greenberg, author of *On Women and Judaism:*
A View from Tradition

"Bob Abrams has pursued a more just world. Proudly a public servant, he was unafraid to challenge the status quo while keeping the interests of everyday New Yorkers always front and center. He pioneered the way for State Attorneys General to hold corporations and government agencies accountable, a legacy from which we continue to benefit. Abrams's talent for storytelling and his zest for the work shine through every page. If you read the first few pages, you will be propelled to the end."

~Mary McCormick, President, Fund for the City of New York

"You don't have to be a New Yorker to appreciate Bob Abrams's career, which repeatedly demonstrated leadership, grit, perseverance, integrity, and capacity to stand up and do the right thing. As the former executive director of the National Association of Attorneys General with more than

twenty-five years of work with Attorneys General, I got to know them all up close. Bob is a standout. Through his creative initiatives, he strengthened the role of Attorney General and provided the blueprint for the modern public lawyer office. Bob's story is a refreshing profile in courage, demonstrating commitment to principle . . . an especially worthwhile read in today's hyper-politicized times."

~Lynne Ross, former Executive Director,
National Association of Attorneys General

"*The Luckiest Guy in the World*, beautifully written by one of the most powerful and visionary state attorneys general of our time, is a fascinating primer about the true stories and intrigue behind the scenes of many of our country's major political and legal battles over several decades. Former New York Attorney General Robert Abrams has given us both a rare glimpse into the world of politics, the legal profession, and public service, as well as his personal example of good citizenship."

~Bonnie Campbell, former Attorney General of Iowa

"This book is compulsively readable. Bob Abrams might well be the greatest raconteur I know. Abrams's writing draws the reader in . . . the reader feels like a fly on the wall. All along the way, Abrams gives us deep insight into how government works."

~Joseph Telushkin, *New York Times* bestselling author

"I've admired Bob Abrams for many years. Reading his spirited and inspiring memoir has increased that admiration. He's one of New York's great warriors."

~David Paterson, former Governor of New York

"This book should be required reading. It's the model of how to be a good politician, a good citizen, and a good human being. It's an enthralling personal and political memoir. It is a story of courage and political adventures by a man who believes all people are created equal, and is willing to stand up for minorities in their struggle for justice. Abrams's DNA wouldn't let him settle for anything less than fighting for truth, freedom and justice regardless of the personal or political consequences he might suffer . . . *The Luckiest Guy in the World* is a fascinating must-read memoir, one that will stand the test of time."

~Don Siegelman, former Governor of Alabama

"*The Luckiest Guy in the World* is a classic tale of a Bronx boy who did good! Abrams's life of public service is a reminder to us all that it *does* matter who holds public office. In today's political zeitgeist, where progressives search for champions on issues such as human rights, LGBTQ rights, women's rights, immigration reform, combating corporate greed, and supporting Black and Latino candidates, Abrams's story makes it clear that he was a man ahead of his time. I strongly recommend that you treat yourself and give it a read."

~**Ruben Diaz Jr., Bronx Borough President**

"Bob Abrams's journey in politics was not only New York's journey, but America's. New York's resources were our country's resources. Bob also shared his wisdom and led by example. A good read, and the photos are priceless."

~**Frankie Sue Del Papa, former Attorney General of Nevada**

"Bob Abrams was blazing a trail on acid rain issues, on toxic exposure issues, on cleaning up Love Canal, cleaning up rivers, protecting the Adirondack Park . . . He was about twenty years ahead of his time."

~**Judith Enck, former Regional Administrator of Region 2 of the US Environmental Protection Agency; Visiting Professor and Senior Fellow at Bennington College**

"Thanks to Bob Abrams for wanting to let his grandchildren know about his career. He has written a book that reminds us all that politics can be a noble profession, that it is possible to use an incisive knowledge of the law and a commitment to equity to make a difference for the general public. Abrams emerges—in the book and in real life—as an elected official who worked on our behalf, took risks, stood up for what he believed, challenged power, and was able to retire with distinction to continue working for the public good."

~**Ruth Messinger, Global Ambassador, American Jewish World Service**

"As a staunch supporter and defender of a woman's right to choose and the rights of the LGBTQ community, with this engaging and well-written memoir, Bob Abrams secures his place in American politics as a progressive pioneer."

~**Deborah J. Glick, member of the New York State Assembly (first openly LGBT member of New York State Legislature)**

"I met Bob Abrams shortly after becoming the District of Columbia's first elected Attorney General. I was looking for guidance, and found a mentor. Bob provided me with the blueprint for success: 'Treat everyone with kindness, decency, and respect. Use the law to make your jurisdiction and our country more fair and just for all regardless of class, race, gender or religion.' There is much for tomorrow's leaders to learn from this book, including how immense humility, love of family, and love of God can be the driving forces of a successful life and career in public service."

~Karl Racine, Attorney General of the District of Columbia

"Bob Abrams uses his memoir as a joyful bully pulpit . . . He celebrates pride in public service with a plea for its restoration, so the Nation might soon again feel young, hopeful, and idealistic anew."

~Joseph W. Bellacosa,
Judge of the New York State Court of Appeals (retired);
Dean and Professor, St. Johns University School of Law (retired)

"Bob Abrams has chosen exactly the right time to publish his memoir. Abrams's passion for civic life and his commitment to democratic values reminds us all what it means to serve in the public interest. There are challenges and disappointments in Abrams political journey, but there are also great policy successes, extraordinary experiences, and real joy. This is a book that should be taught in every Intro American government course. Abrams tells an inspirational story that is just what we need to be reading now."

~Ester Fuchs, Professor of Public Affairs and Political Science, and
Director, Urban and Social Policy Program, Columbia University
School of International and Public Affairs

"A vibrantly written book, which not only sheds new light on Bob Abrams's most important precedent-setting cases, but also beautifully and movingly captures the energy and creativity generated by one man's democratic spirit engaging fully with the democratic tenets of this country. The voice in this book is immediate and human, infused with a belief in the law and its capacity for bettering peoples' lives."

~Elana Greenfield, Whiting Award–winning playwright; author,
At the Damascus Gate: Short Hallucinations

"Buy this book! Give it to your kids who don't want to get into government and politics . . . Abrams fought through the cruelty of machine politics and beat the bosses. His only special interest was the elderly, the disabled, and everybody who needed help. He built the best public legal office in the country. He had one more fight that he wasn't supposed to win—a very bad cancerous tumor which weighed twenty-five pounds. He told his daughter on the way into surgery, 'I'll dance at your wedding,' and he did."

~Neil Hartigan, former Lieutenant Governor and Attorney General of Illinois

"Bob Abrams's stories of his journey in politics make for wonderful reading. Anyone will be able to enjoy these stories, but lawyers especially will not be able to put this book down."

~Michael Turpen, former Attorney General of Oklahoma

"This exceptional memoir reminds us that a true leader must embody intelligence, integrity, and independence. In a world desperately seeking role models, New Yorkers and those around the country were the luckiest people to have, in Attorney General Robert Abrams, someone who demonstrated these special qualities."

~Joseph Potasnik, Executive Vice President, New York Board of Rabbis

"During my tenure as a Republican Attorney General from Kansas, Bob Abrams was a leading force for legal and legislative initiatives and took steps to unite State Attorneys General across the country. This book demonstrates that the rule of law resulting in justice should be the goal of all public servants."

~Bob Stephan, former Attorney General of Kansas

"Bob Abrams offers an inside view from his decades at the eye of the storm in New York's politics, from the ferment of the 1960s to the turmoil of the Trump era. This fascinating book traces his leadership in reform and progressive politics and what it's like to campaign against larger-than-life figures like Geraldine Ferraro, Al Sharpton, Al D'Amato, and Elizabeth Holtzman all in one election!"

~Richard Gottfried, member of the New York State Assembly

THE
LUCKIEST
GUY IN THE
WORLD

THE
LUCKIEST
GUY IN THE
WORLD

MY JOURNEY IN POLITICS

ROBERT ABRAMS

SKYHORSE PUBLISHING

Skyhorse Publishing books may be purchased in bulk at special discounts for sales promotion, corporate gifts, fund-raising, or educational purposes. Special editions can also be created to specifications. For details, contact the Special Sales Department, Skyhorse Publishing, 307 West 36th Street, 11th Floor, New York, NY 10018 or info@skyhorsepublishing.com.

Skyhorse® and Skyhorse Publishing® are registered trademarks of Skyhorse Publishing, Inc.®, a Delaware corporation.

Visit our website at www.skyhorsepublishing.com.

10 9 8 7 6 5 4 3 2 1

Library of Congress Cataloging-in-Publication Data is available on file.

Cover design by Brian Peterson

Print ISBN: 978-1-5107-5878-0
Ebook ISBN: 978-1-5107-5903-9

Printed in the United States of America

The anchor of my life has been my family. It is at the core of who I am. Public service has been a driving force but family is front and center.

This book is dedicated to my family:

Diane Schulder Abrams, my wife of forty-six years; my daughter Rachel Pear, her husband Ian Pear, and their five children, Gavri, Mimi, Darya, Eli, and BJ; my daughter Becky Greenwald, her husband Dan Greenwald, and their three children, Kobi, Sara, and Hana.

They inspire me to move forward every day of my life.

TABLE OF CONTENTS

Foreword
by
New York State Attorney General
Letitia James

THE SOUL OF THIS NATION HAS been shaken to its core. In the midst of the chaos and confusion, we find ourselves asking—who we are, what do we stand for, and how do we want to be remembered?

As I ponder these questions, I recall the face of a young woman, an immigrant woman, who approached me one day seeking legal assistance. She stepped shyly toward me, wringing her hands, with her eyes cast downward as she spoke haltingly about her legal status; she faced the possibility of deportation to a country she did not know, having left as a child with her parents. Now, as an adult with children of her own after a failed relationship, she worried about the future; the tears welled up in her eyes as she thought about the prospect of leaving her children behind. My heart was heavy as I told her I would help her find counsel. I recall mentioning to her that the actions of some leaders do not represent the values of this country, and that we—in the spirit of President Kennedy—are a nation of immigrants.

This chance meeting occurred during the same time I was weighing a decision about running for New York State attorney general. The encounter made it abundantly clear to me that now was the time to use the law both as a sword and a shield in defense of those hiding in the shadows, but I needed a mentor, a northern star.

When you walked into 120 Broadway, the then office of the New York State attorney general, you got the sense that as attorney general, Robert

Abrams was larger than life. His legacy was manifest not only in New York, but across the nation. As the former president of the National Association of Attorneys General, his scholarship and influence loomed over the office. His memoir reflects that and the intersection of faith, service to the community, and legal acumen that engulfed his life.

Our lives are markedly similar: humble beginnings, close family ties, and a deep religious bond coupled with a proud historical tradition. I admired him because he was grounded in his beliefs; his very hardy and disarming laugh filled a room. I recall my first visit to his office. Bespectacled and unassuming, he talked about the impact and rigors of the office and the importance of upholding ethical principles and rejecting a course of self-interest for the public good. He offered his view of the law as a tool for righting wrongs, to advance the cause of justice in society. I left recognizing his sense of noblesse oblige and his steady and unflinching commitment to the rule of law.

His memoir begins with his early days as a young child growing up in the Bronx. His formative years were shaped by days and nights helping his parents at the family's luncheonette. A melting pot of customers gave him insight into a world filled with diversity and awe. Civics in high school and college taught him the framework of government policy. Local retail politics allowed him to engage in the machinery of elections and develop a platform of issues as he mounted a campaign against an entrenched incumbent for a seat in the assembly. And after failing to secure an interview with an absentee congress member as a part of a school assignment, Abrams was off to the races and has never looked back, until now. Winning the assembly seat and then serving as Bronx Borough president, he then embarked upon the office of attorney general.

Transforming the office, aided by a stellar team focused on social justice, Abrams hit the ground running. From antitrust litigation, defending civil rights, to enforcing environmental regulations, to standing up for reproductive rights, to championing marriage equality, to regulating charities, this book is a blockbuster providing powerful page-turning stories that will help the reader appreciate the outsized role that Abrams and the Office of the Attorney General played in our state and nation. Abrams battled the Reagan administration and some of the issues mirror what we face today. Efforts to defend the Constitution and represent the interests of all Americans, as well as marginalized and disenfranchised individuals seeking freedom and opportunity in a land where the rule of law

matters, against the entrenchment of the federal government are central themes, themes that tragically play out today. The tenets that permeate the pages of the memoir are markers that now guide me during dark and tumultuous times. This book is a nostalgic look back in a lot of ways, but the question of who we are, our values, and matters worth fighting for are evident. It will cement your belief in the nobility of public service and engender great respect for a man—my mentor, who has dedicated his career to no greater cause.

~New York State Attorney General Letitia James
August 2020

Introduction

The Yankees Are Leaving the Bronx

IT WAS 1969, AND I HAD just won the Democratic nomination for Bronx Borough president in a hotly contested primary campaign. The general election was a virtual certainty because the Bronx voted overwhelmingly Democratic.

I was reading with increasing frequency stories about the possibility of the Yankees leaving the Bronx to build a new stadium in New Jersey, so I said to myself, "This will be a disaster for me and my borough. This is going to be my legacy? I can't allow the Yankees to leave the Bronx on my watch!"

Yankee Stadium was one of New York City's most famous landmarks and the Yankees one of its great symbols. The Yankees had become an illustrious franchise, the most famous sports team in the world. The stadium, sometimes called "The House That Ruth Built" and "The Cathedral of Baseball," was magnificent at its opening in 1923, but had fallen into disrepair since Jacob Rupert, then-owner of the Yankees, built it.

The team was fed up because of inaction over complaints about the massive traffic jams due to poor road access to the stadium, shortage of parking spaces, and inadequate police presence.

Knowing I had to do whatever I could to stop this from happening, I placed a call to Michael Burke, president of the Yankees, in his office at the stadium.

"Mr. Burke," I said, "my name is Robert Abrams. I hope you don't think I'm presumptuous. I'm the Democratic candidate for Bronx Borough president, but because the Bronx is a Democratic bastion, the reality is I'm going to be the Borough president in a few weeks. I'm calling because

I want to know if there is any truth to the stories about the possibility of the Yankees leaving the Bronx."

"Oh, yeah! Absolutely!"

"Mr. Burke, can I come to see you?"

A few days later, I was seated across from Burke in his office. He was a colorful guy, a former US Navy officer and CIA agent. He recounted his grievances.

"But did you talk to the mayor about this?" I asked.

"Sure—but he never does anything about our issues."

He filled me in on the background in his no-nonsense Navy officer manner. "For the last three years, the mayor has attended the Mayor's Trophy Game," he said, referring to the annual Yankees vs. Mets charity game. "Every year I talk to him, he takes out a little blue card from the vest pocket of his shirt, jots down notes about my complaints, and then puts the card back in his pocket." Burke continued, "I'd never hear from him again! I'm done. We're not gonna take any more of this!"

"Oh, Mr. Burke, don't do anything hasty!" I urged. "I'm going to be your advocate. We'll win this battle; we'll get this done."

He didn't make a commitment one way or the other, but I left feeling there still might be a way to avert this crisis.

As expected, I was elected Bronx Borough president and Mayor Lindsay was reelected in a come-from-behind victory for a second term. John Lindsay was a charismatic progressive who brought fresh blood and bold ideas into city government. He ran on the Liberal Party line against the Democratic and Republican candidates after losing the Republican primary. The Democratic candidate, Mario Procaccino, came out of the Bronx political machine and was a Neanderthal. I bolted my party and supported Lindsay on the Liberal line.

Shortly after Lindsay won, I went to City Hall to meet with him. As I sat down on the couch in his office, I said, "Mr. Mayor, I supported you for reelection. I went out on a limb. I thought you were the better man for the job and deserved to win. I think you owe me one. As I'm sure you know, the Yankees are threatening to move. The city of New York cannot afford to have the Yankees leave. It would be absolutely devastating! The Yankees are an economic generator. Think of the revenue the city stands to lose."

The mayor, sitting forward in his chair, was nodding in agreement.

"For me and my borough it would be a crushing blow," I continued. "The Bronx is already struggling for survival. You've got to help, Mr. Mayor!

Here's what I'm proposing. The city gave $24 million to Queens to build a stadium for the Mets. The Bronx deserves no less."

The mayor listened patiently as I presented my case and then, looking me straight in the eye, said, "You're right about the Yankees. What you said makes a lot of sense. There's been some discussion about this here at City Hall." He paused for a moment and then said, "You've got it!"

I grabbed his hand and, pumping it several times, said, "Thanks! It's the right thing to do!"

The mayor subsequently reached out to Michael Burke and began a series of protracted discussions, which culminated in $24 million placed in the budget to rehabilitate the stadium. The renovations took two years. View-obstructing posts and pillars were removed to create better seats, the stadium top was lifted, more parking spaces were added, and new ramps for increased highway access were created. The project was not without controversy. Many New Yorkers felt that government shouldn't spend so much money to build a sports stadium for a private enterprise. But cities across America were spending proportionately more for their major league teams knowing that better sports facilities attract more tourists. I felt it was an appropriate expenditure to keep New York City as the number one sports capital of the nation.

Keeping the Yankees in the Bronx and improving Yankee Stadium was a precursor of the kinds of battles I would engage in as New York attorney general—only the stakes were much higher.

It's been a wonderful odyssey for me. Never expecting to be involved in politics, I was drafted as a twenty-seven-year-old kid into running an underfunded, David versus Goliath, grassroots campaign for state assembly in 1965 against the powerful Democratic Party machine. That race and unexpected victory set the tone for future battles against the bosses and the way I functioned as a reform-minded officeholder.

As attorney general, I tackled issues relating to civil rights, environmental justice, and the protection of a woman's right to choose. I served as special prosecutor in the explosive Tawana Brawley case, where an African American teenage girl alleged rape and brutality by a group of white men that included law enforcement officials.

I was privileged to be able to help transform the office of attorney general into a powerful protector of people's rights, which were being eroded by the policies of the Reagan administration. Those actions

established the basis for similar efforts by today's incumbent attorneys general in the era of Trump.

If you continue to turn the pages of this book, you'll read about the behind-the-scenes stories, struggles, fun, excitement, highs, and lows of a career in public service.

The values that led me to choose a public path, and that made me want to fight for the rights of ordinary people, can be traced back to my early days in the Bronx and so that is where this story has to begin.

PART ONE

EARLY DAYS & ENTERING
PUBLIC OFFICE

Chapter 1

The Shtetl

I WAS BORN IN THE BRONX IN a place that doesn't exist anymore, the Bryant Sanitarium, on the Fourth of July in 1938.

My parents, Dotty and Ben Abrams, were polar opposites in appearance and demeanor. My father, who was much shorter than my mother, was shy, soft-spoken, and gentle. He had reddish blond hair and a light complexion. My mother was an outgoing woman with a strong voice and dark hair. She was feisty, salty, and direct. They met on a blind date and were married six weeks later. My parents were the most loyal and giving people I have ever encountered. My sister, Marlene Kitrosser, who is ten years younger than I am, agrees. There was nothing that Dotty and Ben Abrams wouldn't do for their children.

When I was a year old, we moved from the South Bronx to a neighborhood in the northeast Bronx called Pelham Parkway. That's where my memories begin.

The southern side of Pelham Parkway was a working-class neighborhood, a densely populated enclave, three blocks wide, nine blocks long, with perhaps 20–25,000 people packed together living in six-story apartment buildings, with some private homes on its edge. The south side bordered on the Bronx Zoo and the north side on the Bronx Botanical Garden.

My family was a significant part of my life from an early age. Coming from Pinsk in Belorussia on my father's side and Vitebsk, in the same region, on my mother's side, they all ended up together in the Bronx. My father's sister Aunt Rose and her husband Uncle Nat lived in our building, one floor above us. My Grandma Ida, my father's mother, lived a few blocks

away, in the same apartment as his other sister, Aunt Faye, and her husband Uncle Sol. Grandma Kaplan, my mother's mother, also lived in the neighborhood, a block and a half away. She spoke only Yiddish and visited us almost daily to watch television and babysit my sister and me. Three other aunts and uncles and their families lived nearby in other parts of the Bronx. We got together often and there was no shortage of lively conversations about the family, politics, and the state of the world. There was always lots of singing of Yiddish and American songs played by my father on the piano. He played by ear—you'd name the song and he would play it for you.

My father's parents worked originally in the garment trade making boys' knee pants and caps in their crowded tenement apartment on the Lower East Side. I remember stories that my father and my grandmother would tell about selling clothing in the 1920s from a pushcart to Jewish and Italian immigrants, speaking Yiddish to their Jewish customers and Italian with their Italian customers. My father told me how his parents sympathized with those working in garment factories and their need for union organizing to improve working conditions. Years later my father's parents opened a luncheonette and my father dropped out of high school before graduation to help them in their new store.

By today's standards, Pelham Parkway was unique. It was like a transplanted shtetl, a small town or village where Jews had lived in Eastern Europe, except in this case, we lived there by preference, not proscription. Like the traditional shtetl, this modern-day version was a self-contained community. On the Jewish holidays, there would be hardly more than a dozen kids in the local public school, which normally accommodated at least a thousand.

My parents, like most people in the neighborhood, were the children of immigrants who had come to America for a better life. In Russia, their parents and grandparents had been subjected to discrimination by the czars who kept the peasantry down in general and the Jewish community in particular. Jews were prohibited from living in certain areas and from pursuing many occupations. Life could be disrupted at any given moment by a bloody pogrom. My grandparents had heard in general terms about the United States; in Yiddish they called it the *goldena medina*—the golden land.

Like most people living in Pelham Parkway, my family was culturally but not religiously Jewish. However, I attended the Roosevelt Synagogue

Hebrew School on Wallace Avenue and was bar mitzvahed at age thirteen, delivering my speech in Yiddish. I still remember parts of it.

We rarely needed to go outside the neighborhood since it had everything we required for our daily lives: grocery stores, kosher butchers, delicatessens, fruit and vegetable stores, bakeries, hardware stores, pharmacies, shoe stores, and clothing stores. There were two banks, two movie theaters, a post office, two bus stops, an elevated subway station, six doctors whose offices also were their homes, and three synagogues plus a shtiebel (a small Ultra-Orthodox Jewish prayer house.) Around the corner from where we lived was Moishe's supermarket where we did our shopping. Moishe's had sawdust on the floor. I remember a pickle barrel near the door, with a handwritten sign: "Two pickles for a nickel."

Everyone in the neighborhood knew each other and often in the heat of summer, neighbors sat outside their buildings on the sidewalk in beach chairs, scrutinizing those who walked past. *What's he wearing? Is he with a girl? Which one is she?* My mom and dad called those people "the jury."

The men and the small number of women who worked had mostly working-class jobs, either in the garment district in Manhattan or as salesmen, storekeepers, furriers, postal workers, librarians, teachers, and accountants. My father worked in a luncheonette in Manhattan with his brothers. People weren't destitute but life was a struggle. They worked hard to make a living.

My parents didn't have extravagances of any kind, but around the time of the emergence of television, in 1950, they bought a ten-inch RCA Victor TV, which had a wooden chassis that cradled a tiny screen. Every Tuesday night just before eight o'clock, our doorbell would ring and people from the building would flock in to our living room to watch the Texaco Star Theater featuring Milton Berle, the most popular show on television at the time. Upwards of fifteen people gathered together around our little TV.

In America, families did special things during the summer and my parents sought to avail themselves of that opportunity as well. For a number of years, they had a summer rental in Rockaway Park adjacent to the boardwalk and the Atlantic Ocean. They paid $250 for the season. It was a single room with an icebox and we shared a bathroom on the floor with other families. The bonus was the big front porch lined with rockers and the house's proximity to the beach, just down the block.

One of my vivid early memories is of being at the beach as an adventurous eight-year-old and building a device that we called "the sifter." I'd

get some orange crates and wire mesh to build the body and handles for this device and I'd take it to the beach to sift sand, looking for things that might have fallen out of the pockets of people who were using the beach. People who came from the city would rent a locker at Curly's Bathhouse on 116th Street, and then they'd go on to the beach. Some men, to avoid the cost of a locker, would have their bathing suit on under their pants and would take their pants off on the beach near their blanket and sometimes coins would fall out of their pockets. When there were no people left on the beach at the end of the day, I would sift the sand to collect whatever money I could find. The sun would be going down, and it would be at the same time when my father would have arrived after a hard day's work in the city. He would run in to take a swim and he'd come out, put his pants on, and watch me. My father would ask, "Hey, Bob, how are you doing?"

I'd answer, "This is all I found!" And I remember showing him my seventeen cents or whatever it was. I'd already been out there with my sifter for about an hour.

He'd say, "Where have you been doing it?"

"Over here."

He'd point to a different area. "Well, why don't you go over there?" I'd sift the sand in that location and lo and behold there'd be a quarter and I'd look up at him, convinced he brought me luck, and say, "Where else should I go?"

"Try over there . . ."

Of course, I realized years later that he was dropping the quarters and dimes in the sand for me to find.

* * *

Eventually my parents decided to buy a luncheonette of their own, in Pelham Parkway. We called the luncheonette "the store." It was down the street from our apartment building, right past PS 105, the elementary school I had attended.

My father got to the store at 5:30 a.m. to make the coffee and set up the breads, rolls, and cakes for the early morning customers. The store sold everything from candy, magazines, newspapers, and comic books, to cigars, cigarettes, razor blades, and playing cards. We sold school supplies, toys, greeting cards, ice cream sundaes and frappes, sandwiches, pie,

Danish pastry, and bottles of soda. Behind the counter, we made fountain drinks: egg creams, cherry Cokes, ice cream sodas, and malted milks.

My father was the food man, making the sandwiches, grilling the hamburgers, and dishing out eggs in the morning. My mom took care of the sodas, the coffee, and cake and was at the cash register ringing up sales.

Their marriage was truly battle-tested when they worked side-by-side for so many years. They came through with flying colors. Their love for each other was strong and enduring.

My formative years were spent helping my father and mother in the store. My mom would be there most of the day at my dad's side, and then she'd go home in the late afternoon, and I would come in the early evening to help my dad. On those Saturdays that I would be at the store, I rotated between different tasks—restocking cases of soda from the basement, replenishing the supply of cigars and cigarettes, mopping the floors, painting the stools, and washing windows with a squeegee at the end of a long pole.

In today's world, people talk about trillions of dollars, but back then every penny counted. A pretzel was two cents and two pretzels sold for three cents. I learned about the value of a dollar and how hard it was to make a living.

Grandma Ida always showed up at the store toward the end of the day to do odd jobs and refill the boxes of candy on the counter. She always wanted to be helpful and productive.

Speaking Yiddish, she and my father discussed politics often. She was progressive, always rooting for the little guy, the ordinary working person. This early political foundation and liberal outlook that passed from my grandmother to my father to me helped shape my own core values and outlook on life.

Grandma Ida did not have an easy life. She came from Russia to the United States when she was a teenager and helped her parents in their business. She never had formal schooling in America and could barely scratch her own signature, but she was nonetheless one of the smartest people I've ever known. She experienced a lot during her lifetime: happiness and fulfillment, yet also tragedy such as when her husband went to buy a bottle of milk on a wintry night and never returned because he was killed by the drunk driver of an ice truck. Through it all she remained dignified and full of zest for life.

When I was in high school, my mother would give me my father's dinner to deliver to him each day at 6:00 p.m. He would often eat standing up behind the counter, gobbling down his food—and then together we'd get ready for the factory workers, the 7:30 night shift, to start coming through the door. He'd serve sandwiches to the people who worked at the Delicia Candy factory up the block.

Working in the store gave me my first view of the larger world beyond Pelham Parkway. Most of the customers came to work from other communities and from backgrounds different from those in my small Jewish enclave. Puerto Ricans, blacks, and Irish were among the men and women who hurriedly ate their soup and sandwiches during their half hour break. When they finished, my dad and I would clean up, close the store, and walk home together, catching up on each other's lives. We'd often talk about our favorite sports teams—the Yankees and the Knicks.

One day, I remember saying, "Dad, how about us going to a Knicks game at Madison Square Garden?"

I'd found out that with my Columbus High School card, which identified me as a student of the school, I could get tickets at half price.

Dad said, "Isn't that discount only for students at the school?"

I said, "No, the holder of the card can buy the tickets at the reduced price."

He wasn't buying my interpretation, but I really prevailed upon him, giving him total assurances that it would be okay.

On the way over to Madison Square Garden, my dad kept asking, "Are you sure this is not a problem?"

I said, "I'm sure" and that, in fact, I'd checked with some students at school, and they told me that they used the cards with friends all the time.

We got to the box office and I said, "Two tickets, please, with the discount." I showed my Columbus High School card to the man behind the window. He peered over at my father and said, "What grade are you in, sonny?"

My father's face turned bright red and, clenching his teeth, he gave me a menacing look, but the ticket agent then said, "Okay, okay. Here are your tickets, enjoy the game." And we did.

* * *

In the years when the family did not go to the Rockaways, on blazing hot days, someone in my family would ask, "Is it time to go to Tar Beach?" Tar

Beach was the tar-covered roof of our apartment building. To escape the heat, we'd spend the night up there with a pillow and a blanket (or sometimes even on the fire escape); at least it would be a little cooler there than in the dense, torrid apartment. As time went by, I remember my parents bought an air conditioner and on scorching hot nights my sister, Marlene, and I would sleep on the floor on blankets in my parents' bedroom where the air conditioner was located.

The parental bonding was strong. After hours of working hard in the store, my mother would devotedly type my high school and college term papers on the family's Royal portable typewriter. What an ordeal that was. I remember the sound that was made when, because of an error, she'd have to pull the piece of paper out of the typewriter and start anew. (It was obviously before the computer where a single backspace can remedy a mistake.) My mother was also a great knitter. She knitted me long- and short-sleeved cable sweaters, which I loved. On Friday nights she would have her weekly mah-jongg game with four of her friends. I recall to this day the voices of the players calling out:

"Four bam!"

"Three dot!"

"Two crack!"

I can still hear the distinct sound of the tiles when at the end of each hand all the players would put their tiles in the center of the table, turn them over, and mix them up.

I remember trying to be a good big brother to my sister, who at the time was seven years old, by attempting to get her into the Peanut Gallery of the *Howdy Doody* TV show, but I failed because it was like trying to get into Harvard. I did manage to get her to appear on the set of *The Rootie Kazooti* program, which was also popular with kids. She was thrilled. I'm proud of my sister, who went on to become a dedicated teacher in the New York City public school system and advanced to the position of assistant principal.

Through it all, my mom and dad always showered my sister and me with unconditional love.

* * *

Although my parents were not active in local politics, they had strong views and ideological beliefs. They were left-leaning Roosevelt Democrats, progressive in thought and instinct.

They were appalled at the way blacks were treated in the South, and even in New York City. They didn't go to rallies or march on picket lines, but in their guts, in their essence, in their conversations, that's who they were. They felt that all people should be treated fairly and should have an equal opportunity to achieve a better life. Discrimination of any kind was repugnant to them.

On Election Day, my father would cast what he liked to call a "protest vote." He always discussed his voting decisions with me, and many times he'd take me as a boy into the voting booth with him. He was a Democrat, but he thought that the Democratic Party didn't go far enough, wasn't left enough, and so he registered his protest vote on the Liberal Party line, the trade union party. Very often, Democratic candidates ran with Liberal Party support, so his vote on the Liberal Party line was a statement more than anything else. It was evidence of a little bit of rebellion, independence, resentment—that the Democrats were not delivering enough in terms of their promises to really help the people. Sometimes he'd vote for American Labor Party candidates.

I remember it was a big event in the neighborhood when Henry Wallace came to Pelham Parkway in 1948. Wallace was FDR's vice president from 1941 to 1944 and previously served in Roosevelt's cabinet as secretary of agriculture and secretary of commerce. He was dropped from the Democratic ticket in 1944 in favor of Harry S. Truman, and in 1948 he was running for president on the Progressive Party ticket, which had a platform that included ending the Cold War, universal health insurance, and ending segregation. My father took me with him to see Wallace speak at the rally. There must have been five thousand people crowded into the intersection.

He also took me to May Day rallies held on the mall on Pelham Parkway attended by a few hundred people. I remember speakers holding large megaphones and talking about how working-class people were not getting their fair share of the benefits of this wealthy and great country.

These early experiences demonstrating the importance of family, enthusiasm for politics, and the respect for hard work, as well as support for the working class, all helped shape my way of seeing the world.

Chapter 2

Beyond the Neighborhood

FOR THE SEVENTH AND EIGHTH GRADES I had to attend a school in a different neighborhood, which meant leaving the shtetl. My new school, PS 34, was in the nearby Italian neighborhood, Van Nest, and I remember I was terrified because I'd heard all the stories about the tough Italian kids. *How was I going to do as a Jewish kid coming into a new school?* But it turned out to be a terrific two years. I loved the teachers, I loved the students, I learned a lot, and I had a great time.

At Christopher Columbus High School, I succeeded academically and was eventually elected to be the president of my class, a big deal at the time. I made a campaign poster at home which said VOTE FOR BOB—HE'LL DO A GOOD JOB.

When it came time to apply to college, I got into a free tuition school, Queens College, based upon my high school GPA. Then I received an acceptance letter from Columbia College, but the tuition was $750. I asked my father, "What should I do?"

He said, "Son, *Columbia*—you go to *Columbia*! Don't worry about the money. Your mom and I will help with the tuition." They wanted the best for me.

During freshman week in my first year at Columbia, I was in awe of the intellect and talent in my class. It was very intimidating. I remember us gathering in Low Memorial Library where Assistant Dean Edward Molloy took the microphone and said, "Let me tell you about yourselves." He began to disclose a daunting array of statistics. I don't remember the precise numbers, but it was something to the effect of: "You are twenty-four valedictorians, eighteen salutatorians, five captains of the basketball team,

six captains of the football team, eleven editors-in-chief of your high school newspapers, seven editors of the yearbook of your high school." I began to slump more and more in my chair. *Oh my God! How do I fit into all of this?*

Doubt about my ability to succeed or even survive was setting in. The challenging curriculum made matters worse. For one course, the stack of required books was nearly four feet tall, including works by Homer, Aristophanes, Sophocles, Aristotle, Thucydides, Plato, and Euripides. Pretty soon I was having a tough time keeping up with all of the reading. Several nights a week, I'd walk out of the library, veer left toward a big room with pay phones, and call my father for reassurance. "Daddy, I don't know if I'm going to make it. This is not easy. This is not Columbus High School. There, I was a big fish in a small pond; here, I'm a tiny fish in a huge pond. I'm not sure it's going so well. I'm having a hard time. These guys are all very, very smart. I have all this reading to do."

"Son, just keep plugging away," he'd say. "You've always done well. You've got ability—just do the best you can. That's all your mother and I can expect of you." His support was like a booster shot and it always encouraged me to keep going.

Students from all over the country and all over the world were in my class. I learned about classical music, art, and poetry—things that I'd never been exposed to before.

By my second year, I was working at various jobs around campus to cover college costs. One job was in John Jay Dining Hall working two hours a day behind the steam table in exchange for my three daily meals. I gave oversized portions of roast beef and scoops of mashed potatoes to the guys I knew as they came by on the line. One day I felt a tap on my shoulder. A tall man wearing a suit said in a firm voice: "Young man, I'm from Portion Control and you have a *very heavy hand*."

In addition to my dining hall job, I delivered the school newspaper, the *Columbia Daily Spectator*, to bins around the campus. I also sold magazines at Broadway and 116th Street for the Columbia Student Magazine Agency, barking, "Step right up, sign up: thirty-five issues of the *New Yorker*—for three dollars. *Time-Life* magazine—one year for four dollars, two years for seven dollars!" On weekends, I went home to help my parents in the store.

During the summer was when I earned the bulk of my tuition money. (I didn't want my parents to have to cover the cost.) I worked at Zeigers

Hotel in the Catskills, which was later renamed the Eldorado. That part of upstate New York was affectionately called the "Borscht Belt" or the "Jewish Alps."

There were no days off in the nine weeks of the summer season, but I'd come home with over a thousand dollars in cash—enough to pay my year's tuition. I worked breakfast, lunch, and dinner in the dining room; I served drinks in the nightclub on Saturday nights during shows; and I worked in the late-night coffee shop until three in the morning, where the nightclub crowd went to sober up.

In the dining room, I learned how to handle myself under pressure and how to get along with people and quickly advanced from busboy to waiter. I found the experience to be very important because it taught me about hard work. It was survival of the fittest: who was going to get the most guests (and tips), who was going to get the best station, who was going to get the mattress in the bunkhouse where we slept that didn't have holes and bugs in it. You learned how to adjust to all these conditions.

The kitchen was divided into domains and the chef was the king. In the pantry, Sol the Salad Man was in charge. He started the season with a clean white shirt but several weeks in, it was green. Sol was a smoker and as he was making coleslaw, scooping gobs of mayonnaise with his bare hand from the huge jar, the cigarette ash from the cigarette he was smoking was getting bigger and bigger, and we'd all watch, knowing that at a certain point the ash would fall into the coleslaw and would become part of that delectable dish.

Guests would ask for "fresh orange juice." There was no fresh orange juice. In the kitchen there was a huge vat into which would be thrown frozen concentrated orange juice which would then be mixed with water coming from a rubber hose, and then cans of pits were cast into the orange juice to make it seem freshly squeezed. The concoction was mixed with a canoe paddle from the boathouse at the lake.

As waiters, our job was to keep everyone happy—from the hotel guests who wanted scorching hot coffee (dip the cup into boiling water), to the guest who wanted a three and a half minute boiled egg (grab one from the soft-boiled pile and hope for the best), to the ones whose roast beef was never rare enough.

"Bob, I wanted my roast beef rare," the guest would say. "This isn't really rare!"

But you can't go back to the chef and say, "I wanted it rare and this is not rare!" He has that big knife in his hand and he'd cut your head off. The solution I devised was to take the plate to the kitchen, turn the roast beef over in the juice it was sitting in, and then go back out and say, "You wanted yours very rare, here it is."

And the guest would look down and say, "*Just* the way I like it!"

Then there was Mama Zeiger, the founder of the hotel. Like Jenny Grossinger, she started with a farmhouse which grew into a significant resort. Mama Zeiger must have been well into her eighties. She had hotel work in her blood. She had to continue to do something, so she took it upon herself to guard the bread machine.

There was a basket of bread on every table. The guests would finish the bread and signal for me: "Bob, can we have some more bread?"

So I'd try to refill the bread basket, but there's Mama Zeiger, standing in front of the bread machine. She'd give me two slices of bread.

I'd say, "But I have a whole table—"

"Two slices of bread. Two slices!"

I'd try to reason with her. "Please! It doesn't look nice. It doesn't look good for you, and it doesn't look good for me. I can't bring this tray back with only two slices of bread."

She'd stare right back at me, her arms folded in front of her chest, and shake her head from side to side: "*Two* slices!"

Again, the job constantly tested your resourcefulness. I'd go into the dining room, put the two slices on a plate on the floor in a corner, go back to where she was guarding the bread machine, and say, "See, they finished the bread. I need you to fill the bread tray." She stood her ground and gave me only two slices. So I had to do this twice more and then with my full tray of bread, I went to serve it to the table.

We did what we needed to do to get by.

We looked forward to "Palm Sunday" each week because most guests stayed for a week and left on Sunday afternoon. At the end of lunch, we got our tips before a new group came in at dinnertime for the next week. The guests who were leaving would call you over and put a crumpled-up bill or collection of bills in the palm of your hand. You'd never know what you were going to get. Sometimes a very nice person would be a very nice tipper; sometimes a very nice person would be a terrible tipper; sometimes a terrible person would be a terrible tipper, and sometimes a terrible person would be an excellent tipper.

Working in the Catskills rounded out my college education. It built a lot of character and taught me how to relate to all different kinds of people.

There were 250 hotels in the Catskill Mountains. With the advent of the jet plane, city dwellers began to have more options for their summer vacations. The number of hotels began to shrink. A whole civilization, gone now.

The Catskills were an important part of the lives of many people in New York. When I was campaigning, I'd often find common conversation with constituents who had a Catskills story of their own.

* * *

Back at Columbia, I was struggling to overcome my doubts about my ability to master the curriculum and to succeed. Fortunately, a couple of things happened which boosted my confidence. I was elected president of my fraternity by my fraternity brothers who had much better grades than I did. I thought, look at this—these guys elected me to this highly coveted position! I must have something going for me for them to entrust me with the mantle of leadership. Another important boost came when I was selected to be a member of Nacoms, one of Columbia's two elite secret senior societies which tapped only ten students for membership each year. My mother would often use a Yiddish phrase: *allas in kanim nishtor in ainem*—everything in everybody is not found in one person. Each person has strengths, and each has weaknesses. It was important for me to keep a balanced perspective.

But it was in my junior year, when I was taking a course in American government, that something occurred which in hindsight altered the direction of my life. "Government 31-32" was taught by a very distinguished professor, textbook author, and future dean of Columbia, David B. Truman. He gave us an assignment for which each student had to research his congressional district and write a paper on everything from the geographical boundaries to the socioeconomic makeup to the various neighborhoods within the district. We also had to learn everything we could about our district's congressman. In addition, Professor Truman required us to interview our representative in Congress.

Charles Buckley, the member of the House representing my district, was a thirty-year incumbent, chairman of the Public Works Committee,

and Democratic leader of the Bronx. New York City was a Democratic stronghold, with a storied history and reputation, including legendary Tammany Hall in New York County, with its myriad of abuses. There was a Bronx machine which also was notorious. Ed Flynn, a Democratic county leader in the Bronx, wrote a book called *You're the Boss* that I remember reading in high school. Flynn ultimately became a confidante of Franklin D. Roosevelt and Charlie Buckley succeeded Ed Flynn. It was an old-line Irish machine. There was a tradition of ethnic succession in different lines of work with the new immigrant groups that came to New York City in the late 1890s and early 1900s. The Irish immigrants successfully gravitated toward politics, which was a vehicle to get them jobs in the police department and government. Charlie Buckley was the epitome of this. He had an eighth-grade education and was a contractor by profession before he was elected. I was intrigued by the prospect of interviewing him to learn more about his rise to Congress and his efforts for the Bronx.

To set up the interview, I tried to call his district office but discovered there was no district office. So I called Buckley's office in Washington, DC—several times leaving messages—but got no response. As my paper deadline was quickly approaching, I was becoming apprehensive about being able to get the interview.

I was at the store with six weeks to go before my paper was due when my dad asked me how things were going at school. I told him I was concerned about getting an interview with Congressman Buckley. He said, "Oh, Bob, I have an idea—Sophie Karpman. She can help you. You know Sophie."

I said, "Yeah, I know her. She comes in the store. She always gets a cup of coffee and a toasted bagel."

He said, "We'll ask Sophie Karpman because she's a captain in the local Democratic Club."

So my dad spoke to Sophie Karpman, who said, "Benny, no problem! For you, for Bob—no problem! Absolutely!"

She came to the store regularly, but my father didn't want to bug her. After ten days went by, he asked, "Sophie, were you able to do anything about getting Bob the interview?"

She said, "I'm working on it, Benny."

Some more time went by and then my father asked her again and she was embarrassed. She said, "Benny, frankly, I'm not getting anywhere. I'm not sure I'm going to be able to do this."

Eventually time ran out and I had to submit the paper. I think I was the only one in the class who couldn't manage to get an interview with his congressman, and it cost me a high grade.

I graduated from Columbia and went to NYU Law School. There was a growing disdain in New York City for the entrenched machine politics displayed by the leaders of the Democratic Party. The autocratic machines in Manhattan, Brooklyn, and the Bronx were thumbing their noses at their constituents, ignoring their needs and tending only to the personal aggrandizement of the bosses and their cronies. An effort was underway to try to reform the party, to open it up and build in some competition against the old-line Democrats. That effort was being led by two well-respected octogenarians, Herbert Lehman and Eleanor Roosevelt. Francis Adams, a former New York City Police commissioner, who was part of that group, invited all NYU law students to a reception at his apartment to discuss what was happening.

Adams told all of us who attended, "You are going to be lawyers, but it's not enough for you to just be a lawyer. You should be active in your community, and you should get involved in politics, because that's a way in which you create social change and bring about reform." I've never forgotten that message.

The motivation for those organized efforts to oust the old-line Democrats was to end the rampant corrupt practices such as no-show jobs. People were put on the payroll but would never show up in Washington, Albany, or City Hall and yet got a handsome salary. Nominations for public office and judgeships were given to club loyalists with little regard for qualifications, temperament, or desire to work hard at the job.

After the Adams event, my name was forwarded to the local Reform Democratic club in my district. Throughout the city, reform clubs were opening in opposition to the regular Democratic clubs. The reformers were trying to oust the regulars from office by putting up competing slates of candidates in primaries for relatively low-profile party positions such as county committee, district leader, and state committee. These posts were important for holding on to the power within the party structure. They were also competing for other positions of public office: state assembly, state senate, and Congress.

A few weeks later, I got a call from the Bronx Pelham Reform Democratic Club. The caller said, "We're at 708 Lydig Avenue, up the steps from

the Chinese restaurant, and we'd like you to come and work in the campaign."

I said, "Well, thanks for the call but I'm very busy. I'm still in law school, and I also help my dad in his store. I don't have the time to do this."

The voice on the other end said, "Well, you should really be part of this effort. We're involved in some exciting contests."

I responded, "Well, as I told you, I really don't have the time."

The caller kept badgering me. "But we have a lot of good races. We're running for party office; we're running for public office. We're giving a challenge to the congressman in the district, we're running against Charlie Buckley—"

I blurted out, "What did you say?"

He said, "We're challenging Charlie Buckley, the congressman for the district. "

"Oh, *that* son of a bitch!" I said. "Okay—you got me. What's involved? How can I help?"

Chapter 3

Entering Politics

THE REFORM-BACKED CANDIDATE RUNNING AGAINST CHARLIE Buckley in the 23rd Congressional District in 1962 was David Levy. Before setting out on the campaign trail, I asked to spend some time with him. He was an able lawyer, a nice, decent man, not widely known, but he was running against Charlie Buckley, and that's all it took for him to win my support.

It was my first political campaign. Levy and I went on walking tours throughout the district. I gave out lots of literature and introduced Levy to voters. I'd say, "Hi. Say hello to David Levy, reform Democratic candidate for Congress." And Levy would shake hands with the voters. On primary night, it was a strong showing, but he didn't quite make it. He lost by 2900 votes.

I finished law school and began working in my uncle's law office. Two years after the Levy challenge to Buckley, I received another call from the Bronx Pelham Reform Democratic Club. "We'd like you to come back and work on a campaign again," the caller said. It was another challenge to Buckley, but this time they had a stronger candidate, Jonathan Bingham, who was more likely to win. I got to know and admire Jack Bingham as a result of many hours of campaigning with him. His primary generated a great deal of enthusiasm with large numbers of volunteers working on his behalf throughout the congressional district. His integrity and message of independence catapulted him to be a victor on primary night. It was an important moment for the Reform movement in the city, especially in the Bronx, because two members of Congress were ousted. Reform candidate Jim Scheuer defeated veteran Jim Healey and Charlie Buckley's thirty-plus-year tenure in the

House finally came to an end. It was exhilarating. Bronxites felt empowered. They were able to dislodge entrenched machine members of Congress who were impeding progress for their communities.

After the Bingham race, a veteran member of the club approached me to become campaign manager for the Johnson/Humphrey/Kennedy/Bingham team, the Democratic ticket in our district. After President Kennedy was assassinated, Lyndon Johnson ascended to the presidency. Now he was running for a full term. Hubert Humphrey, a very popular, progressive Democratic senator from Minnesota, was running for vice president. Robert Kennedy had come into New York State to run against upstate Rochester Republican Senator Ken Keating. Jonathan Bingham was running to win his first term seat in the House.

I agreed to do it, and helped organize literature distribution and drum up interest for the ticket in the assembly district. The Democratic slate won overwhelmingly on election night, not only in the Bronx but across the country. In fact, it was a landslide with Johnson defeating Barry Goldwater.

The Bronx Pelham Reform Democratic Club, where I was spending more and more time, was typical of other Reform Democratic clubs in New York City. It was made up of a combination of idealistic older people who were passionately committed to progressive values, younger voters who opposed the Vietnam War and were interested in political reform, and families who focused on local issues like landlord-tenant problems, maintenance of Little League baseball fields, and street cleaning. Out of 125 members, only thirty-five to forty people showed up for the meetings, a ragtag group trying to fight against the machine.

When the longtime president of the club announced that he was stepping down, members urged me to be his replacement. I didn't have to campaign for the job. No one wanted it. It was a thankless undertaking because the president had to worry about getting the rent paid, sending out meeting notices, and chairing those raucous, contentious monthly meetings. Club members always argued about everything. After some initial resistance, I relented and accepted the job.

As fate would have it, a couple of months later, the US Supreme Court handed down a monumental decision declaring the current New York State legislative districts unconstitutional. The Supreme Court mandated a special election for 1965, when the entire state assembly and state senate would be reelected under newly drawn district lines.

The main decision for the upcoming primary for the club was deciding who we'd support for mayor. There were two front-runner choices for left, reform-minded voters, William Fitts Ryan and Paul O'Dwyer. But the Bronx reformers made a pragmatic choice and ended up supporting an alternative ticket headed by Paul Screvane for mayor, Oren Lehman for controller (a grand-nephew of former New York governor and US Senator Herbert Lehman), and Daniel Patrick Moynihan for president of the City Council. They thought this would be a stronger ticket in the Bronx.

Given the US Supreme Court decision about electing a new state legislature, members of the club suggested that we should run a candidate for the assembly. Normally, it's hard to generate a lot of energy and enthusiasm for the local races of state assembly and state senate, but this primary was expected to generate tremendous interest and visibility. The club felt that since the mayoral race would provide a large turnout, we should take advantage of that momentum and run a candidate for the state assembly. As president of the club, people started looking at me and asking, "Well, Bob, why don't you run?"

"Me run? Are you kidding?"

"No, you should do it, we'll work hard for you."

I remember talking about this with my parents, who said, "*Our* son? *You're* going to run for the state assembly?"

It was a bold thought for me too. I had never considered running for public office.

I learned about the theory and structure of government in high school and college, knew about interpreting laws from law school, and had begun to get involved in campaigns, but I never imagined that I would be a candidate. I started asking myself loads of questions. *Do I have the ability and experience to go to the assembly to be a lawmaker? How can I run if I don't have any real community or governmental background? What's the detailed record of my local assemblyman?* He was a seventeen-year incumbent and chairman of Ways and Means, the most powerful committee in the state assembly. *Am I going to have a chance to win that race?* The incumbent, John T. Satriale, was a Buckley machine guy with lots of power, patronage, and clout. *Who am I?* At this point, I was twenty-seven years old, two years out of law school. I didn't have a lot of money, so how would I stand a chance?

I started thinking about all the issues to be fought for in the Bronx: air pollution, election reform, tenant protections, and greater equity for

working people. If I took the risk, maybe I could raise enough money for some posters and give it my best shot. I probably wouldn't win the election, but I'd at least have the memory of the race. I was still a bachelor. I thought that if I ever got married and had a child, I'd pull out a frayed poster from the back of the junk closet and show it to my kid. *Your daddy actually ran for public office. Look at this! Here's the poster that's the living proof!*

One other thing was running through my mind. I had helped out the club's candidate for the assembly, Eugene Brodsky, during the Levy campaign. Eugene lived up the block from me on Holland Avenue and was a nice guy. When we were campaigning in the Tremont part of the assembly district, we had two big loudspeakers on the roof of my car, which we called a soundtruck. I was on the microphone urging voters to come and meet Eugene Brodsky: "Vote for the Reform team! We gotta beat Charlie Buckley and all his cronies! He's here, ladies and gentlemen, he's here— the Reform Democratic candidate for the state assembly! Come and meet him. He's interested in your issues and your problems. Come say hello!"

Eugene was sitting in the car and people were approaching us—pretty soon a small group had gathered.

"He's here, ladies and gentlemen—Eugene Brodsky!" I leaned into the car and in a low voice said, "Eugene, you gotta get out of the car, there are people here. You have to meet these people." Eugene was a relatively shy guy and he didn't want to get out of the car. After my pleading with him, he finally did. So it crossed my mind now with the state assembly race looming, *Eugene ran for the assembly. He didn't want to get out of the car. At least I'd get out of the car, I'd shake some hands.*

As I mulled over the decision, I also remembered when I was at NYU Law School and my classmates and I gathered in front of the television in Hayden Hall to watch the inauguration of John F. Kennedy in 1961. It was such an inspiring moment to watch a young, handsome, idealistic new president brave the cold weather without an overcoat and take the oath of office. I turned to my friend, Avram Weisberger, and said: "You know, public service should be an inspired goal for all of us."

After lengthy reflection and deep soul searching, and with the support from my family, friends, and the reform club, I decided to push aside my doubts. I said to myself, *Okay, I'll do it. I'll run.*

Chapter 4

Regulars vs. Reformers

THE REGULARS DID EVERYTHING THEY COULD to keep the reform candidates from getting on the ballot and securing a political foothold. If a reformer did manage to get on the ballot, the regulars would resort to all kinds of dirty tricks to undermine your campaign. Of course, they would much rather keep you from becoming a candidate in the first place.

To qualify as a candidate, you had to get a certain number of enrolled Democrats to sign a petition, so I organized a combination of reform club volunteers, family, and friends to help me.

My parents were my most loyal and effective campaigners. Every single night they carried petitions throughout the district in both elevator buildings and multi-story walk-ups. They were totally dedicated throughout this process and maintained their senses of humor. My mother told the story of how one night she knocked on someone's door. "Who is it?" asked a voice from inside.

"It's Dotty Abrams, your neighbor; my son is running for the assembly. I want you to support my son."

"Lady," the woman said as she opened the door and faced my mother, "I have enough trouble supporting my own son."

I told that story when I delivered my mother's eulogy at her funeral.

We ended up filing many more petitions than we needed as an insurance policy against the inevitable attempts by the opposition to invalidate the signatures and get me knocked off the ballot. I qualified and was officially in the running, but I was still an impoverished candidate, not having been able to raise significant campaign funds.

Then, I got lucky and things started to happen. Herman Badillo, the first Puerto Rican commissioner in New York City, decided to run for

Bronx Borough president as a reform candidate. One part of my assembly district, the Tremont section, had a growing number of Puerto Rican voters, so this alliance helped me. Two state senators in the Bronx broke with the regulars and were running as independents; they were now aligned with the reform slate. One senator was Abraham Bernstein, a popular incumbent from Pelham Parkway, the Jewish part of my district, and the other was Joseph Marine, from Belmont, the Italian part of my district. This was a big boost for my campaign.

In addition, one of the benefits of the reform movement in the Bronx supporting the Screvane/Lehman/Moynihan ticket was that the Screvane campaign had some resources which they were willing to share with us. They included my photo and campaign platform on their literature.

Until then, the only piece of campaign literature I had was a flyer produced on a mimeograph machine from an electronic stencil. It was a photo endorsement showing Congressman Jonathan Bingham shaking my hand with warm words of support for my candidacy. Bingham had become a popular, recognizable figure and so this was a valuable message to communicate.

I ran a vigorous campaign. I'd get up at five o'clock in the morning, Monday through Friday, and go to subway stops, accompanied by Jack Abrams, a friend of mine from Columbus High School. He volunteered his time to devotedly meet me at the crack of dawn. We went to different subway stops where, at the bottom of the platform, he handed out our piece of literature, telling people, "Meet Bob Abrams, reform Democratic candidate for the assembly." I was at the top of the steps reaching out to shake people's hands and introducing myself.

I came up with an idea to order ten thousand Chinese fortune cookies with a message inside and handed them out to elderly people sitting on park benches.

They opened the cookie and the slip inside said: "Your good fortune would be Bob Abrams in the assembly." Most people chuckled and loosened up, giving me an opportunity to relate to them, shake their hand, and talk about the race and the issues.

We bought one-inch buttons for the campaign that said ABRAMS FOR ASSEMBLY in black letters against a yellow background. It was the smallest button you could imagine. I couldn't afford anything larger.

My grassroots campaign involved talking to mothers at playgrounds during the day, traversing busy streets to talk to shoppers and passersby,

and shaking hands at the subway stops not only in the mornings but in the late afternoons when workers were coming home. I campaigned outside movie theaters as the lines formed before a showing on Saturday nights and I'd stand outside bakeries on Sunday mornings, introducing myself to those waiting on line for fresh bagels. People volunteered their apartments for me to present myself at coffee klatches. I'd do two or three every night, telling those present about the need for changes in the divorce and abortion laws, election reform (including increasing the hours for voting in primaries), proposals for air pollution abatement, particularly the exhaust coming out of buses, and improving municipal services including police, sanitation, and parks.

In those days, shopping bags were a big staple of local politics. Candidates placed their names in big letters on both sides of a paper shopping bag which they distributed at busy neighborhood shopping intersections. At 5.7 cents each, I couldn't afford them, but the Screvane campaign provided us big white shopping bags with "Screvane for Mayor" in blue letters on them. There was a lot of white space on the bag, so I had my ten-year-old supporters stamp them in several places with a rubber stamp that said ABRAMS FOR ASSEMBLY.

Grandma Ida turned out to be one of my greatest assets in the campaign. In her eighties, she had tremendous energy and was prepared to do whatever was needed. She sat on a folding chair passing out literature, day after day, at the busiest intersection of the neighborhood, White Plains Road and Lydig Avenue. She wore a large homemade button made out of cardboard: VOTE FOR MY GRANDSON, ROBERT ABRAMS FOR ASSEMBLYMAN. Other candidates who were aligned with me asked her to wear their buttons, which she did, and she even passed out shopping bags for them, but she would always say: "You can take these shopping bags, but don't forget to vote for my grandson!"

My campaign was picking up steam and I was making real headway as a direct result of what I called "hand-to-hand combat"—shaking hands, giving out material, and talking to people from morning till night. That kind of campaign is rarely seen today.

Eventually I raised enough money to print my own formal piece of literature, which was designed by the alumni adviser to my college fraternity who ran an advertising agency.

The regulars saw that my campaign was gaining strength, and it started to worry them, so they tried an underhanded tactic. They had

circulated petitions and got enough signatures to place David Blatt as a candidate for state senate on the ballot. When they saw that I stood a chance of winning they took Blatt's name off, replacing him with a bet-ter-known figure, Rabbi Schulem Rubin, the local rabbi at the Young Israel Synagogue of Pelham Parkway, hoping to attract voters to the regu-lar ticket because my name for the assembly was right below the state senate candidate, the well-known incumbent Abraham Bernstein. Because many voters were likely to vote an entire slate, from top to bot-tom, they wanted to draw people away from the reform column and back to the regular column.

Schulem Rubin, an eloquent, handsome, charismatic rabbi, was prac-tically a celebrity. Channel 13 used to have a Sunday evening weekly religious hour. The Catholic Church had the first half hour, which fea-tured Bishop Fulton J. Sheen, and the second half hour featured Rabbi Schulem Rubin. Most rabbis stayed aloof from political campaigns because they didn't want to mix religion with politics. But Rabbi Rubin was very susceptible to the importunings of the regular Democrats to be their can-didate. He agreed to let the regulars put his name on the ballot at the last minute as a substitute for Blatt, the candidate for whom the regulars had obtained signatures. Blatt was then designated to run for judge.

But the regulars' plan backfired.

People started questioning why a rabbi was running for a public office and suddenly it became a citywide issue. The *New York Post*, which was at that time a liberal newspaper, ran editorials describing this as scandalous behavior and the worst kind of chicanery. They said the regulars shouldn't be bending the rules in a manipulative way to put a different candidate in the race at the last minute and also pointed to the issue of the separation of church and state.

The regulars' ploy became a *cause celebre* in the neighborhood. The president of Rabbi Rubin's synagogue resigned in protest and came to work for my campaign. This added excitement to our race and put our campaign on the map. We stepped up our efforts, bringing in more volun-teers and creating a huge phone bank for the final week of the campaign. Thousands of calls were made in the final few days before the primary because my college classmate, Rene Plessner, arranged to have his com-pany volunteer the phones. Anybody who had signed my petition, who had come to a coffee klatch, or who had shown any interest in me on the campaign trail would be called to remind them to vote.

The regulars continued to stoop low right through primary day when they sent in people to break off the levers from the voting machines in areas of my strength, causing senior citizens to wait hours for the machines to be repaired, or covering up my name with chewing gum—doing whatever they could get away with to keep people from voting for me. But on primary night, my exhausting efforts at wooing voters paid off. I scored the biggest upset in the state—a victory of 4,300 to 3,400.

Two months later, as the Democratic candidate, I was elected to the assembly in the general election in November 1965. It was an exciting moment. I was about to take the oath of office as the youngest member of the New York State Legislature, brimming over with enthusiasm and ideas for bills to be filed and to try to help improve the lives of my constituents.

The troopers continued to keep low right through yesterday, when they sent in people to break off the levers from the voting machines in areas of new strength. Enough syringe systems to want liquid for the machines to be repaired, or covering for my noise with a little hosing, gun-acting all—ever they could get away with to keep people from voting for me. But on primary night, my exhausting efforts were rewarded when I scored the biggest upset in the state—closing to 4,160 to 3,102.

Two months later, as the Democratic candidate, I was elected to the assembly in the general election in November. 1972. It was an exciting moment. I was about to take the oath of office as the youngest member of the New York State Legislature. Returning over and off, filaturing and knew. As Sick, to be glad and to try to help improve the lives of my constituents.

Chapter 5

The Assembly

IN JANUARY 1966, I WENT TO Albany as part of a delegation of five newly elected reform and independent members of the assembly from the Bronx. Several reform candidates from Brooklyn and Queens also won seats in the legislature as evidence of this growing reform movement taking hold in New York City.

In a way, the reform movement was an expression of the rebellious spirit of the 1960s. We were living during an important time when change was everywhere. The civil rights movement, the women's movement, and the beginnings of the anti-war movement were all presenting serious challenges to the status quo. It was exciting to be engaged in the struggle to bring about change to programs and policies in our city and state. I started introducing bills and got involved in two of the significant causes being debated at that time—things we take for granted today.

There was a major effort to change the divorce law because, at the time, laws were so restrictive that one of the only places you could go to get a divorce was Reno, Nevada. I felt people shouldn't have to either go to Nevada to get divorced or perjure themselves (the only ground in New York for divorce was adultery). Jerome Wilson, an East Side Manhattan reform Democrat in the state senate, was the leader of the divorce reform battle and I assured him that he could count on my support.

Those were also the early days in the struggle over a woman's right to exercise control over her body. Like so much of the country, New York had a very restrictive abortion statute. *Roe v. Wade* was still seven years away, and women were being subjected to inhumane circumstances—back-alley abortions, mangling themselves with coat hungers, and bleeding to death

or dying from avoidable infections. I submitted a resolution to create a Joint Legislative Committee to study the abortion laws and build a record so we could document the desperate need to change these laws in New York State. In the assembly, Al Blumenthal, a Manhattan West Side Reform Democratic assemblyman, was leading the abortion reform fight. I had a meeting with Al and told him I'd support him and his efforts.

At the same time, I understood the wisdom of the old political adage that House of Representatives Speaker Tip O'Neill liked to quote: "Everything in politics is local." It's what you do in the district for your constituents that means the most. I worked hard on issues that would have a direct impact on my constituents. I wanted to be the antithesis of arrogant, aloof politicians like Charlie Buckley, so I decided to write and send newsletters to inform constituents of my efforts regarding local concerns like traffic lights, sanitation pickups, and broken park benches as well as my efforts in Albany on the legislative front. I'd be in my office till late at night working on these newsletters.

One day I had an extended conversation with Julie Sabatino, a member of the assembly who was from the regular organization in Queens. I met him at the elevator in the state capitol, adjacent to the assembly chamber, and he said, "Kid, I see you're working very late hours. What's keeping you so busy?"

"Well, Julie," I said. "I'm doing a lot of things. I want to find out what bills are going to be on the calendar the next day so I can be prepared to vote. And I work on my newsletters—"

"*Newsletters!* You send out *newsletters?*" He was incredulous.

"Yeah, I've been sending out newsletters. It's important to me."

"Are you kidding? You send out *newsletters?* If you send out a newsletter, you gotta say something in the newsletter, right?"

"Yeah."

"You gotta talk about a bill, you gotta talk about a proposal. Right?"

"Yeah."

"Well, some people are for the bill, and some people are against the bill. Don't you know that?"

"Of course," I replied.

"So, if people are against the bill, they're not going to like you. You're going to annoy and anger them and get disapproval from a certain number of people. And from what you're telling me, you're not talking about only one bill in your newsletter—you're talking about *a lot* of bills. So you got a

second bill, and they're gonna find out what that bill is about. Some people are gonna like it, but some people are *not* gonna like it. And some of the people not liking the second bill are different from the people not liking the first bill. And then if you discuss a *third* bill, you're gonna have a *third* set of people not liking that one. And if you keep that up, you're gonna have enemies all over the place and you're gonna lose your next election."

I said, "Well, Julie, you make an interesting argument."

Julie was an old-line guy, a clubhouse Queens Democrat. I didn't want to be disrespectful concerning what he had to say, so I said, "I hear you. I'll think about your advice, but I believe my constituents like the idea of my being in touch with them and reporting on what I'm doing. I think being a responsive and diligent legislator is a good idea."

It became obvious to me that there were very different attitudes and philosophies floating around Albany.

* * *

During my years in Albany, I shared an office suite with Shirley Chisholm and Sam Wright. We became fast friends because they also won their seats as insurgents running against the Brooklyn machine. Chisholm went on to become, in 1968, the first black woman elected to the House of Representatives and, in 1972, the first black woman to run for president. A schoolteacher by profession, she was not only wise and gutsy but also a lot of fun to be with. I have a vivid memory of Shirley dancing with Sy Posner, one of the reform assemblymen from the Bronx, at a reception, with Sy balancing a glass of water on his head, and the rest of us standing by, applauding.

One day during my first year in the assembly, I came across an article describing how every year, thousands of New Yorkers were significantly injured and disfigured when they walked through glass doors and glass panels, not realizing they were transparent due to lack of signage. I introduced a bill that would require any owner of property where there were glass panels or glass doors to affix a decal or a marking "reasonably calculated to warn."

I worked hard to get the bill out of committee in the assembly, lobbying the chairman of the committee to get it on the agenda, voted on, and reported out. I provided each member of the committee with statistical data underscoring the need for the bill: the number of accidents, the

nature of the injuries, the economic and social costs to the state, and the fact that other states had passed such a bill and how the number of injuries decreased. The bill passed the assembly and then it was sent over to the relevant senate committee. I did the same thing on the senate side. It was approved by the committee and reported out for consideration by the full senate. I kept watching its progress on the printed calendar and when it was getting late, toward the end of the session, I saw that a star had been placed on the bill in the senate calendar. That star meant it had been given a death sentence. It meant the bill went into limbo and would never get onto the floor for a vote. It was indefinitely postponed.

Determined to get this bill passed, I did what I could behind the scenes, even visiting the Republican majority leader of the state senate, Warren Anderson from Binghamton. He was a very dignified, well-spoken, and intelligent man. Here I was, a twenty-seven-year-old kid in his first term approaching this powerful veteran legislator. I believed it was an important bill. It wasn't the most significant bill introduced that year, but thousands of people who might otherwise be injured would be protected.

"Senator Anderson,"I said. "I don't think you know who I am. I'm Bob Abrams. I'm a freshman legislator over in the assembly, and I've got this bill, it's been starred, and I really urge you to take a look at it and try to have the star removed." Knowing that the Republican majority in the Senate was very tight with banks and insurance companies, I added, "Senator Anderson, this bill has the support of the insurance industry."

"Are you sure? How do you know that?" he asked.

"Well, I can show you letters that I've received from insurance companies strongly endorsing the bill because they are paying out millions of dollars for these injuries and if there were fewer claims, they wouldn't have to make those payments. Look, Senator Anderson," I continued. "You'd be doing me a huge favor. It's not going to hurt the Republican Party, and there's no Republican opposition in my district."

Nodding his head, Anderson said, "Yes, I know."

"Help a nice Jewish boy from the Bronx," I said with a smile. "Remove the star, and let this bill be considered."

He laughed and said, "Okay, get me the material about the insurance companies—and I'll look it over."

I raced back to my office to get him the letters I had collected supporting the bill. The star was removed, the bill was passed, and the governor signed it into law. It's been a law ever since, and I think it's been a salutary

thing. It's not a piece of legislation that will earn me a Presidential Medal of Honor, but it does save pain and anguish for many people who might otherwise have to live with these disfiguring scars.

I introduced many other bills with varying degrees of success, some becoming law and others dying in the senate. For example, a bill requiring banks to pay interest on checking accounts never came out of committee. Another proposed bill sought to halt the sleazy pratices of those who were paid to serve summonses on people. It was discovered that in many instances the process servers, instead of serving the summonses, threw them away—in some cases down a sewer, hence the term "sewer service." That proposal passed the assembly and drew editorial support, but went nowhere in the senate. A bill increasing reporting responsibility to help prevent child abuse was passed into law.

Being in Albany as a freshman, I learned about keeping an open mind and not being rigidly judgmental. You can't just blindly adhere to labels and assume that all reformers are the good guys, and all regulars the bad guys. There were, for example, two assemblymen from Brooklyn: Joe Kottler and Lenny Yoswein. They came from regular Democratic clubs, but they were very progressive and very smart. They were among the best legislators I had seen in Albany. They did their homework. They had a social conscience. They were thoughtful in their approach. When they spoke on the floor, they made sense and the members listened. They certainly rivaled Jerry Kretchmer and Al Blumenthal, who were terrific reform legislators from the west side of Manhattan. So I learned you have to have a nuanced approach in life. I found out that sometimes there might be a reformer who stands for the right thing but might not be the best human being in the world. And then there might be people like these two guys, Kottler and Yoswein, regulars who were great human beings, stood for the right values, and also showed a certain degree of independence. When it came to a crucial issue where the leaders wanted a certain outcome, maybe they would be inclined to try to support what the speaker wanted, but they were also independent enough to stand up to the leadership if necessary.

* * *

The assembly was a very controlled place—an ugly reality permeated the whole atmosphere. I saw how well-connected special interests like banks

could, with votes delivered by county leaders, pass or defeat legislation. My colleagues and I rarely had a complete picture of what was going on. Sessions ranged in length from three to six months. And since shockingly 85-90 percent of the legislation was passed within the last forty-eight hours of a given session, we were in the dark a lot. We never knew how long we'd be staying in Albany—whether it would be a three or four-day week. We couldn't predict what time the assembly itself would be called into session during periods of tense discussions by the leadership on controversial legislation. You were sitting there waiting and wondering, then suddenly the bells would ring. It was as if we were schoolchildren. The sound of the bells ringing meant that you'd better report now because the session's going to start. The bells would ring, and you'd go in. The assembly, though it's gotten a little better over the years, was and still is a less than perfect place.

* * *

When it came time to run for a second term, I found myself facing a new challenge. Due to another reapportionment and redistricting, I had to run in a new district.

In an attempt to prevent the reformers from retaining their seats, the regulars chopped up our districts. Mine in particular was an abomination. It looked like a dinosaur—I called it an Extended Regularus Buckleysaurus. The new district was made up of sections of what had been five different assembly districts. They diluted my strength in Pelham Parkway by giving a part of it to a different district. But through hard campaigning and meeting new voters, I was able to win a primary challenge by the regulars. The general election was no problem. When I ran for a third time, two years later, I was challenged again by the regulars and was able to increase my margin of victory, followed again by an easy general election.

In the middle of that third term, I became aware of an exciting opportunity looming ahead.

Chapter 6

Borough-Wide

A s 1969 APPROACHED, IT BECAME CLEAR that Herman Badillo, the Bronx Borough president with whom I had campaigned in 1965, was going to run for mayor. This gave me the opportunity to run for Bronx Borough president. The race would be in the middle of my term, so I could run and if I wasn't successful, I would still retain my assembly seat.

This was a chance for me to expand my sphere of influence and be able to talk to a wider audience about reform issues. Many neighborhoods in the Bronx were facing significant middle-class flight while the South Bronx was becoming a symbol of urban decay. Serving as Bronx Borough president would provide me a significant challenge dealing with those issues as well as a new experience of working in city government. It was an exciting opportunity but, as with my initial decision to run for the assembly, it created a pit in my stomach. Ultimately, I decided to run despite my self-doubt and fears.

Running for Borough president while I was an active member of the assembly was more than challenging, and I quickly felt it bordering on the impossible. It created insane pressure for me given my responsibilities in Albany and the requirements of being an effective candidate in the Bronx. But I was determined to do both.

While I was known in my assembly district, there were now eleven other assembly districts that I would have to worry about. The people in these other areas didn't know who I was. To compete in those districts required waking up at five in the morning, campaigning at local subway stops, then making the three-hour drive up to Albany and returning to New York City in the late afternoon. I would do this three or four times a week in order to be able to register my vote in the assembly.

I was thirty-one years old and a high-energy person. I knew that I was much younger than my opponent in the primary, William Kapelman, and I thought that I could outrun him. I knew the toll campaigning could take.

The stress finally caught up with me and almost ended my life. Driving to the Bronx, I fell asleep at the wheel, lost control of my car, and veered onto the northbound lane and down an embankment. Luckily, there were no other cars coming northbound. The car spun around, and the back of the car hit a tree and crushed my trunk, which had popped open.

The most amazing thing was that I walked out of the car without a scratch—no blood, no broken bones—but I was totally shaken up. I had to calm myself down. I walked around to get my bearings. I said to myself, *I must be the luckiest guy on earth to still be alive.* I looked up at the sky and said, "Thank you. I will try to repay you. I'll try to do good things for people. I promise to be a good person."

Then I looked for a rope in the trunk to tie it down. I walked back to the car and sat behind the wheel. I tried to start the car but it stalled. I tried the engine again, and it clicked on. There was no one around. No one saw this happen, no car had stopped. I decided to continue the trip back to the Bronx. I got onto the road, moved to the right-hand lane, and proceeded home slowly with a new perspective.

I told no one about the accident except for my father. It was his car.

After that close call, I was much more cautious about my schedule and more strategic about my campaign, carefully evaluating the importance of every potential trip from Albany to the Bronx, the importance of being at a particular meeting, and the value of doing a given subway stop. For the subway stops to be effective, my campaign believed we'd have to repeat them, but we were more conservative going forward.

At the same time, we believed it was vital to continue to meet voters, shake hands, and have meaningful conversations with them when possible.

For me, this act of shaking hands was crucial. It wasn't a perfunctory campaign ritual. I think of it as almost an art form, the art of shaking hands.

People might look at it casually and believe that all you do is reach out your hand and shake. Some people might think that baseball is easy—just get up to the plate and hit the ball or go to the mound and throw the ball.

Of course it's not! The majestic timing and swing of Ted Williams, Mickey Mantle, and Willie Mays; the pitching of Sandy Koufax, Tom Seaver, or Mariano Rivera—or getting on a stage to sing a song, there's a method and panache a la Barbra Streisand, Frank Sinatra, or Billie Holliday. Or as the *New York Times* once pointed out—slicing lox—it's not just picking up a knife and slicing away. Those guys at Zabar's on Manhattan's West Side have a special technique in getting those thin slices of smoked salmon just right. And there is also an art to shaking hands.

That sacred experience of saying hello, eyes meeting eyes, and hand in hand with a warm smile was a powerful moment in the campaign for me to make a connection. Each encounter had to be personal and individualized.

The timing is important—when to extend the arm, when to get hold of the hand, the firmness of the clasp. I wanted to send a message of strength. Reaching out and touching someone is a powerful act and makes a meaningful statement. And you have to do this in a split second.

I believe that voters are smart, savvy people. They may not all have advanced college degrees, but they have solid instincts about other people. When I reached for someone's hand, I sought eye contact. I tried to convey to voters, *I understand who you are and want to represent your interests. I want to do the right thing, to make changes, and to improve our neighborhoods.*

* * *

My primary opponent was formidable and I was the underdog candidate once again. William Kapelman had been a veteran assemblyman from the Mosholu Parkway area. When he served, he was considered the most able member of the Bronx delegation and was referred to as the "silver tongued orator." He was rewarded with a judgeship from which he resigned to run for the office of Borough president. He had funding and experience. I was only thirty-one years old. My campaign lacked money for mailings. There was no money for polling, radio advertising, television advertising, newspaper advertising, or staff. It was all volunteers and high energy, so foreign to today's politics which is all about raising and spending huge amounts of money.

It didn't take long for me to understand just what an enormous challenge it was to try to run county-wide. The Bronx was huge, with 1.5

million people. Its population was larger than fifteen states in the union, bigger than every city in America but four, and bigger than countries that have membership in the United Nations. It was a huge metropolis with different communities, different ethnic groupings, and different problems.

Going from neighborhood to neighborhood was fascinating. Different kinds of people who lived in different neighborhoods—Throggs Neck, Pelham Bay, Country Club, Edgewater Park, Harding Park, Van Nest, Morris Park, Kingsbridge, Williamsbridge, Mott Haven, Port Morris, St. Mary's Park, Melrose, Longwood, Hunt's Point, Crotona Park, Bathgate, Highbridge, Tremont, Morrisania, Belmont, West Farms, Soundview, Castle Hill, Clason Point, Parkchester, Pelham Parkway, Mosholu Parkway, Allerton, Pelham Gardens, Eastchester, Bedford Park, Fordham, Marble Hill, Grand Concourse, Norwood, Riverdale, Fieldston, Spuyten Duyvil, Van Cortlandt, Edenwald, Baychester, Westchester Square, Woodlawn, Wakefield, City Island, and Co-op City—there were dozens of neighborhoods in the Bronx.

We had a Republican assemblyman in the North Bronx where there were Germans and Italians, more conservative voters than the Jewish, black, and Puerto Rican voters elsewhere in the Bronx. Then there was Co-op City in the northeast Bronx—15,372 units of union-sponsored housing with over 55,000 people living in thirty-three buildings. There was Riverdale, a more affluent part of the Bronx. I had never set foot in any of these neighborhoods before my campaign started.

It was important to get to know the northeast Bronx, aka the Italian sections. I knew a little bit about enclaves of people who were Italian from my assembly district because it covered Belmont, but that was not the northeast Bronx, which included Throggs Neck, Pelham Bay, and Country Club. And then there was Soundview, which was a middle class black and Hispanic area. I had to campaign in the East Bronx, the West Bronx, as well as the South Bronx.

I can remember in those early days campaigning in all those different neighborhoods, becoming aware of the smells of cooking, the sounds of different languages, and the nonstop beat of music.

My race for Borough president was intertwined with Herman Badillo's race for mayor. We were mutually supporting each other.

Running with Herman Badillo helped me in the Hispanic areas of the Bronx. I had Hispanic constituents in my assembly district, but there were

far more Puerto Rican voters south of my assembly district, in the true South Bronx. Herman brought out huge numbers of Hispanic voters in that race because he was the first Puerto Rican to have been elected Borough president, and he was the first Puerto Rican running for mayor. His candidacy became a great source of ethnic pride. *El Diario*, the daily Hispanic newspaper, went on a rampage. His picture and his name would be in headlines on the front page of *El Diario* every day and follow-up stories and photos would be on pages 2, 3, and 4. It was a war, a crusade, a clarion call for participation and involvement in the Puerto Rican community. His posters were in every bodega, in community centers, and at subway stops. Everywhere you turned in the South Bronx you would see—HERMAN BADILLO FOR MAYOR!

Herman brought to New York the mayor of San Juan, Puerto Rico, to campaign—Mayor Dona Felisa Rincon. In addition to campaigning for Herman, she campaigned for me as well. She was an unbelievably dramatic, colorful, vibrant woman who generated adoration on the campaign trail. Neighborhood people would just come streaming out of their apartment buildings and out of bodegas where they were shopping when they heard that she was there. Throngs would be running toward us, as she'd walk down the street with me, as a campaign aide with a bullhorn blared, "*Dona Felisa dice—voten por Roberto Abrams por presidente del condado del Bronx!*"

El Diario turned Herman into a cultural and national hero. He was like the George Washington of the Puerto Rican people because he was the first to break through New York's political system and penetrate its power structure. It was an interesting phenomenon to witness and to be a part of. Those were some of the most memorable moments of street campaigning in my career.

I tremendously enjoyed this part of politics, the opportunity to meet different kinds of people due to the great diversity of the Bronx. I learned so much about human nature and the individual lives of people. The longer I stayed in politics, the more my social conscience was expanded.

* * *

My Borough president's race provided me the opportunity to redeploy something that had worked well for me in my first campaign. I was going to use fortune cookies again. This time, because of the increased size of the constituency, I ordered 25,000 fortune cookies with a message that said: "Your

good fortune would be Bob Abrams as Borough president." I began handing them out on the park benches in the new neighborhoods in which I was campaigning, and they again were a hit. People smiled when they read the message and invariably gave me a high-five.

One day, my campaign manager called to report that thousands of the fortune cookies were attacked by mice in the campaign headquarters. It was New York City, after all, and our headquarters was in an old run-down building. Luckily, we were able to save approximately 15,000 of the cookies, which we effectively distributed during the balance of the campaign.

As the campaign was getting into gear, one of my fellow assemblymen, Tony Stella, came to me and said, "Bob, you've become my friend. I want you to win. So, I'm gonna have my brother Johnny work for you." I had no idea what that meant, but I thanked him and gave him the green light.

Johnny, a strong, tough guy, came over to see me and said, "This is what I can do for you: we're gonna make signs, big signs—Abrams Boro Pres. We're gonna make these signs and hang them all over the Bronx."

He got sheets of cork which he cut into squares, four feet long by four feet wide. On white paper the same size he had the words ABRAMS BORO PRES printed in large bold letters. He also gathered barrels of paste and lots of brushes, the kind you see the guys in subways using to paste ads to the walls of the station. He would paste the ABRAMS BORO PRES sheets on each side of the cork. ABRAMS would be the top line and BORO PRES would be under it.

My Uncle Al got his cousin to lend me a panel truck for the campaign. One day, I looked out the window of the campaign headquarters and gasped—I saw that Johnny had cut the top off of the truck like you cut the top off a can of tuna fish. He was preparing to do battle. He had produced hundreds of these signs, and he was now getting ready to hang them. He placed a ladder inside the panel truck from which he climbed lampposts and traffic lights to attach the signs. (It was undoubtedly in violation of city ordinances.) Johnny worked alone all night putting them up, from midnight to 6:00 a.m. People woke up up in the morning to signs everywhere, like when you get up after a snowfall and see snow everywhere. It didn't take long before the people of the Bronx knew that Abrams was running for Borough president. My opponent and the Bronx Democratic regulars were going crazy and ripping down my signs every chance they could. This only infuriated Johnny, motivating him to work even harder.

Johnny had a temper and a sadistic sense of humor. He was very angry about the opposition tearing down our signs and so when they began to put up their signs, which were different from ours—they were expensive hand-painted canvas signs posted on a four-sided wooden frame that said Kapelman for Borough President—he would cut out the "K" and the "L." So instead of taking down the sign, he would just leave it there, with the sign now reading: ape man for Borough President.

I didn't have money for the usual campaign infrastructure. I just had volunteers—my classmates from law school, college, high school, even elementary school, friends from the neighborhood, and the family. And, of course, Johnny Stella.

I won the primary and defeated William Kapelman 60,360 to 50,174 by a 55–45 percent margin: a decisive win resulting from a creative and lucky formula for an insurgent victory.

The general election against the Republican candidate, because the Bronx was so overwhelmingly Democratic, was an easy ride to victory.

Johnny had a temper and a satiric sense of humor. He was very angry about the opposition to taking down our signs and so when they began to put up their signs, which were different from ours—they were expensive hand-painted canvas signs posted on a four-sided wooden frame that said Kaufman for Borough President—he would cut off the "K" and the "B." So instead of taking down the sign, he would just leave it there, with the sign now reading aufman for Borough resident.

I didn't have money for the usual campaign infrastructure. I just had volunteers—my classmates from law school, college, high school, even elementary school, friends from the neighborhood and the family. And, of course, Johnny Stella.

I won the primary and defeated William Kaufman 60,300 to 50,174 by a 53–45 percent margin, a decisive win resulting from a creative and lucky campaign. It was an insurgent victory.

The general election against the Republican candidate, because the Bronx was so overwhelmingly Democratic, was an easy ride to victory.

Chapter 7

The Bronx Pressure Cooker

I WAS INAUGURATED AT MY ALMA MATER, Christopher Columbus High School. The school was a key part of my life: it was on the north side of Pelham Parkway adjacent to my old neighborhood, the place where it had all started—my childhood, my education, and my political run for the state assembly. I knew the school would be proud and I hoped the event would send a message to the current student body that if you take school seriously, you could succeed and even become an elected official one day.

Newly reelected Mayor Lindsay attended, to much excitement, as did most elected officials from throughout the borough, and even some of my old teachers. It was amusing to take note that for the entire day before the mayor's appearance, a Department of Sanitation convoy of mechanical sweepers patrolled the area. The streets around the school were cleaner than at any other time in living memory.

My family occupied one long front row of seats. Grandma Ida, ordinarily a modest dresser, was wearing an elegant black dress with a brooch, necklace, and earrings. Every time I looked at her, she was beaming.

While I and others were gathering onstage in preparation for the ceremony, someone came up to me and said: "We have a demonstration out front. Father Gigante is there."

A wonderfully charismatic guy with visionary ideas for improving the community, Father Louis Gigante had created a highly effective organization, SEBCO, the South East Bronx Community Organization.

I exclaimed, "Oh my God! Let me go out and talk to him."

When I got to the front steps of the school, I saw Father Gigante and a number of his followers picketing the event. The message they conveyed

with their handwritten placards and their chanting as they marched back and forth was clear: the South Bronx, which had the largest Puerto Rican population in America, desperately needed help. It was a seriously deprived community with endemic problems, which had been steadily getting worse for years—a severe housing shortage, lack of basic nutrition, high drop-out rates from school, high unemployment, drug addiction, and crime.

I went up to Father Gigante, whom I had gotten to know in the course of the primary and general election campaigns, and said, "Look, Father Gigante, as you know from our previous conversations, I intend to be the Borough president for *all* parts of the Bronx. I am truly sensitive to the needs of the South Bronx. I want to work with you on getting people the services and the help they need." He was satisfied with our exchange and even came inside for the ceremony.

The inaugural program went smoothly. I delivered a short but heart-felt inaugural speech saying in part: "The Bronx sorely needs additional public resources and public facilities. I intend to be an aggressive advocate of the needs of my borough. I welcome the challenge offered me by the people of the Bronx to provide forceful leadership in the 1970s and to vigorously seek solutions to the bleak despair of poverty, the exodus of the middle class, and the fear, frustration and decay that grip too many Bronx neighborhoods."

My encounter that night with Father Gigante was one of many I would have with activist Catholic priests in the Bronx during my time as Borough president. I learned about the committed social activism of the Roman Catholic Church, and went on to work with many dedicated members of the clergy, such as Bishop Patrick Ahern, Father Mario Zicarelli, Father Robert Bonome, Father Timothy Collins, Father Paul Brandt, and Brother Patrick, Sister Anunziatta, Sister Lorraine Riley, and Jesuit seminarians Jim Mitchell and Roger Hayes. Monsignor Gustav Schultheiss from St. Raymond's parish in Parkhester was older and not an activist, but a dedicated loyalist for his community, and I worked closely with him as well.

Although I was already aware of and committed to doing whatever I could for the South Bronx, Father Gigante's appearance at my inauguration was auspicious. We became close friends and worked together on many projects. I tried to be a resolute voice, focusing on the intractable problems that the inauguration ceremony protest underscored. I was going

to do my best to break through the wall of indifference, dismissiveness, and outright bigotry that characterized the response of the government bureaucracy to the needs of the people of the South Bronx.

Around the time I was elected, American cities were going through a period of rapid economic decline. The factory jobs that had historically been a mainstay of working-class communities were steadily disappearing as manufacturers left for other parts of the country, where labor was cheap and where unions had no real power. At the same time, middle class whites were fleeing cities in record numbers for the suburbs, further erod-ing the tax base that had traditionally paid for basic municipal services. The gulf between the urban poor and everyone else continued to expand, and cities were becoming increasingly volatile. The mounting tensions were a result of widespread poverty, job-related bias, the longstanding practice of discrimination in housing that had created de facto segregated neighborhoods, and the periodic use of excessive force by white police officers working in minority neighborhoods. Occasionally, triggered by some unexpected catalyst—the assassination of Martin Luther King Jr., a blackout that suddenly plunged an entire city into darkness—some poor neighborhoods would erupt into sudden violence by rioting and looting. But more often these tensions simmered just below the surface.

In the South Bronx, two problems that had particularly devastating effects were rampant heroin addiction and an inordinately high number of fires. Many of the fires were set by arsonists-for-hire so landlords could collect insurance money on properties doomed to decreasing value. Van-dals would then remove the copper and brass piping and sell it on the black market. Fire engine sirens echoed throughout the night. During the day you could see the results of those nightly fires: whole city blocks that were ravaged, charred buildings with gaping or boarded-up windows, and empty lots where buildings, which had since been demolished, had once stood.

The people of the South Bronx and other impoverished areas responded to these unacceptable conditions in a variety of ways, ranging from hard-fought political battles, strikes, and demonstrations to more dramatic actions taken by radical groups. During this period, the Young Lords, a Puerto Rican radical social action group, occupied government offices and municipal buildings, while members of the Black Panther Party armed themselves with weapons in anticipation of the violent revolution that they claimed was inevitable.

The South Bronx was like a pressure cooker, a cauldron of repressed anger. I wanted people to know that I was fair, attentive, and interested in helping them find solutions to their problems. I was a young, new Borough president; in fact, I was the first Jewish Borough president and not a member of the minority community. It was a very dicey and delicate situation, so I worked hard to win confidence and trust.

With emotions running high in a lot of communities, the office of Borough president functioned as a kind of safety valve during these tense times. There was a lot of finger-pointing, with one community claiming that it was not getting its fair share of resources. It was a challenging responsibility to represent all the diverse groups that were part of the borough. New York is a great social experiment with so many different people coming together to live in one place at one time, in relative equanimity. But there are times when tensions and rivalries are inevitable. It was important for me, as Borough president, to keep the peace and be a sensitive voice for all the people I represented.

Getting stronger housing code enforcement, a traffic light on a dangerous corner, ridding a park playground of drug pushers, guaranteeing reliable garbage pickups, and getting more police out on the street were all fundamental for neighborhoods to be livable. I spent long hours at meetings, sometimes well into the night, to show my concern and commitment and to demonstrate my respect for what was being said.

One of my key priorities upon entering the Borough president's office had been to focus on Lincoln Hospital. A replacement for the dilapidated, inadequate hospital had been on the drawing board for decades. It was constantly being delayed. I had several meetings with local South Bronx community groups to discuss what could be done to make that replacement hospital a reality. Then, an event took place that focused public attention on the problem, which presented an opportunity to put additional pressure on the city to take decisive action.

Just before dawn on July 17, 1970, members of three activist groups, the Young Lords, the Revolutionary Health Movement, and Think Lincoln, slipped in through some lower level windows of Lincoln Hospital and announced to the on-duty staff that they were taking over the hospital for the good of the neighborhood. They alerted the press and set up a free clinic where neighborhood people could be tested for lead poisoning. The hospital was soon surrounded by police and the occupation of the building eventually ended peacefully. But it succeeded in calling attention

to the deplorable conditions prevalent at the only local hospital available to residents of the South Bronx.

Lincoln Hospital had been the subject of exhaustively documented complaints for years. The city repeatedly cited it for health and safety violations. Patients told of unsanitary conditions, rats running through the hospital's overcrowded emergency room, and disrespectful treatment at the hands of hospital staff.

The hospital was also criticized for its inadequate response to the health problems that plagued the neighborhood, including high rates of lead poisoning, tuberculosis, asthma, pneumonia, and addiction. In my campaign for Borough president, I had called attention to the issue of lead poisoning, indicating how this was a pernicious problem affecting children in poor families. Old buildings had lead paint flaking from their walls, with children inadvertently ingesting it. Severe injury, including brain damage, resulted from lead poisoning. During my first year in office, I argued that only half the children who were potential victims had been tested and that the city had an obligation not to continue to neglect these 80,000 indigent children. I fought to get an additional three million dollars in the budget to test preschool children.

When it was announced that Lincoln Hospital was seeking to hire a new director, members of the community let it be known that they wanted to see that job filled by someone who was not only competent and experienced, but who would also be sensitive to the community and its needs. The search culminated with the appointment of Dr. Antero Lacot, who had directed a maternity hospital in Bayamon, Puerto Rico.

Some took Dr. Lacot's appointment as a signal that things were about to change for the better at Lincoln. But it didn't take long for the New York City Health and Hospitals Corporation, which ran and controlled the city's health-care system, to raise objections to his appointment, claiming that Dr. Lacot was not qualified for the job. After meeting and being impressed by Dr. Lacot, I added my name to the long list of his supporters, among them prominent doctors at the respected Albert Einstein College of Medicine, which was located in the northeast Bronx and affiliated with Lincoln Hospital.

In the wake of the takeover of the hospital, the city had once again renewed its promise to construct a new hospital. I held a meeting with Dr. Lacot and local leaders in my office to discuss the best response to this latest announcement. After lengthy discussion, I decided that the only

way to get the city to honor its promises was to put on a full-court press. We held meetings with Health and Hospital Corporation officials in my office in the presence of community leaders and local elected officials every two weeks in an attempt to keep their feet to the fire to make sure that the promises and commitments made were going to be kept and that the schedules of planning and construction progress were going to be honored. The city finally began clearing the site where it had been decided the new hospital was to be built.

When the financial crisis hit, Mayor Abe Beame's ax swingers started looking for where cuts could be made so that the city could save money. Those axes were swung first in the direction of the city's most vulnerable population. They went after programs and institutions that served the poorest parts of the Bronx. They swung at Lincoln Hospital, which was already under construction, but I and others made sure that the city fulfilled its commitment to complete and open the hospital. I intensified the pressure by sometimes having the president of the Health and Hospitals Corporation come to the meetings to articulate and reaffirm timetables and resource commitments. After years of those sessions in my office and pressuring the bureaucracy to complete design drawings and to implement those plans, the new 554-bed hospital built at a cost of $200 million on a ten-acre site was opened in 1976. We stood our ground and, today, the hospital continues to function as a major component of the health-care system of New York.

My office made repeated efforts to get the federal government to pay more attention to the South Bronx and the challenges it was facing. We were in touch with the US senators from New York, relevant federal agencies, and the White House itself. In fact, we sent a report and housing proposal to both the Department of Housing and Urban Development (HUD) secretary and the White House. We received no response, so when President Jimmy Carter made his surprise visit in October 1977 to Charlotte Street, focusing on housing and other South Bronx issues and asking his staff for a plan to deal with the massive housing problems he saw, we contacted the White House and said, "You guys already have a plan and proposal that our office submitted to you." Jack Watson, a key White House domestic policy adviser, was designated as President Carter's liaison to follow up on his visit and so at last some focus and progress was made as a result of the president's intervention.

* * *

I frequently characterized the Borough president as the senator and advocate for the borough, the bridge between a remote downtown City Hall and a local community. We were living in one of the largest, most complicated, and most sophisticated cities in the world, governed by a mayor with tremendous power who appointed commissioners to handle everything from police and sanitation services, to education and social services, to recreation, planning, and transportation. But the mayor's office was way down at City Hall, and it was my responsibility to be the voice of the Bronx.

I knew in order to get all levels of government to care about the various issues facing the Bronx, I needed to find a way to get more visibility for the Bronx.

One day while rummaging through some paper in boxes that I'd found stored in a room in the Borough president's office, I came across a flyer about "Bronx Day" in the 1930s. It was presided over by then Bronx Borough President James J. Lyons, who served in that post for twenty-eight years. That flyer suddenly triggered something within me, and I decided to make it my goal to bring back Bronx Day. With Bronx Day, I thought, I could help unify the borough, develop community pride, and put the Bronx on the map.

It was hard to get coverage for the Bronx in the New York City newspapers because they tended to focus on Manhattan. But despite this obstacle, our newly instituted Bronx Day was a huge success and achieved significant media attention. Thousands of people in the various neighborhoods came together to celebrate and showcase what their communities had to offer. A large parade down the Grand Concourse featured marching bands and thousands of participants from throughout the borough and beyond. Bronx Day eventually became so popular that it morphed into Bronx Week and, to this day, over forty years later, is still celebrated.

Yet, notwithstanding the additional press coverage, there were still ongoing struggles.

Chapter 8

Being Borough President

S HORTLY AFTER I TOOK OFFICE, SANITATION Commissioner Griswold
Moeller came to see me. "Mr. Borough President," he said, "we are
going to extend the life of the Tallapoosa Landfill and keep it open for
another twenty years."

Without a moment's hesitation, I said, "Commissioner, I'm going to
fight you every inch of the way!"

Tackling the problem of garbage and waste disposal was a big issue.
The city was generating a massive amount of refuse every day and it was
running out of space to deposit it. The city's landfills had reached their
limits and indeed were receiving daily shipments well beyond the timeta-
ble set for their closure. The Staten Island landfill was beyond its capacity
and because of its height and smell, it posed a huge political issue with the
residents of that borough.

In the northeast Bronx there was an ongoing controversy concerning
the date when the eighty-acre Tallapoosa landfill would finally be closed.

The heavy truck traffic with its noise and fumes, in addition to the
odor emanating from the landfill, was a pressing concern to the commu-
nity. The city had previously developed plans to create an additional four
hundred acres of landfill. The forceful leadership of local City Council-
man Mario Merola and strong community opposition, along with the sup-
port of environmentalists, helped to defeat that proposal. Merola was able
to have the council pass, and the mayor sign into law, two bills establish-
ing the Thomas Pell Wildlife and the Hunter Island Marine Zoology and
Geology Sanctuaries, covering 489 acres of the 2,800-acre Pelham Bay
Park as well as an offshore zone to guarantee that these areas could not be
used for landfill at some point in the future.

I let the public know that once again the city intended to renege on its promises by dumping more garbage in the Bronx.

While I was busy heading off the Sanitation Department, Sanford D. Garelick, the president of the City Council and fellow Board of Estimate member, entered the fight.

Garelick issued a press release outlining his plan for dealing with the citywide problem of garbage disposal. He wanted to erect a 2,500-foot mountain of compacted and sanitized garbage in Pelham Bay Park which would be turned into "a recreation mountain and ski resort second to none."

I was furious. I called him up and in strong, earthy language, said, among other things, "It's outrageous—absolutely outrageous!—that you would put forward a proposal like that without even discussing it with me first. And by the way, on the merits I think the idea is absurd."

Pelham Bay Park, which is three times larger than Central Park, had already suffered greatly as a direct result of the city's practice of dumping garbage there. It was a wildlife preserve which was being destroyed. A number of expert studies had been undertaken to document the threat that the dump posed to flora and fauna.

So I put out a biting, tongue-in-cheek press statement incorporating an analysis by my civil engineer indicating what the dumping proposal would mean. The mountain would be three times as high as the Eiffel Tower, six times higher than the Pyramids of Cheops, and twice the size of the Empire State Building. It was comparable to a 250-story building. In the press I called it a "Matterhorn of Muck." It would cover up parks, athletic fields, sections of the New England Thruway, the Hutchinson River Parkway, the New Haven division of the Penn Central Railroad, private homes, and portions of Co-op City.

Soon after the press release, the Garelick proposal died a quick death. We also thwarted the city's plan to extend dumping at Tallapoosa for an additional twenty-year period by mobilizing vociferous opposition.

Making use of the bully pulpit was one of the ways in which I augmented the inherent limitations of the office. The Borough president did not have executive authority as in other counties in New York State and across the country, but the press responded to the title. As Borough president, I could draft reports about the borough's needs, mobilize people around given issues, and call press conferences, knowing that there would be a reasonable chance that members of the press would attend. That kind of attention could be helpful in advancing or opposing a specific proposal.

The Borough president's role on the Board of Estimate also presented an opportunity for influence, and I tried to make the most of it. The Board of Estimate was a unique governmental body made up of eight people: three city-wide officials, the mayor, the comptroller and the president of the City Council, and the five Borough presidents. It had significant powers—joint responsibility with the City Council to pass New York City's budget, zoning authority, and the obligation to act on all contracts valued over $10,000 that the city entered into.

One of the most important powers that I had as Borough president was the opportunity to get line items in the capital budget, a document which contains a commitment to build physical facilities for communities in each of the five boroughs such as parks, schools, police stations, and firehouses. I devised a system to get these items in the budget. At community board meetings in the Bronx, encouraging and helping board members to develop a list of priorities, I made it clear that I needed the community's support in order to go to City Hall to make a case for the funding of these facilities. Community boards are made up of citizens who serve without compensation to provide advice to the Borough president and other city agencies and officials on issues relating to budget, zoning, planning, and service delivery. This level of coordination and communication between the Borough president's office and the constituents fostered a new level of trust within the community. In order to be their voice, I needed the Bronx's strong, contentious, and courageous statements as part of the record. It worked. Bronxites came down to Board of Estimate meetings in droves and we won commitments for an unprecedented number of projects.

For example, there was a desperate need for a new high school in the South Bronx and I set a goal in those budget negotiations to create one. Against bureaucratic resistance, I made my arguments at the Board of Estimate and worked with community groups to get them to come out in force to support and advocate for the proposal. We were successful in creating the South Bronx High School with Nathan Quinones serving as its principal. Quinones was a wonderful, sensitive educator who, as a result of the good work he did as principal of the school, was selected a few years later to be the chancellor of the entire New York City school system.

Another battle we waged was securing funding to establish the Bronx Museum of the Arts. There was an empty rotunda at the Bronx County Courthouse, where the Borough president's office was located, that would

be a good start for a first-time museum for the Bronx. Despite naysaying bureaucrats, we were able to allocate $77,000 in the City's capital budget to get the museum off the ground. There was a reservoir of cultural strength in the Bronx emanating from the Bronx Council on the Arts headed by Irma Fleck, with whom I worked closely.

Within a short time, a director of the museum was hired and internationally renowned works, as well as those of local artists, were placed on exhibit. We developed a relationship with the Metropolitan Museum of Art and it arranged for the world-famous Lehman Collection to be shown. Under the aegis of the nascent Bronx Museum of the Arts, programs for local schools were organized. This was a small but significant battle won and it paved the way for—indeed was the foundation of—a great institution.

My successors as Borough president, together with the Board of Estimate and with private foundation support, have built the museum into an important institution not only for the residents of the Bronx but for all. In 1982, the museum acquired a permanent home at the Grand Concourse and 165th Street, a building that was formerly a synagogue. Several years later, the footprint of the museum increased with an innovative design of a building at a cost of nineteen million dollars. It now features galleries, an outdoor terrace, and classrooms for educational programming, as well as a permanent collection of over one thousand pieces of art, with a strong focus on collecting works by artists of African, Latin, and Asian ancestry.

My efforts on behalf of the community would always begin with a huge bureaucratic struggle with the relevant agencies—the Parks Department, the Board of Education, the Health and Hospitals Corporation—but overcoming their habitual intransigence didn't necessarily mean the battle was won. Part of my job as Borough president was to monitor the Bureau of the Budget. If it didn't deliver on the commitment that the City of New York made when it placed that line in the budget, it was my role to make noise, to call them out, to embarrass them, and to keep applying pressure until the funding was effectuated.

As a result of galvanizing the various communities in the Bronx, we were able to have twenty-five new primary and intermediate schools built, new firehouses, police precincts, libraries, and an occupational training center. We also achieved park rehabilitation projects throughout the borough including the construction of a long-awaited new park, Seton Park,

with tennis courts, baseball fields, basketball courts, and jungle gyms, as well as the construction of new skating rinks in Pelham Bay Park and St. James Park. Little League fields were built and upgraded (some with lighting), the old Fiftieth Police Precinct was converted into a community center, and freestanding neighborhood family care and health-care centers were built as well as similar centers in public housing projects. Housing was a crucial issue and tens of thousands of rehabilitated and new units were constructed.

As the youngest Borough president ever elected in the Bronx, I felt it was important for me to give young people access to government decision making, so I created the Bronx Borough President's Youth Advisory Commission. Any young person who wanted to be a member of the Commission could write to my office to join. We received dozens of responses so the Commission was formed; it elected officers, met on a periodic basis to weigh in on proposals, and I met with the leadership of the Commission. I also was committed to having high school and college students appointed to the Community Boards, so I now had a reservoir of talent from which I could draw for those appointments.

Sometimes it took a while for big proposals to take hold and come to fruition. As Borough president, I fought for a mass transit link for Co-op City, which was a community that was isolated. I proposed that the adjacent railroad tracks on which Amtrak and suburban railroad trains operated should be utilized for Bronxites living in Co-op City and Parkchester to connect with Manhattan. Some forty-five years later, Governor Andrew Cuomo has announced that Amtrak and Metro North will build train stations at Co-Op City and Parkchester using those tracks.

We also offered proposals with citywide implications, some of which received support from unexpected quarters. One such idea was a response to the constantly rising price of public transportation. A subway ride used to cost a nickel. The price of a token was constantly going up—from five to ten cents, from ten to fifteen, fifteen to twenty, and twenty to thirty cents and, of course, subsequently much higher.

I wrote a *New York* magazine cover story advocating that the city should provide its residents with free public transportation. To some, this seemed quixotic, but it was successfully instituted elsewhere with a compelling rationale. I argued that for New Yorkers, public transportation was inextricably tied to daily life and was no different from police or fire services or access to the park system, which did not require a specific

payment every time that service was utilized. If you needed to call the Fire Department, they would arrive at your door, put out the fire, and you wouldn't expect the fire department to leave you a bill of $69.95; the cost of that service was covered by the taxes that you paid. I proposed that free access to mass transit could be paid for by a citywide surtax to compensate for the loss of revenue from the fare box. The *New York Times*, in an editorial ("Abolish the Turnstiles?") expressed an understanding of the argument and supported my efforts. As I was concluding this book and the coronavirus pandemic hit, I saw a temporary fulfillment of my dream for free access to mass transit when the MTA established free fare on New York City buses for a several-month period.

During my term as borough president, we were beginning to establish some improvements that made a difference, but the borough still had enormous unmet needs. Not only did I have to fight for affirmative gains, but I also had to wage battle to defend the Bronx.

Chapter 9

Defending the Bronx

O NE DAY I GOT A NERVOUS call from my father. "Bob," he said, "did you see what they're doing to you? Full-page ads attacking you!"

The Dollar Savings Bank, which was the largest bank in the Bronx, was running full-page ads in every Bronx weekly newspaper, including the *Daily News*, stating "A Bronx Politician Wants Us to Start Taking Risks with *Your* Money." I told my father, "Don't worry, Dad. My charges against the Dollar Savings and other banks obviously hit a raw nerve and they are retaliating. We're on the right side and we'll get through this."

Henry Waltemade, the president of Dollar Savings Bank who was well-connected to the Bronx machine, decided to target me in a frontal and intimidating way because I publicly called attention to his bank's anti-Bronx investment policy. The Bronx's housing stock was declining dramatically due to the actions of banks in the Bronx. Dollar Savings and its sister banks were systematically taking money from Bronxite deposit accounts and investing it elsewhere across the United States, instead of using the funds to support the Bronx. Landlords were not getting funds from Bronx banks to renew their mortgages or improve their properties. As a result, the Bronx was being drained of its basic cash resources, which it desperately needed for maintaining its housing stock.

This practice of refusing to invest in a specified area is called "redlining." Using a red marker, the banks outlined areas on a map where they would *not* invest. And in this case, that area was virtually the entire Bronx. It was ironic that during this period in the 1970s when Bronxites' money was being shipped to the Sun Belt, our tongues were hanging out for the rehabilitation of our own local apartment buildings. The banks

were consistently turning their backs on the Bronx. After exhaustive research and analysis, I issued a report on redlining, with detailed data exposing the practices of the Dollar Savings Bank and other banks based in the Bronx.

The ads labeled me as "a politician seeking reelection," and neglected to show the banks' meager record of investment in the Bronx. Our office's reports exposed the banks with hard numbers and they were unable to refute the facts. They merely denied that they were engaged in redlining, saying that they "consistently invested in mortgages which our experience dictates will be sound. This sensible policy has enabled Dollar to pay over $69 million in dividends to our 420,000 depositors in the past six months alone." They didn't say where they were making these mortgage invest-ments and the truth is they were not making them in the Bronx, but instead were investing elsewhere throughout the country. They simply sidestepped the issue.

Community organizations came to my aid, and as a result of stinging public criticism, Dollar Savings and other banks began to alter their poli-cies and became more responsive to the needs of the Bronx.

A good example of greater sensitivity of Bronx banks toward investing in the borough involved a plan I had helped to implement to build a per-forming arts center and library at Lehman College which was going to be a mini-Lincoln Center. Steel was put up for the frame of the structures and then the fiscal crisis hit and the city halted construction, with some officials even proposing that the steel skeleton be torn down.

Working closely with the school's president, Leonard Leif, we were able to get local banks to commit to purchasing the bonds to enable the project to be resurrected and completed. Today the Performing Arts Cen-ter offers great programs of music and dance not only to Bronxites but to people throughout New York City.

Another effort to defend the Bronx from an assault came in response to a 1972 proposal to publicly auction North Brother Island, a twenty-acre island with an interesting history, off the coast of the South Bronx at 148th Street. At one time, North Brother Island housed Riverside Hospi-tal, which was established in 1885 to house people with smallpox who had to be quarantined as a public health and safety measure. The infamous Typhoid Mary, a cook who transmitted typhoid that killed several New Yorkers, was quarantined on North Brother Island for almost twenty-five

years until her death. As time went on, individuals with other communicable diseases, including tuberculosis, were also treated in the facility. After World War II, the hospital and other buildings were used to house returning veterans. It was later utilized as a treatment facility for drug addicts until the hospital closed in the 1960s. The buildings on the island were abandoned and suffered severe deterioration, thus leading to the auction proposal by Mayor Lindsay and NYC Comptroller Abe Beame. I arranged to tour the island to muster arguments in support of its retention in public hands.

A small boat took me and several members of my staff to the safest docking point on the island. We were warned to exercise extreme care in order not to sustain injury because the entire island was overgrown and the buildings were in a state of gross deterioration. It was like going through a jungle. Although the former hospital, the nurses' and doctors' residential facilities, and other buildings were in horrible shape, I was convinced that it was a mistake to blindly sell the island. Just a stone's throw away from the Bronx, the island was a unique commodity, and with some creative vision and commitment of resources, I was sure it could be used for a valuable public purpose. The views from the island provided a breathtaking look at the Manhattan and Bronx skylines. My goal was to preserve it and maintain it in public custody and to create educational or recreational facilities or housing. I feared that if the island were sold at public auction, an oil company could buy it and convert it into an oil depot and place ugly storage tanks all over the island. I was able to persuade the other Borough presidents and the remaining citywide elected official, the president of the City Council, to join with me. We won, defeating the mayor and comptroller's proposal at the Board of Estimate. The effort to sell the island was thwarted and it stayed in public control.

For forty years, nothing significant occurred concerning North Brother Island until 2016 when the J. M. Kaplan Fund provided resources for the University of Pennsylvania's Graduate Program in Historic Preservation and School of Design to undertake planning studies for the island. The Parks Committee of the City Council continues to push for public access to the island so it can be used as an environmental educational resource. It is comforting to know that some thought and leadership are currently being given to the future destiny of North Brother Island.

* * *

What was probably the most memorable case of defending the Bronx started with a call I got in early 1973 from Robert Moses.

"Mr. Borough President!" he shouted into the phone. "Let's have lunch. I want to have lunch with you!"

I said, "Okay. Where are we going to have it?"

He replied, "At my place, of course."

I asked, "What are we going to talk about?"

"You just come here, come down!" he said. "I want to have lunch."

At that point, Robert Moses was one of the legendary giants of New York state governance. He had had a heralded career. He held multiple titles and played multiple roles at the same time. The twelve public positions he held included New York City Parks commissioner, New York City Planning commissioner, chairman of the Long Island Parks Commission, chairman of the Triboro Bridge and Tunnel Authority, president of New York's World's Fair, the New York State Parks commissioner, and New York State Power commissioner. Much has been written about him; he was a larger-than-life character. His stamp on New York was enormous. He had been responsible for the construction of the George Washington Bridge, the Whitestone Bridge, the Throggs Neck Bridge, the Triboro Bridge, the Verazanno Bridge, the Cross Bronx Expressway, Jones Beach, and the 1964–65 World's Fair.

I hung up the phone and called my public information officer, Ethan Geto, into the office and told him: "We're having lunch with Robert Moses."

The lunch was to take place in Moses's palace. Where was his palace? On Randall's Island in the Triboro Bridge and Tunnel Authority administrative building underneath the Triboro Bridge.

On the day of our lunch, Ethan and I drove in my car and cleared the toll booth of the Triboro Bridge heading toward Manhattan. Then we took a ramp from the side and went down a curve and came to this imposing limestone structure. As soon as we entered the building, it was clear we were entering the busy, outsize world of Robert Moses. Just past the door, he had models on display of the different projects that he was involved in and that he was planning.

Moses was always enmeshed in controversy. He had planned to build a cross-Manhattan expressway along Canal Street, which was thwarted, as was his attempt to have a four-way road slice through Washington Square Park. Prior to my time as Borough president, he had successfully

built the Cross Bronx Expressway, which cut entire Bronx neighborhoods in half, gutting them. Moses had also begun to build the Sheridan Expressway off the Bruckner Expressway, which was going to cut through Bronx Park, but because of opposition it was truncated.

At around the time of our lunch, I had interviewed Moses about his latest proposal on my television show, *The Urban Challenge*, which was broadcast on the municipal television station, WNYC-TV. He wanted to build a bridge that would connect Long Island to Westchester County. Many critics said the construction of the proposed twenty-five-mile-long bridge would have created traffic jams on the Westchester side and endangered fish life in Long Island Sound. It was never built. Interestingly, Governor Andrew Cuomo recently resurrected the idea for public discussion. Moses's secretary opened the door to his office and there he was, seated behind a massive desk facing a huge set of windows that offered an unparalleled view of New York's skyline. With him was eighty-seven-year-old Peter Grimm, a major real-estate executive. At the time of this meeting, Moses was eighty-four years old. He had a gruff manner and spoke with a gravelly voice. His words would flow in bombastic clusters. He gave me a nice welcome, offering a bit of a hug.

"You know, Mr. Borough President," he said almost as soon as I had taken a seat, "we're going to move the Bronx Hall of Fame. Have you any concerns or objections?"

I said, "Excuse me?"

He said, "We're gonna move the Hall of Fame. No one goes there. It's out of the way."

The Hall of Fame of Great Americans was one of the signature landmarks in the Bronx. It was a colonnade with a hundred busts of great Americans, located on a bluff overlooking the Harlem River, on the uptown campus of New York University. It was a world-renowned institution designed by Stanford White and completed in 1900. Every five years a new person was nominated and a new bust was placed there. Among others, it featured busts of Thomas Jefferson, Harriet Beecher Stowe, Henry Longfellow, and Wilbur and Orville Wright.

"Where are you going to move it?" I asked.

"We're going to move it to the New American wing of the Metropolitan Museum of Art during the celebration of America's bicentennial in 1976."

I said, "Mr. Moses, you can't do that! You just can't do that. I'm not going to *let* you do that!"

"What?" he blustered, leaning forward. "What are you saying?"

I continued protesting: "The Hall of Fame is synonymous with the Bronx; it's one of our major institutions."

He said, "No one goes there. It's inaccessible!" He started getting belligerent, raising his voice and even shouting. He slammed his hand down on his desk, saying, "In the winter it's freezing up there. People don't want to go to an open-air terrace during the cold months."

I said, "Let's talk about *that* then. Let's talk about how we can make it more accessible, how we can advertise it more, how visitors and others within the city can know more about the Hall of Fame. Let's raise the money to enclose it with a glass casing —but not *remove* it."

His eyes were fixed on mine. He was not saying anything yet, but I could see he was seething. My arguments meant nothing.

I continued: "Mr. Moses, what you are advocating is counter to the trend of what's happening in New York City." I told him about the arrangement I had made with Tom Hoving of the Metropolitan Museum of Art whereby the museum loaned the Lehman Collection to the new fledgling Bronx Museum. "We had 150,000 visitors to the museum since it opened about a year ago!" I said.

His response was another slam of his hand on the desk. "Damn it, Mr. Borough President!" he said, glaring at me. "Paris is Paris!"

And he regaled me with a story about how in the 1700s there was a proposal to build a Pantheon that would serve as the burial place for France's great leaders. "And the pipsqueak, squirt mayors of Marseille and Lyons," he said, "started to advocate that the Pantheon be built in their cities. And just as reasoned judgment prevailed there, so must reasoned judgment prevail here.

"Paris is Paris and in the United States, Mr. Abrams," he concluded, "Manhattan is Paris."

Peter Grimm, piggybacking on Moses's earlier objections, raised the accessibility argument again, asserting that the Hall of Fame was not near a subway.

I was getting increasingly frustrated and annoyed and retorted: "Look, why don't you guys move the Statue of Liberty to Times Square right adjacent to the subway, then?"

I was flabbergasted by Moses's response: "No, we can't do that—it's federal property and so we just can't do that!"—taking my off the cuff comment literally.

He absolutely insisted that he was going to move the Hall of Fame. At one point, he brought a bunch of his cronies, his staff of loyal bureaucrats, into the room. They were like his own personal Greek chorus, and soon enough they began to chime in about the frigid, wintry weather. One of those guys, to please his boss, said, "Maybe the Borough president is an Eskimo."

The others nodded their heads and laughed, repeating: "An Eskimo."

"Yes, he's an Eskimo!"

I stood my ground. "You're not going to do that. I'm not going to allow you to do that."

Fortunately, the tension was broken at that moment because Moses's secretary came in and announced that lunch was ready.

The conversation over lunch was a treat because Moses and Grimm kept spinning out stories that involved some venerable New Yorkers. They told about their experiences with Jimmy Walker, Al Smith, Franklin Roosevelt, and Fiorella LaGuardia.

As we were leaving, Moses turned on the charm by embracing me again. "Now, Mr. President, give some thought to this. I know you're a reasonable man."

During the car ride back to the office, Ethan teased me, asking: "Have you ever been called an Eskimo before?"

I responded, "Politics is a tough business and I've been called a lot of names, but never an Eskimo."

Complicated man that he was, Moses showed graciousness and sagacity by sending me about a week later an autographed copy of his autobiography, an 893-page tome titled *Public Works: A Dangerous Trade*. This was at about the same time as the publication of *The Power Broker*, Robert Caro's Pulitzer Prize-winning 1974 biography, a less flattering chronicle of Moses's career. It painted Moses as an unelected master builder running roughshod over the city's communities to build a road network that often brushed aside the needs of the venues it upended. While I was pleased to get Moses's book (and I still have it on my shelf), it certainly didn't accomplish the goal of getting me to acquiesce.

The slightly illegible inscription reads:

> To the BP of the B
> —with kindest regards,
> R. Moses

When NYU sold its campus in the 1970s, the Hall of Fame remained and became part of the campus of Bronx Community College, a division of City University of New York (CUNY). The Hall of Fame, the first such institution in the United States, continues to represent a challenge. Andy Wolf, a Bronx newspaper publisher, has been a vocal advocate for upgrading the Hall of Fame. It remains underutilized and needs leadership to bring its governance up to date. There has been no election of new members since 1975. The selection process for electing future members should include individuals from more recent ethnic groups who have made outstanding contributions to the life and culture of our nation. As I said to Robert Moses many years ago, "It's a great borough trophy and needs a constituency to strengthen and promote it." It continues to be a unique asset worth fighting for.

Chapter 10

Mississippi

D URING MY TIME AS BOROUGH PRESIDENT, civil rights issues were per-
colating around the country as a result of centuries of systematic
oppression and discrimination against black Americans. As a member of
a religious minority group, the Jewish community, I felt and understood
the significance of prejudice and discrimination, although I realized I
could never truly know the pain of black Americans. America's legacy of
slavery and the pernicious practices of racial discrimination were embar-
rassing and morally reprehensible.

Campaigning in the South Bronx in the race for Borough president
heightened my sensitivity to issues like poverty, inadequate education,
and the way in which these problems were connected to racial discrimi-
nation. What I saw were not overt examples of institutional discrimina-
tion, but rather the impacts of neglectful governmental policies that had
debilitating effects on minority people's lives. I also knew that a sizable
number of African American residents of the Bronx had themselves come
to New York as part of the Great Migration. They set out in search of a
more secure economic future, but in a sense they were also refugees who
had fled the daily indignities—and worse—of the old South. Many main-
tained strong family ties to people in the South and they were inevitably
affected on a deep level by what was happening there.

Early in my first term as Borough president of the Bronx, the Americans
for Democratic Action (ADA) reached out to me to ask if I would be willing
to volunteer to go to Mississippi as part of a special project lending support
to African Americans running for local office. The ADA is an organization
that was founded by liberal giants Eleanor Roosevelt, Walter Reuther,
Arthur Schlesinger, and John Kenneth Galbraith in the mid-1940s after the

death of Franklin Roosevelt, which has advocated and worked for a progressive agenda and supported candidates who adhere to its credo.

The Civil Rights and Voting Rights Acts of 1964-65 provided amplified rights for minority citizens and candidates. Between 1965 and 1971, black voter turnout in Mississippi had increased tenfold from fewer than 30,000 to more than 300,000, resulting in more than 100 black officeholders. The New York State chapter of ADA in 1971 was backing the independent candidacy of Charles Evers for governor of Mississippi and wanted to send a small group to help the Evers campaign by working with his African American activist allies who were running for local office. These activists were the remnants of the Mississippi Freedom Democratic Party, which had been challenging the legitimacy of the Mississippi Democratic Party.

Charles Evers had been elected mayor of Fayette, Mississippi, in 1969, the first African American mayor in Mississippi in the post-Reconstruction period. Evers, a longtime civil rights activist, was the brother of Medgar Evers, the head of the National Association for the Advancement of Colored People (NAACP) in Mississippi who, in 1963, was fatally shot in the driveway outside his home in Jackson, Mississippi, by a member of the Ku Klux Klan.

We were charged with providing advice and hands-on assistance. Since I had been successful in underfunded insurgent races, ADA wanted me to discuss and demonstrate how you can create inexpensive campaign literature, successfully register voters, and mobilize people to work in a local campaign.

Five of us, including Lou Sepersky, an associate editor at a trade magazine, George Mora and Marty Lichtig, two members of my staff from the Bronx Borough President's Office, and Richard Stone, who had managed my campaign for Borough president, constituted the ADA delegation. We all brought different levels of expertise down to Quitman County in northern Mississippi, the second poorest county in the state.

Our meetings were set to take place in the town of Marks. Locals warned us not to call attention to ourselves for fear of word getting out that "agitators from the North had come to town to stir up trouble." We were told not to rent a motel room in Marks, but someplace nearby. We were acutely aware of the ruthless violence that had been a staple of recent Mississippi history as a result of the unchecked power of the Ku Klux Klan and its close ties to local law enforcement: firebombings of the homes of activists, lynchings, and burning crosses to inspire terror in those who were brave and audacious enough to work for change.

Of course, we also had in mind the murder of three civil-rights workers (two of whom were from New York) who had been gunned down in Mississippi in 1963. Michael Schwerner and Andrew Goodman were the New Yorkers who had traveled to Mississippi to help organize civil rights efforts on behalf of the Congress of Racial Equality (CORE), and James Cheney was a local African American CORE worker. All three were viciously murdered and only much later found buried in an earthen dam near Philadelphia, Mississippi.

Before agreeing to participate in this project, each of our group evaluated the risk that would be involved in such an undertaking. As for myself, I knew that our effort was not totally free from risk of violence. But I had lived by a guiding principle that one can't go through life totally avoiding danger and therefore I approached life fatalistically—what will be will be.

I had been through parts of the South before this trip, but never to Mississippi. I had never seen the kind of poverty that was on such visible display as we drove through this rural part of the state. Ramshackle housing was a reminder of the exploitative nature of sharecropping. As we drove through the most run-down areas of town, they seemed to be populated exclusively by African Americans. The countryside looked like a tableau of an earlier period: African American men and women bent over in fields on either side of the road, hard at work in the sweltering Mississippi heat.

I can't remember all of the people we worked with, but a few names remain large in my memory—Reverend A. D. Coleman, our primary contact, Moses Kincaid, candidate for county commissioner, Willie Ware, candidate for deputy sheriff, and Jimmy Edwards, candidate for constable. They were all running in the primary against white establishment Democratic Party candidates.

One of the first things we did was emphasize what rights the newly enfranchised voters had pursuant to the Voting Rights Act—how a voter or candidate could challenge any effort by the local political establishment to deny them access to vote or to wage a campaign. We were aware that while from a legal standpoint the advice we were giving was sound, in following this advice—in insisting on the rights guaranteed them by the federal government—these activists would be putting themselves in mortal danger. They understood this better than we ever could and we couldn't help but admire them for their enormous courage.

The ADA gave us a cash donation for the Evers campaign to go toward renting a school bus to transport voters to the polls. Since the voting was done by paper ballots, we also warned the local activists about the

possibility that ballots of black voters could be thrown away rather than being placed in the ballot box—or that ballot boxes themselves could be tampered with. We highlighted how any assertions of impropriety had to be documented and made in such a way that there was a proper record of the deprivations of these rights.

We helped create and design literature for the candidates that could be inexpensively produced by using an electronic stencil on a mimeograph machine. We also coached candidates to develop stump speeches under-scoring their programmatic ideas while providing voters with encourage-ment to exercise their vote. Since I personally knew how difficult it was to speak in front of others, I worked one-on-one with several candidates to practice their speeches until there was a degree of comfort and confi-dence. Often we accompanied candidates to local churches where groups could gather to listen to them speak.

As we returned at night to our motel, there were times when we sus-pected we were being followed. Cars with honking horns would pass us in the darkness of the night, and on one occasion I was sure that a man in the passenger seat of one of those passing vehicles, which slowed down as it passed us, slid the barrel end of a shotgun pointed in our direction out of the rolled-down window. After a while, that car sped off, one or more voices shouting out something unintelligible, the words drowned out by the revved-up engine, as the car's red taillights eventually faded into the darkness ahead.

I remember that the sparsely furnished motel room where we slept had a Bible and a chipped enamel basin on the night stand, a closet-like bath-room, and a poorly functioning air conditioner. I'd fall asleep at night drenched in sweat to the sound of cicadas and cars passing by.

We wondered whether our assistance would be welcomed and so we were pleased to see those with whom we worked appreciated our presence. At the end of the week, we sat in chairs and on picnic benches in the yard behind the home of one of the local activists, enjoying a spread of home-made southern food—chicken, corn bread, collard greens, and potato salad—that had been prepared especially for us as a show of hospitality and appreciation. While children played in the yard, we sat around giving last-minute tips and encouragement to the men and women who were destined to be in the vanguard of new emerging leadership.

The Mississippi experience was rewarding, as were others, as you will see next.

Chapter 11

Gay Rights

"I HATE TO DELIVER BAD NEWS, BUT you've become the center of a firestorm," my secretary, Peggy Rodriguez, conveyed to me with a shaken voice and grave look. "The phones have been ringing off the hook."

I had just returned to the office after testifying in favor of the gay rights bill. "People are angry. They're saying they will never vote for you again. One man called and said you should rot in Hell."

It was 1971. A few weeks earlier, my public information officer, Ethan Geto, whose advice I respected, informed me that the City Council was to hold public hearings on a proposed gay rights bill. He strongly advised me to testify in favor of the bill, which would protect the civil rights of gay people. The legislation, using the classic language of the federal Civil Rights Act of 1964, sought to prohibit discrimination against gay people in housing and other public accommodations, including the workplace.

Inspired by the African American civil rights movement, women, Native Americans, Latinos, and other marginalized groups, gay people across the United States had begun to organize and fight for their right to be treated as full citizens deserving of equal protection under the law. In the late 1960s and early '70s, there were large-scale street demonstrations, dramatic acts of civil disobedience, and courtroom efforts to usher in change. It was an exciting, dynamic period when one group after another spoke up and made its presence known, ultimately enriching the image that we had of ourselves as Americans.

Ethan knew I strongly believed our system of government was robust enough and the law expansive enough to extend the promise and basic protections of democracy to all citizens. He realized that I would be

supportive of an opportunity to use my authority as Borough president to help improve the lives of a group of vulnerable New Yorkers.

On the other hand, as an elected official with a diverse constituency, I naturally thought about what my support of the bill would mean for me politically. For starters, I had no doubt that the bill would be defeated, and I knew of no other major politician who was likely to testify in favor of it. Going on record to take a principled position might compromise my ability to effectively do the daily work of the office. I needed to consider very carefully whether to take the risk.

I told Ethan that I would need some time to consult other staff members to get their take on the issue. As it turned out, the people on my staff—decent, tolerant people who struggled daily on the side of justice —were almost all opposed to my testifying in favor of the bill.

I remember some of the responses:

"Bob, are you kidding? Don't go anywhere near it."

"Keep your distance, your enemies will try to use this to destroy you."

"I hate to state the obvious, Bob, but think about it. This will stir up rumors. It'll just be more grist for the mill. You're thirty-three years old and a bachelor."

My political opponents had already tried to use my marital status to hurt me politically.

When I first ran for the assembly in 1965, I remember my father calling me and saying, "Bobby, there's this rumor going around the neighborhood. It's the regulars, those lying bastards, they're saying you have a girlfriend, you made her pregnant, and she gave birth to your baby."

And then, a few weeks later, he called again. "Bobby," he said, lowering his voice, "they're at it again, there's another rumor! They say that you're a *homosexual*. You're twenty-seven years old and you're not married."

I said, "Daddy, a couple of weeks ago I had a girlfriend and I had a baby, but now I'm a homosexual. They'd better get their story straight." I added: "We can't control what they're saying. Daddy, this game of politics that I've entered is very tough and ruthless. People will say and do anything to win. We have to brush it aside. You've always taught me, 'The good guys will win in the end.' Try to not let it bother you."

The reactions of my progressive staff reflected just how unpopular the position stated in the bill was at the time. Criminal sodomy laws were still on the books and routinely enforced against homosexuals. The New York State Liquor Authority prohibited serving homosexuals on the basis that

they were, by definition, "disorderly." Mayor John Lindsay's periodic attempts to "clean up" the city used these circumstances to justify increased police raids on gay bars. Since these establishments were illegal, they tended to be run by mobsters who paid corrupt police officers to turn a blind eye. But police still occasionally raided mob-run bars, whether in response to complaints or to pressure the owners to increase the amount of money paid for protection. Patrons were rounded up and often arresting officers would extort money from them in exchange for keeping their names out of the newspapers. At that time, the press regularly printed the names, addresses, and occupations of those who were arrested, destroying many lives and reputations in the process.

Then, in June 1969, during a raid on the Stonewall Inn, a gay bar in Greenwich Village, patrons unexpectedly fought back. Police barricaded themselves inside the bar, awaiting reinforcements, while patrons stood outside hurling bricks and other objects at the windows. Three days of rioting ensued. This event has come to symbolize the time when it became clear to many, in the highly politicized atmosphere of the 1960s, that gay people were assertively thinking of themselves as an oppressed class. The annual gay pride parade on the last Sunday of June commemorates this sea change. In 2019, over 100,000 marchers from around the world gathered in New York City to celebrate Pride Day and the fiftieth anniversary of the Stonewall Riots that launched the gay rights movement.

A few days after our initial conversation about the proposed gay rights bill, I pulled Ethan aside and told him: "It's the right thing to do and I'm going to do it." It was clear to me that testifying was the only appropriate response to such ugly exploitation. Ethan looked visibly relieved.

I wasn't prepared, however, for the hostility that met my testimony at the City Council. The City Council chamber, where the public hearing took place, was crowded, with a packed balcony. Opponents of the bill jeered, hooted, booed, and shouted anti-gay epithets in an attempt to drown me out. An avalanche of criticism streamed down on me.

The telephones in the Borough president's office hardly stopped ringing in the days that followed. For over a week, we received hate calls, threats, and complaints from constituents who felt personally betrayed by my support of the bill. When the calls abated, I remained convinced that I had done the right thing. It would take another fifteen years before the bill finally passed.

* * *

Two years after Ethan first approached me about the gay rights bill, we were gearing up for my race for attorney general. We were walking down the steps of City Hall, about to head back up to the Bronx, when Ethan stopped in his tracks. "Bob, I need to talk to you," he said, and then added, "privately and personally."

We sat down on an empty bench in City Hall Park with no people in earshot. I could see from the expression on his face that whatever it was he was about to say weighed heavily on him. He took a deep breath, launching into what sounded like a carefully prepared speech. "Bob," he said, "I have something really important to tell you. Look—I'm gay and not only am I gay but I won't live in the closet anymore. I just can't do it. I won't do it. I'm not going to make a public declaration—but I'm a gay rights activist and I have a lot of gay friends and now I have a boyfriend and I may want to walk down the street holding my boyfriend's hand. And I feel I have to tell you this because I really want you to win the attorney general race and I realize what consequences this could have, and I'm prepared to resign."

I began to respond but Ethan continued. "I don't think people should *have to* resign," he said. "I don't think people should *not* take jobs or *not* be promoted because they're gay. So, in one way, my offering to resign goes against everything I believe as a gay-rights activist. But I'm so committed to you and I want to see you advance your progressive agenda and you've been so good to me—I really sincerely am willing to resign with no hard feelings." A deep sigh followed.

My reaction was instinctive and immediate. Until that moment I had no idea that Ethan was gay. After all, he had been married and had two children. I was at his apartment in Riverdale many times when his wife and kids were there. We had meals together on numerous occasions. He was my key political advisor. We'd been working together for years and having constant meetings and discussions. Never, ever did it cross my mind that he was gay.

This was just one human being to another, one friend to another, and I knew what I wanted to do and to say: "That's absolutely crazy. First of all, Ethan, you're my friend. Second, I admire you for the courage to say what you just said to me. Third, you're a major part of my political and governmental life and operation. I want you to know that I'm prepared to take any political damage, any setback, and I will stand by you."

He started to speak but I held up my hand to stop him. "Ethan, I wouldn't dream of accepting your resignation. That's a ridiculous idea. I'm

Five years old during World War II.

With my mom and dad, Ben and Dotty Abrams, on the boardwalk in Rockaway Park.

Columbia graduation with Dad and Grandma Ida, June 1960.

My dad and mom in their luncheonette ("The Store") in 1951. (Note that a pastrami sandwich cost forty cents.) Dad has his perennial cigar in his right hand and Mom is making a New York City favorite soda drink, an egg cream.

Working as a waiter in the Catskills to pay for my Columbia tuition. (How about that dexterity in balancing a tray of goblets!)

Receiving election returns in my first Assembly race, Primary Night, September 14, 1965. When this photo was taken, the results were still uncertain which explains why there is not a single smile on anyone's face.

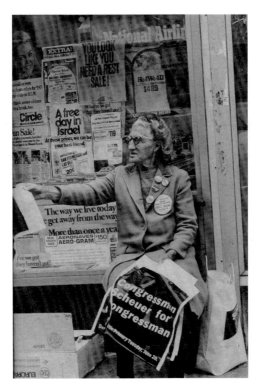

Grandma Ida campaigning for me at the corner of White Plains Road and Lydig Avenue in Pelham Parkway. She's wearing a homemade button that says "Vote for my grandson, Robert Abrams, for borough president."

Rally in Pelham Parkway with Senator Robert Kennedy prior to November 1965 election. I'm between Senator Kennedy and Comptroller Abe Beame running for mayor.

Debating a bill as a freshman legislator in the New York State Assembly. Seated to the left is fellow freshman, David Dinkins, who went on to become New York City's first African American mayor.

Campaign literature for 1966 reelection race for NYS Assembly.

With Governor Nelson Rockefeller at bill-signing ceremony in the Red Room in the Capitol in Albany for one of the bills I sponsored when I was in the Assembly.

ELECT
ASSEMBLYMAN
ROBERT ABRAMS
BRONX BOROUGH PRESIDENT
"PREFERRED" BY CITIZENS UNION

ABILITY · DEDICATION · INTEGRITY

HIS RECORD PROVES THAT HE IS DEDICATED
TO THE PEOPLE, NOT THE MACHINE

VOTE LINE 17

★ ★ DEMOCRATIC PRIMARY TUESDAY, JUNE 17, 3-10 P.M. ★ ★

Campaign literature for borough president's race.

Speaking in support of free tuition at City College.

With Assemblyman Sam Wright (left) and Manhattan Borough President Percy Sutton.

Sharing a light moment with Governor Nelson Rockefeller, Mayor John V. Lindsay and Bronx Borough President Herman Badillo at dedication ceremony in Co-op City.

Joining Cesar Chavez (to my left, looking down) at a Brooklyn demonstration in support of the Farmworkers Union.

The inauguration of Bronx Day. Monsignor Gustav Schultheiss (at microphone), Detlev Bronck (whose ancestors founded the Bronx) and Secretary General of the United Nations U Thant who lived in the Riverdale section of the Bronx.

New York City mayor John V. Lindsay, Yankee president Michael Burke and I are displaying a model of Yankee Stadium with proposed renovations at a press conference at City Hall.

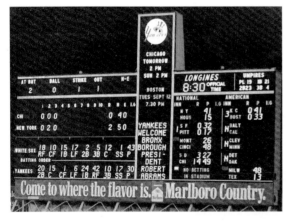

Yankee Stadium welcome.

This photo with an autographed inscription thanking me for my support was sent to me by George Steinbrenner who in 1973 became the principal owner of the Yankees.

I'm in the South Bronx studio that produced the set for the Broadway show, *Two by Two*, starring Danny Kaye (left) with music composed by Richard Rodgers (center).

Rehearsal of American Symphony Orchestra, with conductor Skitch Henderson for Co-op City performance. I narrated *Lincoln's Portrait* by Aaron Copeland.

I'm with Kevin McCarthy, prominent film and TV actor, in preparation for a rally for senior citizens.

U.S. Senator Alan Cranston from California touring the South Bronx with me.

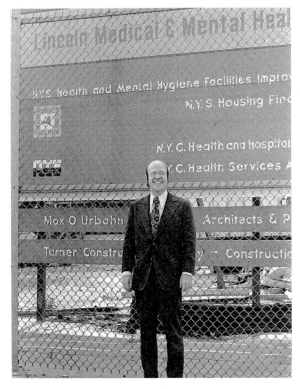

Building a new Lincoln Hospital in the South Bronx was one of my highest priorities.

Press conference at which Hugh Carey and I cross-endorsed each other during 1974 New York State Democratic Primary. Former Mayor Robert F. Wagner is at the podium and former Governor W. Averell Harriman is at the right.

U.S. Supreme Court Justice, William O. Douglas, a naturalist, walking through the Bronx Botanical Gardens.

U. S. Senator Jacob K. Javits and Assembly Majority Leader Albert Blumenthal joined me in the South Bronx advocating for improved health care programs.

Endorsing George McGovern for president at Fordham Road and the Grand
Concourse in the Bronx, August 1971.

I traveled with a delegation of Hispanic leaders to Puerto Rico to attend the
inauguration of newly elected Governor Rafael Hernandez Colon in 1973.

Victorious statewide insurgent candidates the day after the Democratic Primary at Waldorf Astoria, 1974. Left to right: Ramsey Clark for U.S. Senate, Hugh L. Carey for governor, and Mary Ann Krupsak for lieutenant governor.

President of the New York City Council, Paul O'Dwyer, Manhattan Borough President Percy Sutton and I are being briefed on local crime statistics at a police precinct.

Court of Appeals Judge Lawrence Cook administering oath of office for Attorney General of New York.

Attorney General Swearing-in Ceremony Albany, NY, Left to right: Baruch Silvererstein, Pres. NY Board of Rabbis, Howard Hubbard, Most Reverend Excellency Bishop of Albany, Ned Regan, newly elected Comptroller and his wife, Jennifer, Louis Lefkowitz, outgoing Attorney General, me and Diane, Hugh L. Carey, Governor, Basil Paterson, Secretary of State, Mario Cuomo, Lt. Governor. Background: Family of Governor Carey.

With Israeli Prime Minister Golda Meir in her Jerusalem office in 1971.

Governor Hugh Carey delivering the State of the State address, Albany, NY, 1981. Left to right: Assembly Speaker Stanley Fink, myself, Lt. Governor Mario Cuomo, Comptroller Ned Regan, and Senate Majority Leader Warren Anderson.

for you, you stay with me, and I'll back you up. And if this becomes an issue in my campaign for attorney general and causes my defeat, so be it. We're friends, we stand together."

My commitment to advance gay rights was just beginning and the road ahead was filled with enormous potential.

Chapter 12

The McGovern Campaign

I N 1971, THE VIETNAM WAR HAD been raging for years, taking the lives of more than 57,000 American soldiers. The wrongheaded nature of this conflict was evident to millions of Americans as print and TV media ramped up their reporting about the death toll on both sides. Thousands of soldiers were returning home with serious physical and psychological infirmities. The president announced plans to send more troops and there seemed to be no end in sight to the senseless violence. The rationale for the war, stopping the spread of communism, was based on the domino theory that held that if we didn't halt a communist victory in Vietnam, the rest of Asia and other parts of the world would fall to communism, threatening the United States and our freedom-loving allies. But Americans weren't buying it anymore.

Opposition to the war was particularly strong among the youth of the nation. Rallies and demonstrations were taking place across the country. Intellectuals, ordinary citizens, and Vietnam veterans were joining the fight for peace.

I found myself increasingly involved in this struggle to extricate our country from the Vietnam quagmire. I attended and spoke at rallies questioning our country's policy, signed petitions, and lent my name to anti-war efforts. During the 1968 presidential primary three years earlier, the war had been the major issue, with presidential candidates Eugene McCarthy and Robert Kennedy speaking passionately about pulling us out of Vietnam. I supported Kennedy in the primaries only a few short months before he was assassinated. With the upcoming presidential elections, many Democrats were desperate to find a candidate who could

speak with passion about ending the war and realistically capture the presidential nomination.

After Bobby Kennedy's assassination, Hubert Humphrey won the Democratic nomination but ultimately lost to Republican Richard Nixon, who expanded the conflict as the body count grew and the Vietnam War flared on. We needed a candidate who could defeat Nixon and take the country in a different direction.

I started to hear about George McGovern, the senator from South Dakota, a World War II bomber pilot and now a strong anti-war critic, and got involved with his campaign as a co-chairman for New York State.

I knew that to run as a McGovern anti-war delegate and attend the upcoming Democratic National Convention would involve risk and require a lot of hard work. But I was willing to do whatever it took to get McGovern elected because I was convinced that he offered our best chance to end the slaughter in Vietnam. Still, those of us opposed to the war were in the minority and I knew that the potential for victory was not assured.

In August 1971, very early in the political calendar, I endorsed George McGovern at the busiest Bronx intersection, at Fordham Road and the Grand Concourse.

At around 8:00 p.m. that night, I turned to my Public Information Officer Ethan Geto and said, "I wonder what kind of coverage we'll get for this endorsement."

He promptly replied: "Let's go find out."

We raced downtown to get a copy of the *New York Times* because in those days, at around 9:00 p.m., you could get a copy of the next day's edition of the *Times* at one of the newsstands near the *Times* building.

We arrived a little early and were sitting in the car waiting for the paper to be delivered to the newsstand when I happened to look up at the building known as One Times Square. There used to be an electronic board that went around the building and flashed the latest news. "Ethan!" I said. "Oh my God, look at that!" I was flabbergasted to see the electronic crawl say: BRONX BOROUGH PRESIDENT ABRAMS SUPPORTS MCGOVERN IN THE DEMOCRATIC PRIMARY FOR PRESIDENT.

A few minutes later, I was at the newsstand holding the paper and discovered that my endorsement of McGovern was on the front page. He was a long shot and the *Times* must have felt that support from a key elected official might be a turning point for McGovern to pick up valuable delegate strength at the convention.

I worked very hard for McGovern, heading up a slate of McGovern delegates in my congressional district, winning against tough opposition put up by the regular organization. We also opened storefronts on Long Island in the northern suburbs and other parts of the state to attract volunteer support for McGovern.

At a meeting of major McGovern supporters in May 1972, my friend Hilly Gross and I were asked to hammer out elements for a McGovern Middle East platform. We drafted an outline of principles, one of which was that the United States should recognize Jerusalem as the capital of Israel and move its embassy there. Soon thereafter, McGovern enunciated this policy as his own. The Democratic Convention later adopted the following statement in its platform: "The next Democratic Administration should recognize and support the established status of Jerusalem as the capital of Israel, with free access to all of its holy places provided to all faiths. As a symbol of this stand, the United States Embassy should be moved from Tel Aviv to Jerusalem." In 1995, during Bill Clinton's presidency, the Jerusalem Embassy Act was passed to fund the relocation of the American Embassy from Tel Aviv to Jerusalem and called for Jerusalem to remain an undivided city and for it to be recognized as the capital of Israel. The legislation included the ability of the president to waive the requirement of moving the embassy—a waiver that has been exercised by Presidents Clinton, Bush, Obama, and Trump. But President Trump, differing from his predecessors, officially announced US recognition of Jerusalem as the capital of Israel on December 6, 2017.

* * *

In the summer of 1972, I went to the Democratic Convention in Miami and served as one of four co-chairs of the New York delegation.

I had been very involved in the United Farm Workers effort to unionize the farmworkers in California, for them to work under decent labor conditions and to get adequate pay. To dramatically indicate my support for the farm workers, when New York was called during the roll call of the states, I was at the microphone and announced: "Mister Chairman, New York, the state that boycotts scab lettuce, casts two hundred and sixty-seven votes for the next president of the United States, George McGovern."

Unfortunately, the convention was a disaster for McGovern. His acceptance speech, instead of being delivered at prime time, reached television on the East Coast at 3:00 a.m. After the convention, newspapers started providing negative coverage about the vice presidential nominee, Tom Eagleton, a US senator from Missouri, because it was disclosed that he suffered from depression, incurring several hospitalizations and electroshock therapy. A huge controversy emerged about Eagleton's competency to serve if elected, thereby creating sufficient pressure for McGovern to drop him from the ticket. He was replaced by Sargent Shriver, John Kennedy's brother-in-law.

During the course of the campaign, many of the Democratic Party establishment either sat on their hands or walked away from McGovern's candidacy. McGovern was accused of being too strident and tied to left and radical elements in the party.

McGovern returned to New York for a rally at DeWitt Clinton High School in the Bronx during the weekend before the election. The auditorium was packed to the rafters with people standing in the aisles. The excitement of a presidential candidate making a stop in the Bronx was palpable. It was a big thrill for me to introduce him to my constituents. As always, he made a great presentation: his look, his bearing, and the power and precision of his thoughts.

Leaving the rally, I said to myself, *Wow! If only the rest of the country could feel this way.* But it turned out McGovern ultimately carried only one state—Massachusetts. The monumental McGovern loss was the result of many factors, but mainly due to a series of controversial blunders and the national electorate's hesitation for an immediate pullout from Vietnam.

A few months after the convention, I received a call from one of New York's labor leaders, who said, "The president of the United Farm Workers, Cesar Chavez, is coming to the Bronx. He's going to be in the Hunt's Point Market. I know how active you've been in supporting their cause. Would you like to meet him?" I admired Chavez because he was such a humble man who courageously focused the country's attention on exploited people.

I said, "Of course I'd like to meet him! That would be fantastic."

The caller said, "But he's going to be there at four in the morning—that's what time the produce comes in."

I said, "I don't care what time it is, I'm going to be there." I got to the designated place promptly at 4:00 a.m. Soon I saw a large crowd approaching. Cesar Chavez was there with lots of people at his side. Someone next to Chavez said: "Cesar, this is Bob Abrams, the Borough president of the Bronx."

Chavez shook my hand and said, "I know Bob Abrams, he's a hero of mine."

I looked at him with astonishment and asked incredulously: "What do you mean? It's just the other way around. You've been an enormous hero of mine for many years. What are you talking about, Mr. Chavez?"

And he proceeded to tell this story. He was in a jeep with some of his fellow organizers crossing the desert in the Southwest, listening to the 1972 Democratic National Convention. During the state by state roll call, when the secretary of the convention called New York, Chavez said, they heard my announcement.

They stopped, ran outside, joined hands, and danced around the jeep.

He said, "You put us on the map. What you said was heard by millions of people across this country and around the world. So that's why I will never forget who you are."

That was a cherished moment that I savor to this day.

The McGovern Campaign / 79

I said, "I don't care what time it is. I'm going to be there." I got to the designated place promptly at 4:00 a.m. Soon I saw a large crowd approach me. Cesar Chavez was there with lots of people at his side. Someone next to Chavez said, "Cesar, this is Bob Abrams, the borough president of the Bronx."

Chavez shook my hand and said, "I know B.J. Abrams, he's a hero of mine."

I looked at him with astonishment and asked incredulously, "What do you mean? I'm just the other guy around. You've been an enormous hero of mine for many years. What are you talking about, Mr. Chavez?"

And he proceeded to tell the story. He was in a jeep with some of his fellow organizers crossing the desert in the Southwest, listening to the 1972 Democratic National Convention. During the state by state roll call, when the secretary of the convention called New York, Chavez said, they heard my announcement.

They stopped, ran quasi joyously around, and danced around the jeep. He said, "You put us on the map. What you said was heard by millions of people across this country and around the world. So that's why I will never forget who you are."

That was a cherished moment that I savor to this day.

Chapter 13

Blind Date

"I T'S TIME THAT YOU GOT MARRIED and I have the *perfect* girl for you," Rabbi Klaperman said to me. "She comes from a wonderful family. I know her parents; they're members of my congregation. She's extremely attractive, she's very intelligent, she has interests similar to yours—what more could you ask? Here's her name and telephone number."

I knew Rabbi Klaperman, a very prominent and highly respected rabbi, through the Soviet Jewry movement. It was at a rally for Soviet Jewry in 1973 that he pulled me aside to give me this advice, along with a folded piece of paper on which he had scrawled the name—Diane Schulder—and the telephone number of the young woman he insisted was my "ideal mate."

"Thank you, rabbi," I said politely; I was so occupied with my work and my responsibilities that I never got around to making the call.

When I saw Rabbi Klaperman at the next Soviet Jewry rally, he looked at me and said. "*Nu?* And? Have you made the call?"

This went on repeatedly.

I never seemed to be able to find the time. I was thirty-six years old and though I had dated a number of women, with a few bordering on serious, nothing had ever ultimately developed.

At another demonstration, I saw Rabbi Klaperman out of the corner of my eye. "Bob! Bob, over here!" he called out, waving, just in case I was thinking of walking in the opposite direction. And then he said: "So, what's the problem? Why haven't you called that young lady?"

"I'm busy, Rabbi Klaperman," I explained. "I'm doing a lot of things, I'm working very hard."

Shortly thereafter at the Borough President's Office, I looked up to see my secretary, Peggy Rodriguez, standing in the doorway to my office, shaking her head and frowning.

"Mister President," she said.

"What is it, Peggy?"

"It's that rabbi on the phone again," she said, lowering her voice and looking back over her shoulder as if he were about to walk in behind her. "You know what he's going to say. He's going to ask you to take out that girl. Why don't you just take her out for a drink? It's an hour of your time. That way you'll get him off your back and who knows; maybe something will come of it."

"All right, put the call through," I said, sighing.

"So Bob," Rabbi Klaperman said almost as soon as I finished saying hello. "What's going on here? I told you all those great things about Diane Schulder. If you're not careful, you're going to lose a wonderful opportunity. You should call her up. Time is fleeting!"

I made the call. I started the conversation by saying, "We have a mutual admirer in Rabbi Klaperman. He thinks we should meet. Why don't we get together for a drink at the Pierre Hotel?"

"Sure, why not?" she said.

A few days later, we met.

As Rabbi Klaperman had indicated, Diane was quite attractive and we did have similar interests. Like me, she was opposed to the Vietnam War. While I was on the floor of the Democratic Convention the year before, in 1972, supporting George McGovern the peace candidate, Diane had been picketing outside with a group of feminists, all of whom, including her best friend, black activist Flo Kennedy, were fiery protesters against the war.

And there was more to spark and hold my interest in this young woman. She had graduated from Columbia Law School, clerked for Dudley Bonsall, a United States District Court judge in the Southern District, worked for the Legal Aid Society handling arraigned defendants, and had been part of the defense team when prominent civil liberties lawyer Leonard Boudin represented Dr. Benjamin Spock regarding his anti-war activities. Spock, whose baby book had sold more copies than any book in history other than the Bible, was the most famous physician in the world. She also told me about a course she had created at NYU Law School, "Women and the Law," which it turned out was the first course of its kind to be taught anywhere.

I was taken by the fact that she seemed to be a very thoughtful person who was not controlled by the superficialities and banalities of our time.

A few nights later, I was scheduled for a late-night radio interview at a restaurant called Jimmy's, named for the columnist Jimmy Breslin. It was the former Toots Shor's restaurant and had become *the* hangout for political aficionados. The interview was to be conducted by the former deputy mayor of New York City in the Lindsay administration, Dick Aurelio. It occurred to me that maybe this would be a nice opportunity to get together with Diane again and that she might get a kick out of this.

I called her and said, "Hi, this is Bob Abrams. I really enjoyed our conversation over drinks and dinner the other night. Look, I know it's a little sudden and unusual but how about being with me tonight when I do this radio interview?"

She said, "*Tonight?* It's almost nine o'clock and I'm getting ready to watch the ten o'clock news and go to bed."

I said, "You can always do that, but you can't always have this opportunity to be part of a whole scene on the Upper East Side and listen to this interview."

She said, "Oh no, some other time. I need my sleep. I've got a big day tomorrow."

I said, "Oh, come on, that's ridiculous. Come on, you've got to be flexible. It'll be fun! I'll pick you up in an hour, at ten o'clock, and we'll go to the interview."

I was successful in persuading her.

Both of us being the same age, thirty-six, and already having some experience against which to measure these encounters, we were probably reacting in a similar manner. I know that by the end of that second date I was starting to feel: *Gee, this is starting out in an interesting way and maybe our contact and relationship should continue.* Which in fact is what happened. We began to see each other more often, sharing long conversations and events that came up in each other's lives.

I learned that Diane was a religious person and committed to the tenets and traditions of Orthodox Judaism. A considerable amount of our conversation focused on religion and our religious backgrounds.

Diane had a fascinating religious odyssey. She grew up in an Orthodox family, went to a Hebrew day school for the first eight years, strayed from religious observance in her teenage years and then, in the 1970s, returned with strong emotion and conviction. By the time we met, she

had returned to observance of the ritual requirements of the Sabbath and the holidays. She and I had different religious backgrounds and experiences. She grew up in a kosher Orthodox home and I did not. Her family observed the rituals for all of the holidays and mine didn't.

Diane and I had much to talk about in terms of what would happen if we got married. I told her that I had no problem and would indeed be proud to live in a home that was strictly kosher. The more we talked and the longer we knew each other, the more open I was to making the pledge to be home every Friday night for the onset of the Sabbath. I also said that this would be a sharp departure and create a difficult challenge for me. I indicated to her that many functions I attended as Borough president took place on a Friday night, but I was prepared to make that adjustment and commitment.

On the other hand, I couldn't commit to being "shomer Shabbos," which means being home, not traveling, not working, and going to the synagogue every Saturday, praying three times a day, observing every holiday and observing all the rules relating to kosher food outside of our home. Although I respected people who followed this path, it was not me and I just could not do it. Diane accepted that.

I began to worry whether my inability to accept invitations to be with community groups at their functions on Friday evenings was going to hurt me politically. Throughout my career I had demonstrated responsiveness to my constituents by being with them at meetings and special occasions, such as dinners for their organizations. Now I would have to say no and decline those invitations if they occurred on a Friday night. But this was very important for Diane. She felt being together on Friday night was going to be an anchor for our family. She turned out to be 100 percent correct. On my end, I have honored this commitment for more than forty-six years of our marriage. I developed in the office what we called my "Friday night letter" which I sent to organizations that invited me to an event on a Friday night. The letter explained that I made a commitment to my family that I would be home on the onset of the Jewish Sabbath to celebrate the religious rituals associated with a Friday evening and that this was a "sacrosanct" obligation that I undertook. I learned that my constituents respected this practice, did not hold it against me, and indeed admired the faith-oriented principled position I took.

Later in my married life, I saw this play out in a real-life context. I was having a meeting in my office on a Friday afternoon. It happened to be a

group of people from the Black and Hispanic communities. As the meeting continued, and it was getting close to sunset, a man seated next to me leaned over and softly said, "Mr. Abrams, it's getting close to sundown. Don't we have to wrap this up? Don't you have to get home?"

I smiled and said, "Yes." As we were breaking, the man came over to me and said he had read an article in a Bronx weekly that appeared after I was married where I mentioned the commitment I made to my new wife. He said I had made a wise decision.

Diane and I were engaged within a year of our first date.

I told her that I wanted to approach our engagement in a proper way and so I went to her father's office to ask for permission to marry his daughter.

When I sat across from him with Diane at my side, I said, "Mr. Schulder, I want to marry your daughter, do I have your permission?" He responded by emotionally embracing me, at which point I tearfully said, "I will not let you down."

He then picked up the phone and called his wife: "Hilda, are you going to be around in the next couple of hours? I must see you," he said.

"Jack, what is it?" she said. "What is it?"

Mr. Schulder responded, "Just wait for me. I have to talk to you. But I can't discuss it over the phone."

Diane and I accompanied her father to the Schulder home where we gave Hilda the good news. We next went to the Bronx to see my parents and finally to Grandma Ida. I remember when we told my mother that we wanted to become engaged, she raised her hands upward toward the sky and exclaimed: "Thank God! I thought this day would never come!"

As time went on, I saw how much respect Jack and Hilda had garnered in the community because of the way they comported themselves and the quiet leadership that they had demonstrated throughout their lives. While Jack was the leader and front man in the family, there was always Hilda who, quietly working behind the scenes, greatly influenced whatever key decisions were to be made. I felt it admirable that Jack clung to politically and socially progressive values. He would vote against his own economic interests, always supporting Democratic liberal candidates because he felt they were seeking to do social and economic justice.

Although my parents came from a different social and economic setting from Jack and Hilda, the four of them had the greatest relationship with each other. There was tremendous mutual respect and they shared a

core value that they admired and loved their children and would do any-
thing for them.

* * *

Since I was Borough president of the Bronx, I wanted to get married in the
Bronx.

I had said to Diane, "So, what do you think? What kind of a wedding
should we have?"

She'd said, "I don't know, whatever you want."

I had always jokingly said that if I ever got married the wedding would
either take place in Yankee Stadium or in a telephone booth. We began
with the Yankee Stadium model, drawing up a list of potential guests. We
started with categories: relatives, friends, elected officials, party officials,
contributors, religious leaders, civic leaders, and so on. The list was get-
ting to be very, very long and we weren't even halfway finished when I
said, "Oh no, I'm not sure this is going to work, it'll be a zoo!"
So we went in the opposite direction, deciding to have a very small wed-
ding, aka the telephone booth model. It was going to be a private event
with only immediate members of the family and so the invitation list was
kept to forty. We picked the Bronx Botanical Garden, right on the banks
of the Bronx River, as the site for our wedding.

It was an Orthodox Jewish wedding, a very simple but moving cere-
mony, conducted under a chuppah, a canopy held by four people, at the
Lorilard Snuff Mill in the Bronx Botanical Garden. There were no
engraved invitations. The invitation was a simple letter on Diane's letter-
head. There was no professional photographer; a friend of Diane's, Josh
Siderowitz, offered to take the photos. The ceremony was conducted by
Rabbi Gilbert Klaperman, the man who introduced us, assisted by Rabbi
Max Meltzer, the rabbi from my synagogue and Hebrew school in Pelham
Parkway. There was no band. A single accordion player was enough to
create the glorious melodies flowing through the air, which inspired lively
Hebrew dancing, including the lifting of the bride and groom on their
chairs.

The simple refreshments served after the ceremony were sponge cake
and whiskey. The invited guests then left in their cars to drive to Law-
rence, Long Island, for a delicious lunch in Diane's parents' home. There

was more rejoicing, merriment, and dancing to the melodic strains of the accordionist.

The weather was fantastic. It was a sunny, clear, sparkling mid-September afternoon.

Throughout the day, I kept kibitzing with my mother about the perfect weather conditions. Ever since Diane and I had announced that we were going to have an outdoor wedding, several months earlier, I would receive periodic telephone calls from my mother. She would say, "Bobby, go to the window and look outside."

I would say, "Ma, what am I supposed to look for?"

She would reply, "It's pouring outside—what if it rains on September 15?"

I would chuckle and say, "Ma, don't worry. Everything will be all right. It'll be nice." And indeed it was.

PART TWO

ATTORNEY GENERAL

Chapter 14

What's Next?

I T WAS 1974 AND I HAD been Borough president for five years, twice elected. Friends, staffers, and people who shared my agenda urged me to seek a position of greater influence. They were asking with increasing frequency, "What's next, Bob?"

Eventually, I started asking myself the same question. The severe limitations of the office of Borough president were becoming increasingly frustrating for me. I was an activist without the tools at my command to do what was necessary.

The next natural step was to run for mayor of New York, without doubt an important governmental post with the challenge of running the greatest city in the world. But for some reason, the mayoral role didn't get my juices flowing despite encouragement from others and speculation from the media, including a *New York Times Sunday Magazine* cover that featured a number of likely candidates, myself among them. The more I thought about it, the more I set my sights on the office of the New York State attorney general.

The attorney general's office had not been held by a Democrat in decades. Republicans tended to be on the side of the establishment, voted into power by those who had a vested interest in the status quo. It was exciting to think about a Democrat in that office, especially one committed to advancing civil rights as well as environmental justice and consumer protection.

The attorney general's office had the unique ability to get things done, to bring about tangible results, not just platitudinal talk but to obtain concrete action. The attorney general was in a position to have a direct

impact on the daily lives of the state's citizens. This was an office worth pursuing and fighting for.

What good was a civil rights law, passed by the legislature and signed by the governor, if it was never enforced? The attorney general had the unique ability to protect people from discrimination based on physical handicap, age, race, religion, and gender. The attorney general could secure jobs for constituents by demonstrating illegal discrimination and prevent racial steering in the suburbs.

The attorney general could protect consumers by investigating and prosecuting those who were defrauding the public and return money directly to consumers' wallets and pocketbooks.

The attorney general also could protect our environment, making sure that the air we breathe, water we drink, and land upon which we live are free from harmful pollution and prosecute those who poison our environment and endanger our well-being.

The office was held by long-time incumbent Louie Lefkowitz. He was popular, but he was also an establishment Republican who did not maximize the possibilities of that office, rarely tackling big cases. New Yorkers deserved an attorney general who could take on cases that addressed systemic problems affecting significant issues, large numbers of people, and substantial amounts of money.

The obstacles ahead, competing against a strong opponent, going against the regular party, and raising campaign funds, were not unlike those I faced when I ran for assemblyman or Borough president. After considerable reflection and knowing that a favorable outcome was far from guaranteed, I decided I would seek the office of attorney general of New York.

In the months before I formally declared my candidacy, I quietly put together a small staff, working in a modest office, and began to make moves to launch a statewide campaign.

When I ran for Borough president, I had to get to know parts of the Bronx that I had never set foot in before. I was confronting a similar challenge now, but on a massive scale. New York had been my home for my entire life, but I did not know the length and breadth of the Empire State.

New York has seventeen million people, sixty-two counties, and encompasses an enormous land mass measuring hundreds of miles from the tip of Long Island to Niagara County at the Canadian border. People living in Chautauqua County, where Jamestown is located, are closer to

Columbus, the capital of Ohio, than they are to Albany, the capital of New York. Long Island has 2.5 million people in just two counties, Nassau and Suffolk. Westchester County immediately north of New York City has a population of one million. In the southern part of the state, there's a tier of counties along the Pennsylvania border. The Mohawk Valley covers the central part of the state. Then there's the upper part known as the North Country, where the Adirondacks are, and in the west there's Buffalo and Rochester. I had to become familiar with the diverse range of problems confronting the people in all these places, which was hugely intimidating.

I tapped into my network of support from throughout my career and started meeting with party leaders.

My opponent in the Democratic primary for attorney general was Robert Meehan, the district attorney of Rockland County, a suburb twenty-six miles north of New York City. Meehan was trying to take advantage of the growing public concern about crime in New York City and other parts of the state. He would talk about his experience in prosecuting drug dealers and violent criminals, keeping the streets safe for women, children, and the elderly, and his support of the death penalty. The office of attorney general is not the district attorney for the state. The attorney general is the chief *legal* officer and not the chief law enforcement officer. The reality is that the attorney general's office in New York State is essentially a civil office with only marginal white-collar criminal responsibility. One of the challenges I had in my race against Meehan was to educate the public about the role of the attorney general.

The other statewide races were taking shape. Howard Samuels, a wealthy upstate industrialist who had previously sought the nomination for governor, was emerging as the reform candidate for governor. Our campaign reached out to Samuels to see if we could work together and be on the same ticket. He was receptive. As the campaign continued, Samuels was broadening his base and sought and received regular organization support in addition to that of the reformers. He thought he would be able to present himself as the candidate accommodating all elements of the party. With the Democratic Party convention approaching, my campaign manager got a phone call from the Samuels campaign manager, Ken Auletta, who said he had something important to discuss and asked Ethan to meet him for a cup of coffee.

Ethan filled me in later on what was said.

"Ethan," Auletta started. "I have some bad news."

"What is it?"

"Bob can't run," Auletta said. "Bob has to drop out of the race. He can't be on the ticket."

"What are you talking about?" Ethan said.

"We can't have another Jew on the ticket besides Samuels and Levitt," he said. (Arthur Levitt, the long-term comptroller, was running for another term.) "Bob is one Jew too many!"

"That's crazy!" Ethan said, raising his voice.

Samuels had decided he wanted Bob Meehan, an Irish Catholic from Rockland County, on the ticket instead of me "to even things out."

"That makes no sense!" Ethan said. "Bob's put together a great race. He's a popular Borough president, he's well-known, he has a high profile beyond the Bronx— "

"No," Auletta said. "Abrams *has to* drop out. I'm telling you—Abrams is one Jew too many!"

"Oh yeah? Okay," Ethan said, "Well, then it's gonna be *my* Jew that's on the ticket, not *yours.*"

The convention met and the regulars designated Howard Samuels for governor, Mario Cuomo for lieutenant governor, Robert Meehan for attorney general, Arthur Levitt for comptroller, and the mayor of Syracuse, Lee Alexander, for United State senator.

I was so angry at Samuels for stabbing me in the back that I aligned myself with Congressman Hugh Carey, who was running for governor as an independent candidate with the support of the *New York Post.* We cross-endorsed each other and did commercials together. We became political allies and good friends.

The party leaders had put together an ethnically and geographically balanced ticket, but they failed to take into account the public's impatience with boss-controlled politics as contrasted with the appeal of candidates who displayed independence. In a dazzling upset, the entire ticket went down except for Arthur Levitt, who had no primary opponent. Every candidate for statewide office endorsed by the party lost in that primary.

Hugh Carey beat Howard Samuels. Mary Anne Krupsak, a state senator from Canajoharie in upstate New York, beat both Mario Cuomo and Antonio Olivieri, a member of the New York City Council, who was also in the race. Ramsey Clark beat Lee Alexander and Allard Lowenstein. I beat Bob Meehan. The four of us were far from an old-line ticket put together by party

bosses in a smoke-filled back room or a big convention center. We were a ticket selected by the people in an open democratic primary. The morning after the primary results were in, there was an electrifying press conference at the Waldorf-Astoria with the four of us, each excitedly talking about this amazing ticket chosen by the people and not the bosses.

In the general election, Carey beat interim governor Malcom Wilson. I ran a strong, close race for attorney general but lost. I did, however, beat Lefkowitz in New York City, something that had never happened to him before, and cut one million votes off of his previous margin of victory. Lefkowitz was a Republican but also had Liberal party support, which proved to be decisive.

Sometimes when you lose a race your career is over, but in this instance it was clear that I had a strong showing, displaying credibility and potential for the future.

I went back to being Borough president. A couple of weeks after the election, I was in my office when I received a call from Governor-elect Hugh Carey. "Bob!"

"Yes, Governor," I replied.

"Counsel! Counsel! The word is Counsel!" he said.

Sometimes he spoke in riddles and this to me was another riddle. I didn't know what he was talking about. I said, "I don't understand you, Governor. What do you mean?"

"I want you to be my counsel! Counsel to the governor!"

I said, "Oh, Governor, that's very gracious of you. I really appreciate it, but it's not for me. I'm planning to run for attorney general again in four years with the Bronx as my base. I think I'll have a shot."

* * *

A funny incident occurred after the 1974 campaign for attorney general. It was the summer of 1975. Diane and I were sharing a rental house on Shelter Island with my friend Rene Plessner, my Columbia College classmate who had helped me on my campaigns and was the best man at our wedding. It was a beautiful spot on Southold Bay, a small cottage with a couple of bedrooms. I had first learned about Shelter Island during my campaigning with Hugh Carey the previous year. He had a house on the island called Westmoreland Farm, the place that he and his large family went to get away from the hurly-burly of political life.

We were enjoying our last week at the house before Labor Day. The phone rang and Diane answered it. Rene and I were sitting in chairs near the water, reading and chatting. Diane opened the screen door and yelled: "Bob, the phone—it's for you!" As I approached the doorway, Diane said, "It's Pat Cunningham."

As soon as she uttered those words, I started thinking, *Pat Cunningham? Why would he be calling me?* Pat Cunningham was my archenemy. He was the Democratic boss of the Bronx, the successor to Charlie Buckley and Henry McDonough, the old-line bosses of the Bronx Democratic machine. When Hugh Carey got elected, he designated Cunningham to be the Democratic Party's state chairman, so he was now a very powerful force in politics, serving as a confidant to the governor, state party chairman, and Bronx County chairman. I had been very disappointed that Carey selected Cunningham to be the state chairman because that was a bow to the regular organization. Carey had won the primary nomination against the organization leaders.

Diane, who had become not only my partner in life but also my partner in politics and thus got to know everything that was going on in my political life, handed me the phone with a quizzical look and a shrug of the shoulders, indicating, *What's this all about?* Of course, I was wondering the same thing.

I said "Hello" into the phone and the voice on the other end said, "Robert! It's Pat Cunningham."

"Pat," I said, "how are you doing? What's going on?"

He said, "Everything's great with me. How about with you?"

I said, "Same here. I'm back hard at work tackling the tough problems of the Bronx. Everything's good."

Pat said, "Robert, do you know what's happening in a couple of weeks?"

"No. What are you talking about?" I asked.

"Robert! The judicial convention is coming up!"

I said, "Oh."

There's a judicial convention held periodically at which State Supreme Court judges are nominated. It's a very controlled operation whereby the county leader/boss decides who he wants to give the judgeships to and then delegates go to the convention and robotically implement and rubber-stamp the will of the county leader. Throughout my career I opposed this process, saying there should be a more accountable system for selecting judges by either direct election by the voters or through a merit appointment system.

Pat said, "Robert, how would you like to be a Supreme Court Justice?"

I said, "Pat, that's very generous of you but I'm not interested in being a judge. I'm thirty-seven years old. I've got a lot of energy in me and being a judge is very sedentary. Frankly, it's pretty boring. I'm going to run for attorney general again three years from now, in 1978. But look, I really appreciate your offer."

"Robert! *Robert*," he said, "do you realize what I'm saying? I'm offering you the chance to become a Justice of the New York State Supreme Court—for a fourteen-year term. Do you know how many people would kill for this opportunity? The prestige and the power of being a Supreme Court Justice?"

"Pat, I really, really appreciate your offer," I said, "but it's not for me. I'm not interested."

"Robert!" he said. (No one calls me Robert so this whole conversation was slightly surreal.) "Robert—your wife, she's a lawyer, isn't she? Isn't your wife a lawyer?"

"Yes."

"So," he said, "how about two judgeships?"

I burst out laughing, saying, "Pat—Pat, you're most generous but I've got to tell you, I'm not interested."

We both cordially said goodbye and I hung up.

Cunningham was so anxious to get me out of the Bronx, to get me out of his hair—if I vacated the Borough president's office, he would control the filling of the vacancy and put in his guy—that he was offering two judgeships to end my political career. Given the exciting life I had for the next twenty years, I have never regretted not accepting his offer.

Even though I had a very full plate as Borough president of the Bronx, I was able to utilize whatever spare time I had in the next four years to build on the good will established in my 1974 run in preparation for the 1978 race. People began reaching out to me, indicating that they wanted to help in my next campaign. I kept a file of all of those offers, knowing that they would come in handy.

One of the lessons I learned from my 1974 race was that I needed a strong finance chairman in order to raise sufficient funds for both the primary and general elections. Luckily, Larry Buttenwieser, who had an outstanding reputation as a lawyer and who was a community-minded person involved in philanthropic causes, agreed to take on that role. His

participation was a key component to my next campaign's success. Larry helped me conceptualize a fundraising plan, spent untold hours raising money for both the primary and general election, and, by the end of the campaign, became a lifelong friend. Never once in all the years we worked together did he ask me to do anything for him personally. He took me on as a benevolent cause. I was very proud of that and determined to never let him down.

In 1976, I again became active in the presidential race by leading Indiana Senator Birch Bayh's campaign in New York. He had demonstrated a strong ability for a progressive Democrat to win in a conservative Republican state. He had authored two US Constitutional amendments, passed anti-crime legislation dealing with juvenile justice and legislation barring gender discrimination, was pro-choice, and was pro-Israel. This was a good profile for me. Unfortunately, Bayh performed poorly in early primaries and dropped out of the race before the New York primary took place. Jimmy Carter ultimately won the nomination.

* * *

In 1978, successfully building on the base of support I developed in my first run for attorney general, I was going into the Democratic state convention without facing a strong primary opponent. Then, at the eleventh hour, the day before the convention, we heard rumors that the regulars planned to support Judge Dolores Denman from Buffalo, who was serving on the Appellate Division. It felt like a repeat of four years earlier when last-minute deals threatened to undermine my campaign. However, the reform and independent delegates who were committed to me held firm and we squeaked out a 52 percent victory. Denman got more than the required 25 percent of convention votes to qualify to run in the primary.

Despite the fact that Denman was a woman, based upon my record as a strong advocate for women's issues, I garnered support from virtually all of the leading women elected officials in the state. It turned out to be a solid victory with my getting 67 percent of the primary vote. I was aided by the fact that there was a newspaper strike in the New York City area and so my unknown opponent was not able to muster needed coverage and recognition.

In the general election, as hoped, Louie Lefkowitz decided not to seek reelection, which created a genuine opportunity for me to capture the

seat. My opponent was the Republican and Conservative party candidate Michael Roth, who had never before run for public office. He was a well-spoken, Westchester lawyer in his late forties who graduated from Yale and Columbia Law School. His only record of public service was his appointment as chairman of the New York State Liquor Authority where he served for almost four years.

We had several statewide debates during which I emphasized my intention to be a consumer champion and environmental protector, and my commitment to appointing lawyers as assistant attorneys general on the basis of merit as opposed to patronage. Roth pointed to his experience growing his private practice law firm and running the State Liquor Authority. He also emphasized his support of the death penalty, which I opposed.

On election night, my family and significant supporters gathered for drinks and food at the apartment of Ben and Helen Buttenwieser, Larry's parents, as the polls were closing. Afterward, we went to the Warwick Hotel to watch the returns come in and, if all went well, to celebrate.

Our campaign won 56 percent to 44 percent, enabling me to be the first Democrat elected as attorney general in New York State in forty years.

Chapter 15

Fresh Air

O N MY FIRST DAY AS ATTORNEY general of New York, Stan Brooks, a veteran reporter for WINS, the all-news radio station, interviewed me at my office on the forty-seventh floor of Two World Trade Center. He put the microphone in front of me and asked, "What's it like being the attorney general, Bob?"

I said, "Stan, it's thrilling! I'm looking out the window with you now at the Statue of Liberty, and I'm thinking about how my grandparents escaped from Eastern Europe, fleeing oppression. They were on a ship that passed that statue, and now their grandson is the attorney general of New York. What an incredible country this is. It's a true land of opportunity that gives everybody a chance to dream and work toward the fulfillment of those dreams. Of course, who knows if my grandparents actually saw the Statue of Liberty—they may not have been able to get up to the deck to see it. They may have been stuck down in steerage!"

It was also thrilling because I was determined to bring change to the office of attorney general.

Even though my predecessor, Louie Lefkowitz, was a popular guy, his office was not known to uniformly have first-rate lawyers. It was no secret that Lefkowitz had hired a significant number of assistant attorneys general through the patronage system.

I faced a decision about what to do with the Lefkowitz appointees in the office that I was about to inherit. Two attorneys general with excellent reputations and experience in Massachusetts and Michigan gave me conflicting advice. One suggested I take my time to evaluate each of the lawyers I was inheriting before making any decisions, while the other

encouraged me to fire everyone and bring in my own appointees and start with a fresh slate.

My instinct was to take the moderate approach: assess the current staff, find out issues that needed immediate attention, make sure things didn't fall between the cracks, and get a firm grip on the office.

The size and scale of the job was becoming clear and I had a lot to learn. There were large bureaus based in Manhattan at Two World Trade Center that handled a significant amount of work for the office, such as the Litigation Bureau, which had responsibility for the defensive cases—the lawsuits brought against the state. There were also the affirmative bureaus: Antitrust, Civil Rights, Consumer Protection, Real Estate Finance, Investor Protection, Environmental Protection, Charities, and Labor. In Albany, there were a large number of lawyers who handled appellate work, litigation, claims, opinions, and environment. There also was a network of twelve regional offices across the state that handled defensive cases and local consumer problems.

I appointed a three-member blue ribbon panel: Whitney North Seymour Jr., a Republican former United States attorney for the Southern District; Adrian DeWind, a past president of the New York City Bar Association; and Nicholas Scopetta, former investigations commissioner for the City of New York and a former assistant US attorney in the Southern District. I asked the three of them to sit with me while I interviewed every bureau chief that I was inheriting. We spent an hour and a half with each of the bureau chiefs. The judgment of these highly respected lawyers who had decades of experience in the public and private sectors was invaluable. After each interview we compared impressions.

I set out to attract the best people to join the office. I sent out word that a new day was on the horizon and encouraged people to apply for positions. Soon we were drowning in resumes submitted by fantastic candidates from both the public and private sectors. It was impressive to see lawyers who worked in private law firms willing to take big cuts in salary to come to work in the attorney general's office. To help implement the process of merit selection, I created a position of director of recruitment and training whose responsibility it was, together with bureau chiefs and division heads, to review resumes, interview candidates, and make recommendations to me. I made it a point to personally interview every candidate who passed the screening process. By the time I left office, I had conducted 675 personal interviews. There were hundreds of lawyers spread

throughout the state working as assistant attorneys general. Since they were not going to see me that often, I felt it was important that they spend some time with me at the very beginning to get a sense of what motivates me. To this day I meet former staff lawyers who say, "Do you remember that interview? I'll never forget it as long as I live. I sat with you for an hour and you did this and you said that!" And most of the time I do remember.

* * *

Early on, the resume of a man named Peter Yellen crossed my desk. I had never seen or heard of him before, but it was a stellar resume. He graduated from Columbia College and Columbia Law School, spent three years in the Marine Corps in the Judge Advocate General's Office, and served as public defender in Broome County and Monroe County in upstate New York. I arranged to meet him the next day. When he showed up, I saw a man with short cropped hair and a military bearing. I found him to be extremely intelligent and earnest, and I hired him on the spot to help me with the regional offices.

I said, "Peter, here's your mandate and your mission—we're going to make decisions on the merits. Whatever is the right thing to do, that's what we're going to do. I have this large network of regional offices. You're my man reviewing those offices. I want you to go from city to city, from office to office, interview every single person. I want you to talk to the president of the local bar association, judges, district attorneys, public defenders, US attorneys and find out what they think about the head of the office and the lawyers in the office. I want a report for every office."

He got right to work and pretty soon I started to get these reports. Based upon what Peter recommended, I took action.

A few weeks after Peter began his work, he came to me and said, "Bob, I have a test of your mandate to me. The head of the office in Broome County is not so great and I have a recommendation for you based upon everything you told me to do. I'm recommending you appoint as the head of that office John Marshall, who is the district attorney of Chenango County which, as you know, is next to Broome County. But Bob, I want you to understand that he's the elected *Republican* district attorney."

I said, "Peter, I gave you a mandate, you're telling me he's the best candidate for the job, that you've investigated and searched and you feel

he's the man who could do the best job for the people and for me—then that's what we're going to do."

I set up an appointment to meet John Marshall. It was obvious during the interview that everything Peter had told me was true. I offered him the job and he accepted it. He was not flashy but very solid and earnest. John did an outstanding job. He was a sincere, dedicated, loyal, and effective public servant. He worked for me for ten years and in fact died of a heart attack at his desk.

Not surprisingly, the announcement of my appointment of John created a furor within the Democratic Party. The Broome County Democratic Chairman called me on the phone. "What are you doing?" he said. "You're the first Democrat to be attorney general in decades! Are you a madman appointing an elected Republican district attorney? You're a turncoat! You're a traitor!"

I stood my ground, saying, "The people of New York should only be represented by the best talent possible."

Some time later, Peter came to me to discuss the Syracuse office. "Bob," he said, "I've got to tell you, there is a vacancy for the head of the Syracuse office. The county leader has come to see me, the mayor has come to see me—they have a candidate. I don't think that candidate is the right choice. They're applying pressure and trying to foist this guy on you."

I found this out myself soon enough. Mayor Lee Alexander called me and said he would like to come to New York City to meet with me. When he walked into my office a few days later, the Onondaga County Democratic chairman was with him. They indicated that they were supporting someone to head the Syracuse office. The mayor said the candidate had a lot of experience and would be a good choice. Then the county chairman said, "I know we weren't with you in the primary but we worked hard for you in the general election and we're here today to tell you we really want this guy appointed."

They finished making their pitch, which they seemed to think was all they had to do to get their man hired. I said, "Well, I'll have to take it under advisement. You know I have a talent scout, he's interviewed your man and he's not given the highest grade to him. I will talk to him again and get back to you."

As soon as they left, I called Peter and asked him, "Do you have somebody else?"

He said, "Frankly, I don't have anyone."

I came up with an idea. I called the dean of Syracuse Law School, introduced myself, and said, "I have to appoint a new head of the attorney general's office in Syracuse. There are several people who applied for the job, but none of the candidates are of the quality and stature we are looking for. I'm committed to improving the quality of that office. Is there somebody on your faculty you can recommend to me who would find this job interesting and challenging?"

The dean said, "I'll get back to you."

A few days later, he called me back and recommended Tom Maroney, an antitrust professor. I interviewed Maroney, and I liked him a lot. He was not only highly intelligent and experienced, but he had a warm and engaging personality. I appointed him. Tom Maroney turned out to be first rate. He was so highly regarded that after his service as the head of the attorney general's Syracuse office, President Clinton appointed him the United States attorney for the Western District of New York in 1994.

Several months later, Peter called me. "There's a vacancy for a line position in Albany in the Court of Claims Bureau," he said, "and you're going to be sent the resume of Jim King. After you see him, let's talk."

When King's resume arrived a few days later, I couldn't believe what I was seeing. King had been a brigadier general in the Marine Corps and ran the Judge Advocate General program for the United States Marines, which involved over 1,500 lawyers worldwide.

On the day of the interview, in walked an impressive and distinguished-looking man. Graying hair, impeccably dressed, and shoes that were spit-shined. We had a very nice conversation, which rattled me a bit because in every other sentence King would use the word "sir": "Yes, sir!" "No, sir!"

He had these amazing credentials. After college he was commissioned a second lieutenant in the US Marine Corps. When he left active duty, he went to Albany Law School and after graduation he returned to the Marine Corps. Following a tour of duty in Vietnam, he was selected to attend George Washington University to receive an LLM (master's degree in law). Along the way, he earned decorations and citations, including the Bronze Star, and he wound up as the director of the Judge Advocate Division.

I said to him, "You realize that the position that you are interviewing for is a staff line position in the Court of Claims bureau?"

"Yes, sir!"

I said, "Wait a minute—are you understanding me correctly?—you would be a staff lawyer reporting to a section chief who reports to a deputy bureau chief who repots to the bureau chief."

"Yes, sir."

I said, "You're telling me that after being a brigadier general in the US Marine Corps and supervising 1,500 lawyers in the Judge Advocate General Division, you are applying for a simple line position?"

"Yes, sir! I would be honored to be given an opportunity to serve in that position."

I said, "Don't you think you are overqualified for that spot?"

"Sir, there are many things that I would have to learn to appropriately handle those cases."

I countered: "Don't you think you would be bored handling those kinds of cases? The claims filed against the state are generally contract cases or negligence cases for injuries at state facilities, or other situations whereby it is alleged that New York State is at fault."

"No, sir! I would be honored to have such an opportunity. But sir," he continued, "I do have something to tell you if I may—"

"What is it?" I asked.

He said, "Sir, I want you to know that I am a Republican."

I said, "That doesn't matter to me. I'm running a nonpartisan office. I don't ask about people's political affiliations. I hire the best candidates I can find."

"Well, sir, I felt I had an obligation to tell you that."

I called Peter Yellen and said, "King is absolutely a fantastic candidate. Let's give it a shot."

I hired Jim King. Although he had never handled state claims before, he quickly grasped the issues and did outstanding work. When vacancies arose in the bureau, I kept promoting him and eventually appointed him to be bureau chief, a position at which he continued to excel. Eventually he became a Court of Claims judge appointed by the governor.

* * *

Another important message had to be sent about decision-making. Word needed to be communicated to the staff in the clearest way that all decisions were to be made on the merits. It didn't matter who was the subject of

an investigation, whether that person or company was prominent, or powerful, or active in politics, or a campaign contributor to me. Every decision was going to be based on the answer to the question, "What is the right thing to do?" No preferential treatment for anyone.

I did something that no statewide elected official ever did. When it came time for my reelection campaign, I banned contributions by anyone who worked in the office. I put out a memo stating: "It is forbidden for any employee or his or her spouse to contribute to my campaign." The usual practice was to have employees help the campaign of the public officeholder they worked for by either making a contribution or taking responsibility for selling tickets for the officeholder's campaign dinner. I didn't want people to get involved in potential conflicts of interest or feel that someone in the office got promoted to a bureau chief position because he or she sold tables at the attorney general's dinner.

I also sent out a memo discouraging people from being involved in the campaign. I was the politician. I was the one who was going to be out there on the campaign trail. Everyone else in the office was a public servant who should pay attention to their public responsibilities and not be involved in my reelection campaigns.

I picked able people who worked very hard and who were prepared to do good things for the people of New York. I knew that as the head of the office I would benefit from that. The office would compile a strong record of achievement and I could proudly run on that record.

Hiring women was high on my list of priorities. More women were graduating from law school. When my wife graduated from Columbia Law School in 1964, there were only six women in her section and eleven women in the entire class. Today, over 50 percent of students in law schools are women. When I took over the attorney general's office in 1979, this revolution was just starting to take place. With more women becoming lawyers, a problem started emerging that still exists today: How do women who want to be professionals balance their careers with the pressures of starting and raising families?

Women in the office came to me and suggested we start a job-sharing program in which two people on a single line would work with full health benefits.

I had formed an executive committee of high-ranking people within the office, the heads of divisions and my executive assistants with whom I met with every week, and I took this idea to them. We kicked it around

and some were for it, but some expressed hesitation. Those who were for it said, "That's a great idea, it's progressive, that's what we should be doing."

Others were saying, "Sure it's a great idea but we are a litigating agency—how can you have a woman work three days a week? What if there is a month-long trial?

Disagreeing with the naysayers, I challenged many of their arguments and concluded that not only was it the right thing to do, but it was ultimately good for the office because we retained women who normally might have left. We also attracted first-rate women to come to our office because this opportunity wasn't available to them either in the private sector or other public law offices.

It was also important to have the office better reflect the population of the state by increasing diversity. Out of five hundred lawyers, there were only six minority lawyers when I took over the office. I was determined to hire quality lawyers of all races and cultures. By the time I completed my service as attorney general, we had 15–20 percent minority hires and 50 percent of the people working in my office were women. I appointed women and minority community members to the highest posts in the office, such as division heads, bureau chiefs, heads of regional offices, and, for the first time in state history, an African American solicitor general, Jerry Boone, was appointed. When Jerry left the office a few years later, I appointed another member of the African American community, Peter Sherwood, to succeed him.

Another significant effort undertaken was to restructure the office to make it operate more efficiently and more transparently. I called on the Institute of Judicial Administration to conduct a study of the way in which the office was organized and to make recommendations for changes. It issued a report calling for consolidation of existing bureaus and the creation of three separate divisions for the office: Counsel for the State, with the responsibility of defending the state agencies in all lawsuits brought against the state; Appeals and Opinions, to be given the responsibility for handling all of the statewide appellate work as well as the many opinions which would be rendered each year; and Public Advocacy, to launch the major affirmative initiatives such as investigations, reports, and lawsuits relating to protecting the citizens of New York.

* * *

In the statewide attorney general race, I had a few liabilities—I was from New York City, I was a Democrat, and I was Jewish, hardly representative of all the individuals who make up New York State. It was very important for my constituents to get to know me better and to understand my priorities. I made a pledge that during my term, I would visit each of New York's sixty-two counties. I honored that pledge and even visited many counties multiple times. During my upstate travels, I'd stop by the local newspaper to introduce myself to the editors, explaining what I had done since taking office. These appearances early on in my term seemed to surprise people. They expected politicians to make one stop during campaign season every four years to try to get editorial support. Soon, they learned they could count on my regular visits.

As a result of my travels, I saw firsthand there were major issues the office wasn't addressing. For example, farming communities were suffering, so I created a position for a liaison to the agricultural community who could represent their interests.

Every summer from the time I was elected, I took four or five days to drive to different parts of the state with my wife and daughters to visit the local sites. Traveling around the state as a family had the added benefit of bringing us closer together.

On one trip to Chemung County, I remember talking to my daughter Rachel, nine years old at the time, about our upcoming visit to the National Soaring Museum. I said, "So, look, we're going to go to this place where there are gliders. Do you know what a glider is? It's an airplane that has no motor, it has no engine, but it glides—the wind carries it. Gliders were used during World War II to bring troops where they were needed. They used gliders because they're silent. You can get in a glider and cross enemy lines without being noticed." I told her everything I could think of about gliders and then I said, "Listen, we're going to make a stop there, and I suspect the person from the glider museum is going to say: 'Would you like to go up in a glider?' And I don't think we want to go up in a glider. All right? We have a tight schedule with other stops to make so we don't have time for a glider flight. So the answer is no. Okay?"

"Okay!" she responded.

Of course the reason I wanted Rachel to agree was because I was terrified at the prospect of going up in a glider.

Sure enough, the woman from the museum showed us around and then she took us to the field next to the museum. "This is where the

gliders are kept," she said. "How would you guys like to go up for a ride in a glider?"

Rachel said, "Oh, yes! Yes, Daddy—say yes!"

I gave Rachel a *look* to let her know that that was not the answer we agreed on.

Each of us went up in different gliders. I ended up being glad that she didn't listen to me because it was phenomenal being up there. It's quiet, you're gliding along, looking at the rolling hills and the plains and the sky. It was an unforgettable experience.

We also went to minor league baseball games, museums, saw glass blowing displays, visited Mark Twain's home, and toured historic sites such as the National Women's Hall of Fame in Seneca Falls. My favorite stops were at the county fairs across the state—something I never got to experience as a city kid. Those family excursions increased my appreciation for life outside of New York City and helped me better understand those I was serving.

An upstater, John Sullivan, gave me a great idea which we adopted—to have staff from my regional offices go to adjacent counties where there wasn't an office of the attorney general. We did not have the budget to open an office in every county, but this idea enabled us for the first time to give people in every county direct access to the attorney general's office. At a given time on a given day in a fixed location, people would have an opportunity to meet with a representative of the office.

As I eventually ran for second, third, and fourth term reelections, these trips continued to pay off, helping me to win solid Republican counties.

Taking charge of the office and helping shape it to my priorities and my vision was exciting. It was all about bringing fresh air into the office. Ordinary working people did not have the resources and tools to wage the battles I intended to fight. Now, the citizens of New York, through their attorney general backed up by talented and highly motivated lawyers, were going to be ready to enter the fray and even win some of those battles.

But before I get into that, I believe some background and history on the office might be helpful.

Chapter 16

Evolution of the Attorney General's Office

THE OFFICE OF ATTORNEY GENERAL IS a fascinating governmental institution, dating back to the earliest days of the American colonies. After the English seized New Amsterdam from the Dutch in 1664, the Duke of York, on the order of his brother, King Charles II, established the colony of New York. It was determined at the outset that a lawyer representing the sovereign would take care of the king's legal interests including appearing on his behalf in court. A similar pattern occurred in the other colonies.

After the American Revolution, the role of the sovereign's legal representative was carried over, and it was the office of the attorney general that represented the new democratically elected government of the state. That defensive role of the attorney general was carried forth for the next 175 years. During that time, state constitutional conventions took place and in many instances the office of attorney general was changed from an appointed one to an elected post. Today, most states elect their attorney general. (There are a handful of exceptions: In New Hampshire, Wyoming, Alaska, Hawaii, and New Jersey, the governor appoints the attorney general; in Maine, the legislature selects the attorney general every two years; and in Tennessee, the Supreme Court selects the attorney general for a fixed term of eight years.) The fact that the attorney general in most states had to run for office meant that the office would have to answer not just to the state government it was to represent, but also to the electorate at large. As time went on this would have an impact on the role of the attorney general.

In the 1960s, a number of attorneys general, in addition to their defensive work, crafted an affirmative role whereby they were launching consumer, civil rights, and environmental initiatives. State legislatures and the federal government were passing statutes placing authority in the offices of attorneys general to protect the rights of citizens. With these powers in hand, together with constitutional authority and common law principles, attorneys general were empowered to take affirmative enforcement action. The definition of the role played by the attorney general was gradually expanding. The attorney general was no longer viewed as exclusively responsible for defending the state government but also took on the role of protecting the citizens of the state, the people, and thereby the public interest.

Over the past forty years, the office of attorney general has been further and more dramatically transformed from a low-key, back-seat, governmental player to a frontline significant force for change, capable of altering the status quo. I feel privileged to have been a significant part of that transformation.

Two years after I took office, Ronald Reagan was elected president on a laissez-faire platform of getting the government off the back of business. He was true to his word in implementing that policy. His appointees were committed to non-enforcement of federal laws. The chief of the Antitrust Division expressly stated that he was not going to enforce the antitrust laws and indeed advocated repeal of the Sherman and Clayton Acts, which have been the cornerstone ensuring free and open competition for business in the United States for a century, going back to the trust-busting days of Teddy Roosevelt. The administrator of the Environmental Protection Agency (EPA) rolled back and stopped enforcing the environmental protection laws. The head of the Civil Rights Division reversed course on civil rights cases in the midst of key litigation. The chief of the Occupational Safety and Health Administration simply ignored the federal government's obligation to enforce laws aimed at ensuring a safe workplace for employees. The head of the Federal Trade Commission put that consumer watchdog to sleep. In the first six years of the Reagan FTC, not a single false advertising case was brought against a company, a sharp break from the kind of enforcement action that had been a regular staple of the agency in years past.

As the head of a large state attorney general's office, with significant staff and a strong commitment to enforcing the law to maximize the benefit for the citizenry, I indicated to fellow attorneys general across the country

that I was willing to share resources and work cooperatively with them. We needed to bring cases to protect our state's citizens against this national policy of non-enforcement of laws. In a nonpartisan way, my colleagues and I began to launch joint investigations and pursue joint prosecutions. We stepped into the breach at the state level and filled the vacuum that had been created by the failure of the federal government to enforce the law. Just as states had been laboratories for progressive legislation in the early part of the century, so we would become laboratories for legal progress in the latter part of the century. I also informed my colleagues that in New York we were establishing *parens patriae* authority, asserting the right of the attorney general to go to court to protect the rights of citizens in the areas of the environment, consumer protection, and civil rights. The federal courts sustained our right to pursue these cases.

I organized the northeastern states to join together to combat the acid rain that was destroying our lakes and fish life by filing lawsuits against the Environmental Protection Agency for failure to enforce the Clean Air Act. Power plants in the Midwest were burning high sulfur coal and were being allowed to generate huge quantities of sulfur and nitrogen compounds which were carried by the wind and dropped over the lakes of the Northeast.

I also worked with literally every state in the union to file lawsuits under federal antitrust laws to combat consumer fraud, such as "resale price maintenance" (in plain English, price-fixing) which was robbing consumers of the opportunity to purchase products at the lowest possible prices. We shared information with our sister states and brought lawsuits to halt deceptive and false advertising of goods in the marketplace. This cooperation among the states was unprecedented and set the tone for collective action for decades to come.

We put in place a mechanism that enabled this kind of group activity to become a permanent part of the daily workings of offices of state attorneys general. We had regular meetings and conference calls to share information and plans for investigations and lawsuits. We circulated amicus briefs so that multiple states would have their voices heard in precedent-setting cases before the United States Supreme Court. We asked public interest advocacy groups to join as parties in our lawsuits and they did.

These cooperative relationships did not disappear when Ronald Reagan left office. Cooperation and joint enforcement became a permanent

part of the operations and functioning of the offices of state attorneys general and were evidenced during subsequent Democratic as well as Republican administrations.

In the post-Reagan era, as discussed in the antitrust chapter which follows, the states began to work cooperatively with federal agencies such as the Antitrust Division of the Department of Justice, and the Federal Trade Commission, creating for the first time an Executive Working Group whereby information was shared and joint investigations and prosecutions were launched. We designed cross-deputization programs allowing the states to deputize federal prosecutors to work on their cases, and the feds could deputize state prosecutors to work on theirs. We also introduced joint training programs.

Because of the collective power of various states working together, the influence of attorneys general on major public policy matters can be significant. For example, while Congress, the Centers for Disease Control, the American Medical Association, and public health organizations allowed smoking to proliferate in our nation for decades, causing illness and death, as well as extraordinary financial expense to the taxpayers resulting from hospital costs, state attorneys general mounted attacks against the tobacco industry. Several years after I left office, the states, in cooperation with each other, brought individual actions alleging cigarette manufacturers marketed their product while knowing, and without adequately informing consumers, that it was addictive and could cause cancer. The Tobacco Master Settlement Agreement that forty-six states entered into with the companies enabled more than $200 billion to go to the treasuries of the states to compensate for medical costs for citizens with smoking-related cancer conditions and other illnesses traced to smoking.

Just as importantly, it imposed restrictions on the future sale and marketing of cigarettes. Under the agreement, the five major settling tobacco companies could not advertise and promote their products targeting youth. It barred marketing in entertainment media, limited free distribution of cigarettes, and prevented the industry from hiding negative information about smoking. This has had a huge impact on public health by reducing the use of harmful tobacco products.

During the mortgage foreclosure crisis and the predatory lending scandal, the attorneys general, by means of investigations and lawsuit settlements, likewise carved out a significant role in overseeing the activities

of banks and financial institutions. Widespread reforms as well as fines and restitution emerged from the investigations. As a result of these successful activist efforts, attorneys general were given increased standing to become key players in the regulatory process and specific authorization in the Dodd Frank Act to enforce rules promulgated by the federal Consumer Financial Protection Bureau.

Attorneys general through litigation were also responsible for a major shift in the way the pharmaceutical industry priced and marketed its products. Again, this occurred after years of failure by administrative agencies and a gridlocked Congress to take corrective action.

During his time in office, President Trump sought to limit the entry of visitors from foreign nations or immigration from certain countries. His administration pursued the separation of parents from children concerning visa issues. It was the state attorneys general who took the lead to halt these efforts. As the Trump administration, like the Reagan administration decades before, sought to gut environmental, consumer, and worker protection, it was the state attorneys general who sought to block those tactics with officials like Letitia James, the attorney general of New York, taking the lead. Bob Ferguson, the attorney general of the state of Washington, and Doug Chin, the former attorney general of Hawaii, brought lawsuits challenging the Trump administration's Muslim travel ban.

Josh Shapiro, the attorney general of Pennsylvania, issued a grand jury report in 2018 indicating that more than a thousand children were victimized sexually by three hundred Catholic priests throughout Pennsylvania and that the predator priests were protected by an institutional cover-up. Shortly thereafter, New York, Delaware, Florida, Missouri, and other states announced they were opening up statewide investigations into similar issues. In 2019, the pope issued an edict calling Catholic hierarchy from all parts of the globe to attend a summit in Rome to discuss and implement actions to deal with and prevent sexual abuses by priests against innocent children and others. Thus, once again, it was the office of state attorney general exercising leadership to act on an issue of extraordinary importance, which backed up stories emanating out of Boston about miscreant priests which previously escaped scrutiny and action by other institutional and governmental actors.

As the opioid epidemic continues to proliferate, taking the lives of increasing numbers of our citizens, it is state attorneys general who are launching investigations to establish culpability and seek deterrence.

The state attorney general's office has become a major force protecting the average citizen in the country. Attorneys general are now the guardians of basic legal protections that are important every day to citizens in every state. This is a far cry from the invisible, inert office of attorney general of decades past. No wonder that so many attorneys general have been recognized for their leadership and have gone on to higher state and federal office.

The pages that follow recount some of my efforts in various substantive areas, as well as some interesting and diverse cases that we undertook during the fifteen years that I served as attorney general of New York.

Chapter 17

Love Canal

PROTECTING NEW YORK'S ENVIRONMENT WAS A high priority during my
tenure as attorney general and it was important to have the right per-
son to help undertake that effort. In searching for an Environmental
Bureau chief, I gave my staff a general outline of the kind of person I was
looking for. It had to be someone with the competence, moxie, and pas-
sion to blaze a path for strong environmental enforcement.

A few weeks later, I found myself looking at the resume of Marcia
Cleveland. She'd graduated from Wellesley College and Yale Law School,
had worked in Legal Services, and was currently at the Natural Resources
Defense Council, a well-respected advocacy organization, doing import-
ant litigation. I could see why several key aides were convinced that she
was the person we were looking for.

When the day came for the interview, I remember asking myself as
Marcia was escorted into my office, *is this the person who's going to be able
to bring the Love Canal lawsuit?* I knew that soon we would be suing to
clean up Love Canal.

"How badly do you want this job?" I asked Marcia when I interviewed
her.

"More than any other job in the world," she replied. "I know the pow-
ers of the attorney general's office and I know the kind of impact an activ-
ist attorney general can have on the environment for New York and in
helping to shape environmental policy for the country."

I challenged her throughout our conversation. "Look," I remember
saying, "we're going to be up against powerful adversaries. We're going to
be outgunned. The big corporations that we're going to take on will have

the resources to hire the best law firms. They'll outnumber us and will try to intimidate us. Do you think we'll be able to stand toe to toe and not only take them on, but prevail?"

She said, "Absolutely! We may have to fight to get some more resources but I know we can get the job done and become a leader in bringing about policy changes that the country desperately needs. I know we can make a difference."

I hired Marcia in March 1979, and we began to create and implement an important agenda. The first item was Love Canal, a graphic and tragic example of our society's immoral indifference to the destruction of our environment. It was a reminder that careless actions, routinely and reck-lessly taken by corporate executives, endangered health and put many lives at risk.

Love Canal was a neighborhood in the city of Niagara Falls named for William T. Love, a late nineteenth-century entrepreneur from the West-ern Railroad Corporation. Love's plan for a model community included the creation of factories and the construction of a canal. The water flow-ing through the canal would be used by those factories to generate their own electricity, a standard practice at the time. But once Westinghouse and others solved the problem of transmitting electricity over significant distances, there was no longer a need for a local power source and on-site generation. The planned community was abandoned.

Hooker Chemical and Plastics Corporation eventually purchased the canal, converting it and the surrounding area into a sixteen-acre landfill. The canal was drained and the company began using it to bury fifty-five-gal-lon metal and in some cases fiber barrels filled with chemical waste left over from the local manufacture of dyes, perfumes, and solvents for rubber and synthetic resins. Some of the deadly substances in those barrels included benzene, chloroform, toluene, dioxin, various kinds of PCBs, and pesticide residues. Hooker also disposed of large quantities of fly ash that was loose—not in barrels—most of it concentrated in the center section of the ditch. Between 1942 and 1953, Hooker dumped more than forty million pounds of hazardous waste, burying it in close proximity to what would later become the thirty-five-block neighborhood known as Love Canal.

In 1952, representatives of the Niagara School Board approached Hooker with an offer to purchase the Love Canal property to build a school. As internal memos drafted by Hooker board members would later reveal, the company agreed to sell the property because its board

recognized the danger of the toxic dump. Disposing of this property would, some argued, shield the company from the responsibility of future problems that might arise. The deal was approved and Hooker turned the property over to the school board for a dollar, with the stipulation that it would not be held responsible for future claims or damages resulting from the underground storage of chemicals.

The canal was subsequently covered with a thin layer of clay and topsoil. Freshly planted grass belied the dangers lurking below. Over the next twenty years, the school board gradually sold off pieces of the property to housing developers. A total of nine hundred homes and two public schools were eventually built in dangerously close proximity to what had formerly been a huge, noxious dumpsite. Unsuspecting residents went about the ordinary activity of their daily lives. Love Canal seemed to be a safe, peaceful neighborhood, and an ideal place to raise children.

However, there were periodic reminders of the past. Over the years, residents complained of foul odors and of a mysterious black sludge that oozed from cracks in the asphalt that covered the school playground and sometimes even bubbled up in their backyards. Vapors associated with more than eighty chemicals emanated from Love Canal.

The first alarm was sounded in 1976 with the publication in the *Niagara Gazette*, the daily newspaper of Niagara Falls, of an article written by two reporters who had arranged to have some of the sump pumps near the former canal tested for toxins. The results revealed that the pumps were loaded with dangerous chemicals.

The following year, another reporter published an article describing an informal door-to-door survey he had conducted of residents of Love Canal. The disturbing results indicated an inordinate number of people in the neighborhood seemed to have a variety of troubling health problems.

This second article, which emphasized the fact that a public school had been built directly over a toxic dumpsite, confirmed some of Lois Gibbs's worst fears. Gibbs, a twenty-seven-year-old housewife and mother of three children, had long suspected that the pediatricians who examined her five-year-old son Michael were overlooking obvious external causes for his chronic ill health. He suffered from epilepsy, as well as from urinary tract and respiratory problems. Convinced now it was the chemicals buried beneath the school Michael attended that were making him sick, Gibbs went to the school board and demanded that they move her son to another school. The board refused.

Gibbs decided to knock on doors and conduct her own survey to find out if there were others in the neighborhood with persistent health problems. She learned that an unusually high number of neighborhood residents were suffering from liver disease, epilepsy, and asthma. Children who walked barefoot outdoors developed strange rashes on their feet, a significant number were prone to seizures, and some had died. She also heard story after story about miscarriages and birth defects: babies born with holes in their hearts, damaged livers, hearing loss, cleft palates, and excess front teeth.

Convinced that something urgently needed to be done, Gibbs founded, and was elected president of, the Love Canal Homeowners Association. Under her leadership, members worked tirelessly to document the health problems that they were increasingly convinced stemmed from exposure to hazardous chemicals. Among their findings, they discovered that the number of Love Canal residents suffering from a variety of cancers was inordinately high.

The Love Canal Homeowners Association began demanding answers of public officials. Ignored at first and then ridiculed and dismissed, Gibbs and others made it clear they were not going away. An investigation conducted by New York State Health Department officials confirmed some of the statistics that the Homeowners Association had presented. It was increasingly clear that the chemicals buried at Love Canal were slowly poisoning residents.

* * *

Confronted with the data that was being compiled, Occidental, which had bought Hooker Chemical in 1968, strenuously denied that there was any causal connection between the impaired health of residents and the buried chemicals.

Finally, in 1978, the EPA released the results of blood tests of local people that showed a higher-than-average incidence of white blood cells, a precursor to leukemia, and chromosome damage. Other studies showed disproportionate levels of low birth weights and birth defects among local residents. Children were found to have a high incidence of learning problems, seizures, skin rashes, eye irritations, abdominal pain, and stunted growth. Results of tests of soil, air, and homes at Love Canal underscored the dangers the community was facing.

During my campaign for attorney general, based upon briefings and background papers prepared for me, it was clear that, if elected, a good deal of my time and effort was going to have to be directed toward doing something for the abused victims of this community.

Events suddenly began to take on greater urgency. The school that had been constructed over buried barrels of toxic waste was ordered permanently closed. At the beginning of August, the New York State health commissioner declared "A State of Emergency at Love Canal" and ordered the relocation of thirty families with pregnant women and children under age two. Then, President Jimmy Carter announced a federal health emergency and ordered the Federal Disaster Assistance Agency to assist the city of Niagara Falls in remediating the Love Canal site. With this assistance from the federal government, 239 families were permanently relocated, leaving behind their contaminated homes, which were later demolished.

In February 1979, New York State announced that it would pay temporary relocation costs for an additional thirty families at risk for pregnancy-related problems.

Love Canal was becoming notorious nationally and even internationally. *Time* magazine referred to it as a "Toxic Time Bomb," and the community continued to put pressure on Governor Hugh Carey to take further action.

There was increasing interaction between Marcia and the State Department of Environmental Conservation and the governor's office about what was happening at Love Canal, with Marcia indicating that we should be compiling the data for an eventual lawsuit to be brought.

In March 1979, the governor held a press conference in the course of which he said, "I urge State Attorney General Robert Abrams to pursue legal action, to protect public health in the Love Canal area of Niagara Falls." The next day I announced to the press that I and my staff would be meeting with the governor to discuss litigation.

It was clear that new standards of care had to be mandated for disposal of hazardous materials since corporate decision makers were willing to inflict pain on people's lives and saw themselves as answerable to no one.

By putting the power of his office behind our plan to litigate, the governor had, as far as I was concerned, opened the door for a range of future prosecutions. Occidental and Hooker were at the top of a long list of dumpers and polluters who would have to pay for the damage they had already done and, in some cases, continued to do.

Governors have to be careful when it comes to confronting corporations because those companies maintain a leverage which they do not hesitate to use. Asked to take responsibility for their actions, corporations can always threaten to relocate to a friendlier, less litigious state, taking thousands of jobs with them. A governor might be reluctant, even if well advised, to call the corporation's bluff. My job as attorney general, however, was to enforce the law. I was the lawyer for all the people of New York, and I believed it was my responsibility to act in the public interest whenever I could. Since ordinary citizens didn't have the power or resources to stand up to powerful interests, it was my obligation to fight for them.

With the case against Occidental looming, Marcia pressed for a dedicated hazardous waste budget appropriation. The state had by this time already budgeted twenty million dollars in programs aimed at providing relief to Love Canal residents, but nothing for litigation. Governor Carey hesitated, but in the end, he gave us funding so we could move forward in full force.

Meanwhile, tensions continued to mount between residents of Love Canal and various representatives of the government, both state and federal. A federal report released in November 1979 indicated the odds of Love Canal residents contracting cancer were as high as one in ten. As grim statistics continued to be made public, more and more residents saw packing up and leaving as their only viable course of action. They were convinced that staying meant risking their own or their children's lives. Yet, for some, leaving was out of the question because their life savings were sunk in a small piece of toxic property and the contaminated, worthless house perched on top of it. While the state had shown a willingness to assist those whose houses were right next to the canal and were within the boundaries of what was being referred to as the "first ring," it wasn't offering at this point to help anyone outside that ring. Community advocates were urging that more families be relocated, but Governor Carey, mindful of the cost, refused to resettle fifty-four families located on the outskirts of the original containment area. The costs of the relocations were already skyrocketing and would obviously end up being astronomical. The lines of demarcation between those who got help and those who didn't were starting to look increasingly arbitrary.

After conducting a great deal of factual and legal research, we filed the Love Canal case in April 1980, a $635 million lawsuit against Hooker Chemical, Occidental Chemical Corporation, and the Occidental

Petroleum Corporation. The suit claimed that all three were responsible for the Love Canal environmental disaster.

Marcia and I went to Niagara County State Supreme Court to file the lawsuit. Since there wasn't yet a specific law to deal with this kind of phenomenon—the dumping of toxic chemicals into the ground—we used an ancient legal theory of public nuisance. It goes back hundreds of years to English common law. Basically, it asserts that if you create a public nuisance, you can be required to take action to fix the problem and pay for the damage you created.

Our state case eventually went to the federal court after the passage of the Comprehensive Environmental Response, Compensation, and Liability Act (CERCLA), commonly known as Superfund. This law both provided funds for cleanup of toxic sites and gave us a new strengthened statutory basis for prosecuting those responsible. Love Canal was one of the three toxic dumpsites that led Congress to adopt the law. We eventually merged our case with the Department of Justice case, obtaining the benefit of a strong alliance of the state and the federal government joined together.

Tensions continued to mount. On May 20, 1980, two officials from the EPA met with Lois Gibbs and other members of the Love Canal Homeowners Association and presented them with more bad news: blood-test results showed evidence of chromosome breakage. They explained that people with chromosome breakage are at higher risk for cancer, birth defects, and miscarriages. The EPA's representatives went on to recommend that residents take certain precautions—do not plant a garden, keep out of back yards, stay out of your basement. Yet, they could not answer what was the most important question for those who were gathered there that day—if their basements and back yards weren't safe and their children had to be bused out of the neighborhood in order to go to a school that wasn't contaminated, why weren't they being relocated? Was anyone really expected to believe that it was still safe to be there?

The meeting suddenly took a dramatic turn when members of the Homeowners Association filed out of the room, closing the door behind them and locking the EPA representatives inside. "If it's safe for us, then it's safe for you," someone shouted to them through the closed door. "We're going to hold you here until President Carter does the right thing." FBI agents were on the scene not long after that and managed, after five hours, to persuade the group to free those locked inside.

The Homeowners Association members delivered an ultimatum to the White House: You have until next Wednesday to evacuate us. They didn't make clear what would happen if their demand wasn't met, but within two days the federal government agreed to temporarily relocate an additional nine hundred Love Canal families.

In the lawsuit we filed, we agreed upon a discovery schedule. The state had to produce its documents first. Occidental's attorneys served us with their document request and it seemed obvious that they thought they could overwhelm us with the sheer volume of material they wanted. They were flexing their muscles, attempting to drown us in paper. They probably thought that we would not be able to respond effectively because of our limited resources. We had to review half a million pages of documents, which would not be considered much these days with computers doing a major part of the work, but back then it all had to be done manually. We had just two weeks to meet the deadline, which we did, while the Justice Department and the defendants did not make theirs. The ability and passion of a few dedicated public servants can help to level a very uneven playing field.

Thus began a fourteen-year process of discovery requests, production, motions, and trials, as well as negotiations and further trials and more negotiations regarding the Love Canal site.

It eventually came to light that Occidental had also been dumping hazardous waste at four other sites—S-Area, Hyde Park, 102nd Street, and Durez—over a long period of time, with despicable abandon. For example, Occidental had started disposing of dangerous chemicals at its Hyde Park site in 1953, the same year that it stopped using Love Canal as a dumpsite. The dumping at Hyde Park continued until 1974 with 80,000 tons disposed, which far exceeded what was dumped at Love Canal.

* * *

In 1980, the Love Canal Area Revitalization Agency was created by the legislature as a government agency to assist in rehabilitating that area. After containment systems were installed, houses were deemed habitable and thus rehabilitated and resold.

During the early years of cleanup, there was tension and confrontation between my office and the Love Canal Revitalization Agency, the EPA, and Governor Carey. I felt that they were prematurely allowing the

resettlement and resale of rehabilitated homes. We argued that in their haste to move forward these agencies were not accurately reviewing the scientific data. My office continued to monitor the levels of dioxin and other dangerous chemicals found in the area. We made public the results of studies conducted by state health agencies that clearly indicated that it was not yet safe for people to move back. In fact, at one point in 1985, our office sued the Love Canal Area Revitalization Agency and obtained an injunction against it from selling some homes. The court ordered the agency to conduct a medical study and to comply with the New York State Environmental Review Act before any future sales.

We ultimately succeeded in getting Occidental to clean up the toxic mess, not only at Love Canal but at its four other locations, and to radically alter its approach to the disposal of hazardous waste. This meant that it would have to take time and money to see to it that toxic waste was disposed of in a safe and responsible fashion. Occidental was also held legally responsible for monitoring those sites where it had dumped toxic waste.

It took many years and legal battles before we were finally able to go to trial regarding the issue of punitive damages. That trial took place over a period of seven years. Assistant Attorney General Gene Leff, a brilliant and dedicated lawyer, tenaciously represented the state. We argued that when Hooker deeded the Love Canal landfill to the Board of Education as a site for a new school and playground, the company knew that highly toxic wastes buried there would eventually surface and endanger the children and the environment. The state called fifty witnesses to make its case. Occidental insisted that this case was being viewed through "the lens of hindsight," arguing that punitive damages were not warranted. They claimed that the dumping of chemicals was not illegal over the extensive period during which Hooker and later Occidental dumped hazardous waste into the canal. Federal District Court Judge John T. Curtin ruled in favor of Occidental, refusing to award punitive damages.

With the threat of an appeal, the case was finally concluded in an out-of-court settlement in 1994, with Occidental agreeing to pay ninety-eight million dollars. Occidental also paid over twenty million dollars to 1,400 persons who had suffered injuries as a result of the dumping. In December 1995, the Justice Department announced that Occidental would pay the government $129 million to cover the costs of the evacuation of more than one thousand homes, an elementary school, and an entire neighborhood.

Love Canal was a precedent-setting case and it made people around the country aware of the risks of toxic waste. But, sadly, it was only one case of many more to follow. Before I became attorney general, the state of New York had never sued to clean up a toxic waste site. We ended up bringing sixty-five lawsuits that involved illegal dumping, compelling corporations to spend hundreds of millions of dollars to clean up toxic waste sites all around the state. Indeed, Love Canal became a catalyst not just in New York but across the country and around the world for governmental intervention generated by citizen activism in response to the toxic peril.

Marcia left in 1985 after years of outstanding and effective service. She was ably succeeded by Jim Sevinsky, who had served as her deputy, and going forward provided his own brand of leadership regarding Love Canal and other important initiatives the Bureau undertook.

Air pollution was also a major threat to our health and environment and so we focused on chemical or manufacturing facilities that were emitting excessive amounts of toxic pollutants into the air. For example, in the Echota neighborhood in Niagara Falls, residents complained that their lush green trees had suddenly turned brown and shed all their leaves. As a result of tests conducted by our Environmental Protection Bureau, Olin Corporation and the DuPont Corporation agreed to reduce emissions at their plants situated nearby. In another part of the state we required an IBM facility near Binghamton to cut emissions by 90 percent.

While there had been improvements in basic air quality since the Clean Air Act was enacted in 1970, most toxic air pollutants remained virtually unregulated at the time I took office. Those pollutants, which were particularly pervasive in urban areas, included arsenic, benzene, and airborne radioactive matter. They were known to cause, or were suspected of causing, cancer and other diseases.

The EPA had a record of regulating toxic air pollutants only when compelled to do so by federal court orders. To prod the agency to act, my office brought suit against it for its failure to regulate arsenic, a hazardous substance known to cause skin and lung cancers in humans. In that case, *State of New York v. Gorsuch*, the agency acknowledged that its failure to issue regulations violated the law, but argued that it needed more time to study the technologies available to solve the problem before issuing controls. The EPA's constant claim that it needed more time became the agency's mantra. It had turned its foot-dragging into an art form.

In the last chapter I made reference to my efforts at bringing north-eastern states together to halt power plants from having a devastating effect on the region's lakes. One by one New York's lakes were being poisoned. In New York's Adirondack Mountains, 212 lakes were barren of all fish life as a result of acid rain. When the environmental scientists in my office told me the astonishing fact that fish life might never return to those lakes, I felt even more determined to do whatever I could to stop this assault on our environment.

In addition to mobilizing the coalition of northeastern states, we asked national environmental groups such as the Natural Resources Defense Council, the Environmental Defense Fund, and the Sierra Club Legal Defense Fund to join our efforts. They were powerful allies in litigation and in the court of public opinion.

Rachel Carson's *Silent Spring* had a profound effect in calling attention to the dangers posed to the environment by the use of pesticides.

In New York, pesticide issues were a substantial problem. Too often the information placed on the labels of pesticides was unreliable or even, in many cases, completely false. Many of these pesticides, which were used both indoors and outdoors, had not been adequately studied and much remained unknown about their effects on health.

We sued the manufacturers and the distributors of pesticides for misleading advertising. One common false claim was that the product in question was safe for both children and pets. Unsuspecting pet owners were heartbroken to discover that the pesticide they were using was in fact dangerous or lethal to animals. And we heard of too many parents who wound up rushing young children to hospital emergency rooms as a result of exposure.

The unprecedented release of dangerous chemicals at the Union Carbide Corporation's pesticide plant in Bhopal, India, on December 2, 1984 created what was called the worst industrial disaster in history. The plant released thirty tons of a highly toxic gas, killing an estimated fifteen thousand people, with an additional thirty thousand related deaths occurring in the years that followed. It is said that ultimately a total of five million people were affected by the Bhopal disaster. Even at the beginning, the figures were staggeringly incomprehensible. Photographs in the immediate aftermath showed unforgettable images of ominous dark clouds of poisonous gas emanating from the plant, corpses lined up by the hundreds at the side of a dirt road, and a father running for help with his screaming, just-blinded very young son in his arms.

Shortly before the Bhopal disaster, we had a near-miss in New York involving the same chemical, methyl isocyanate, which was accidentally released from an FMC chemical plant in Middleport, New York, forming a dense, ground-hugging cloud which moved with the prevailing winds across the athletic field of a nearby public school. The students were inside with doors and windows closed. But for good fortune and the wind direction of the day, this could have been a true large-scale tragedy.

I found myself thinking about the many potential dangers for New Yorkers resulting from industrial accidents waiting to happen. I knew that those potential incidents were multiplied or made more acute by shortcuts regularly taken by companies which were reluctant to pay the full cost of guaranteeing safer working conditions, by inspections that should have happened but didn't, and by government agencies that were lax in their enforcement of safety regulations or in tabulating reliable statistics.

I made it a priority of the Environmental Protection Bureau to compile data involving toxic chemical accidents in New York and in early 1986 issued a study that listed them. The report, which was critical of serious gaps in state and federal laws to protect the public, pointed out that since 1983 at least 370 people had been injured in more than seven hundred toxic chemical accidents in New York. It also noted fourteen deaths and that more than four thousand people had to be evacuated from the locations of chemical accidents. It indicated that many accidents in New York went unreported, responsible parties were not punished, and communities were not being informed.

The report was the first documented analysis ever published of chemical accidents in the state. The EPA had compiled data related to chemical accidents in the United States which covered the same time period. Of the seven hundred accidents listed in our report, only 150 appeared in the federal report's list of chemical accidents in New York.

Our study demonstrated that most accidents were associated with major companies such as International Business Machines Corporation, Allied Chemical, Consolidated Edison, Long Island Lighting, Mobil Oil/ Chemical, and General Electric. There were an average of five accidents a week during the study period.

The report caused many companies to change their internal procedures and manufacturing processes to minimize use, storage, and transport of chemicals.

I decided that it was important to create an opportunity for the public to tell me what they felt were the key environmental problems in their communities. During my tenure I scheduled and attended forty-seven public environmental hearings throughout the state of New York. We advertised in those communities that the attorney general would be coming to listen to your concerns. I wanted to unleash seventeen million New Yorkers against the polluters. I wanted them to be the eyes and ears of the Environmental Protection Bureau of the Attorney General's office. We coordinated with statewide groups such as the Environmental Planning Lobby and the New York Public Interest Research Group.

These meetings often lasted late into the night. People told us where chemicals were being dumped. Most landfills are only allowed to accept a certain kind of refuse but not chemicals. We discovered that people were paying off the man at the gate. Those who testified told us about the midnight dumpers, the driver of a truck who would pull into an isolated area and dump liquid wastes into a river or stream or creek. They told us of surreptitious illegal dumping at night where contaminated material would be hauled to open fields and of witnessing trucks with open spigots dumping dangerous liquid materials on highways. As a result of this information, we conducted undercover investigations in order to apprehend some of these illegal dumpers and polluters.

I went to the Legislature requesting authority to prosecute environmental cases criminally. An Environmental Felony Crimes Bill was passed and enacted into law in1985 that created a unit within the office to handle these cases. Within a few years we had prosecuted dozens of people, imposing fines of millions of dollars and even imprisonment in serious cases. A powerful message was sent out that if you pollute you would have to pay with your purse and your personal liberty.

In light of the Trump administration's efforts to diminish the role of the EPA and to cut its budget, Love Canal and other environmental injustices stand as a reminder of the crucial role needed for citizen watchdogs and state governmental enforcers to be strong actors ready to protect the quality of our environment and the health of our citizens.

Chapter 18

The Pymm Thermometer Case

THE CASE OF THE PYMM THERMOMETER Company is a story of callous greed, emblematic of the distinguishing features of the Reagan years. It came to our attention when an injured employee applied for workers' compensation and the company that had employed him fought his claim. This led to an investigation that exposed far worse abuses than anyone had originally anticipated.

A doctor brought the claim of his patient, Vidal Rodriguez, to the office's attention in 1985. The doctor noticed that Rodriguez seemed to be displaying some of the classic symptoms of mercury poisoning. Most noticeably, Rodriguez showed an impaired sense of balance, requiring him to use a cane. He also experienced restlessness, sleeplessness, and memory loss, which turned out to be irreversible brain damage. Mercury is ingested through the lungs and circulated through the bloodstream to other parts of the body, including the brain.

Rodriguez worked in the "reclamation area" of a thermometer factory located in the Williamsburg section of Brooklyn, owned by brothers William and Edward Pymm. One of the last local manufacturers of glass thermometers, Pymm had a program in place for unavoidable accidents that regularly resulted in broken thermometers and the loss of mercury. Workers in this area of the plant, including Rodriguez, were instructed to feed the broken thermometers into a glass-crushing machine. The mercury from the broken thermometers was then collected in a nearby sink. The Pymm brothers had been cited several times for health and safety violations and were fully informed of the grave risks posed to the health of their workers. They continued with their mercury reclamation project because they considered it too costly to let the mercury go to waste.

Assistant Attorney General Richard Corenthal, a no-nonsense labor lawyer with years of experience investigating claims of abuse of workers employed in some of New York City's most deplorable sweatshops, headed up the case on behalf of my office. With the assistance of the doctor, he managed to contact the patient and arranged to meet with a group of Pymm workers in a local hall. Most of the employees were Hispanic, so he took along an interpreter.

Many of the Pymm employees Corenthal met were immigrants whose visas had expired, which made them particularly vulnerable. The workers were reluctant to act for fear of deportation. But when the interpreter explained how dangerous and poisonous the conditions were, they were willing to cooperate.

Corenthal was using the "Right to Know" law, which guaranteed a worker's right to be informed of any dangerous chemical associated with a job. This statute justified his involvement in a case that at first glance might seem to belong to the Occupational Safety and Hazard Agency (OSHA), a federal agency. He knew that the local branch of OSHA was understaffed. He also soon learned that OSHA had been negligent and was implicated in the case.

Corenthal filed a Freedom of Information Act request in order to examine the history of OSHA's involvement with Pymm and discovered that OSHA had previously cited the Pymm brothers on several occasions and had given them not one but three extensions relating to numerous violations throughout the factory. By granting the Pymm brothers these extensions, OSHA agents had contributed to the workers' exposure to mercury. As far as we were concerned, they too should be held responsible for the debilitating and in some cases irreversible consequences of that exposure, not only to the workers but to their children. The environment of the Pymm factory was so highly toxic that some of the workers brought home mercury on their clothes. Their children, breathing in the toxic fumes, showed symptoms of poisoning as well.

The Pymm brothers concealed the risks from their employees. They had also concealed the existence of the basement reclamation area from investigators. We discovered this because Rodriguez asked the OSHA investigators why they hadn't gone downstairs. "What downstairs?" one of the investigators asked. The Pymm brothers had persisted in denying that there was a downstairs.

We called these OSHA agents, among others, to testify on behalf of the state when we proceeded some months later, in a pathbreaking criminal case against the Pymm brothers brought by the attorney general and Brooklyn District Attorney Elizabeth Holtzman. The Pymms were charged with assault with a dangerous instrument—mercury—recklessly endangering workers by exposing them to this deadly chemical. We crafted an argument used for the first time that an assault by a dangerous chemical was just as damaging, if not more so, than an assault with a fist, a knife, or a gun, because in this case it could lead to permanent brain injury. They were also charged with conspiracy and falsifying records.

Clive Morrick, head of our Environmental Criminal Prosecutions Section, who tried the case on behalf of the state, remembers the strong reaction of some of the jurors when they learned that the effects of exposure to mercury can be mitigated and even eliminated with proper ventilation. It became clear that the Pymm brothers protected themselves in their private office which had proper ventilation, while there was next to no ventilation where employees worked on the floor of the factory. Jurors also learned that the employees worked alongside boxes loaded with broken thermometers. Though it had been recommended to the Pymm brothers by OSHA that they supply their employees with protective gear, including gloves and face masks, the workers were not provided with even this inexpensive minimum protection.

The jury found the Pymm brothers guilty. The judge, however, dismissed the case, saying that the federal OSHA statute preempted state prosecution. We appealed the judge's ruling and the Appellate Division agreed with us, stating that "the goals of State criminal law complement rather than conflict with OSHA so as to ensure that workers are adequately protected and that particularly egregious conduct receives appropriate punishment." The state's highest court, the Court of Appeals, affirmed that decision.

The case was drawn out over the course of eight years and while the Pymm brothers were forced to close one of their two factories, they were given a relatively light sentence: six months of weekends in jail and a twenty-thousand-dollar fine.

Despite the minimal sentence, which reflects a tendency on the part of courts to be more lenient toward white-collar criminals, this case set an important precedent. The criminal charge of "assault with a deadly

instrument" was held to be a creative use of the law and to be appropriate. New York State could bring cases to protect workers, and assault by dangerous chemicals was a valid exercise of prosecutorial discretion. The case raised the bar for workers' rights, especially those who are easily exploited because of their immigration status.

With both the decline of unionized workers in the United States, thereby reducing the pressure to ensure safe working conditions, and the retrenchment of the Trump administration's enforcement efforts in this area, there continues today to be a need for strong efforts to guarantee workers' rights and employee safety.

Chapter 19

Antitrust

Antitrust enforcement sounds esoteric, but I saw it as a significant bread-and-butter function of the attorney general and sought to vigorously enforce state and federal antitrust laws because I knew we could save consumers millions of dollars each year. By combating anticompetitive behavior such as price-fixing, monopolization, and bid-rigging, the attorney general could promote free and open competition. In turn, this would allow goods and services to be sold in the marketplace at the lowest possible price with the greatest possible choice. Strong enforcement of antitrust laws establishes a level playing field for producers as well as consumers. Because this role was so pivotal, it was vitally important to pick the right person to fill the post of assistant attorney general in charge of the Antitrust Bureau.

Some people thought I was crazy to appoint a Brooklyn legal services lawyer who had never handled an antitrust case to head the Antitrust Bureau, but appointing Lloyd Constantine turned out to be one of the best decisions I made in the attorney general's office. In a short period of time, he became one of the leading antitrust practitioners in the nation and helped shape an agenda that benefited consumers not just in New York but throughout the country.

Constantine began his tenure toward the end of July 1980. This was during the last days of the Carter presidency and just before President Ronald Reagan took office. The Reagan administration was openly hostile toward—and made clear that it had no intention of enforcing—existing antitrust laws. In fact, they even took the position that many monopolies were good.

My reaction to this radical departure was to attempt to fill the void that had been left by the federal government. It had gotten to the point where the feds would actually go to court to try to prevent the states from enforcing antitrust laws. So, I put together a national coalition of state attorneys general, Republicans and Democrats, to work on enforcement of these laws. We trusted each other and agreed that the larger states, like New York, Texas, and California, would share resources with the smaller states like the Dakotas, New Hampshire, and Hawaii.

Before New York got into these national cases, we spent some time on an important local investigation based on allegations about price-fixing by milk companies in the New York City metropolitan area. This was important to tackle because it impacted virtually all consumers. The attorney general could assist a large number of people—especially poor families who were highly affected by the price of milk—by undertaking this single investigation. This high-impact case was the antithesis of the kinds of trivial cases my predecessor had pursued. For example, during Lefkowitz's era, the Antitrust Bureau pursued a price-fixing case in Poughkeepsie wherein five barbershops were colluding to fix the price of haircuts. The milk price-fixing investigation led to a significant round of lawsuits against all of the major milk companies in the downstate area, resulting in forty convictions and guilty pleas as well as millions of dollars in recovery.

Theoretically, this money should have been sent back to individuals who had paid too much for milk. However, given the small, fractional amounts of money per household, we came up with an alternative plan. We told the judge that we had eliminated, at least for now, the price-fixing problem and that the consumer benefitted from the outcome going forward and thus proposed that the majority of the several million dollars that we recovered be distributed to public and private schools across the New York City metropolitan area to help with educational programs related to nutrition. These school districts had been harmed because they were large purchasers of milk distributed to their students. The judge agreed. There was some additional money allocated to the National Association of Attorneys General to enhance states' ability to enforce antitrust laws. That Milk Fund has assisted attorneys general in dozens of cases over these many years and exists to this day some forty years later. This was a prime example of states assisting one another.

When we first started prosecuting antitrust cases, practitioners in the private sector tended to look at the state as a joke. They firmly held that

antitrust enforcement belonged to the federal government and that the states were not qualified to handle such cases. On the one hand, the private bar was delighted to have us step in when they needed something done. On the other hand, they were aghast at state enforcement when we were in opposition to their clients who were benefiting because there was no cop on the beat.

In several cases, private lawyers joined the federal government in seeking to block our ability to go to court. One such case, *California v. American Stores Company*, involving the merger of two West Coast supermarket chains, went all the way to the United States Supreme Court. Our position was that the New York attorney general and the Texas attorney general, as well as other attorneys general, were correct in their assertion that this case was relevant to them. This anticompetitive merger, if allowed to go forward, would set a dangerous precedent, threatening our respective economies. Surely A&P and Grand Union or any of the other dominant players on the East Coast might see a merger on the West Coast as a green light for similar mergers in other parts of the country. In an 8–1 decision, the Supreme Court ruled that the states had the right to act.

As the attorneys general began acting collaboratively, it became clear that some of our cases were bound to have national—and sometimes even international—consequences.

At one point, New York launched an investigation that involved an international insurance conspiracy. Commercial general liability insurance is required for all businesses in the United States. You cannot operate a business without such insurance. During the 1980s, the price of general liability insurance soared, increasing by 1,000 percent, causing businesses and facilities to close.

Similarly, the price of seepage and pollution insurance skyrocketed at around this time.

It appeared suspicious that these two events occurred simultaneously in the insurance industry, so we launched an investigation. A multistate team of lawyers led by New York went to London to investigate what was starting to look like a conspiracy. This resulted in a case against the four largest insurance companies in the United States, all of the syndicates of Lloyds of London, and the two largest reinsurance companies in the world. On the other side of the Atlantic, Her Majesty's government felt the need to file a brief challenging America's right to intervene in these matters. New York

State was leading the charge based on the notion that anything that touched the commerce of New York gave us jurisdiction. There is really nothing that touches the commerce of New York that doesn't also end up affecting international commerce and the commerce of virtually every state. The case ultimately went to the Supreme Court, where we won.

* * *

The Reagan administration claimed the reason they weren't enforcing antitrust laws was that they wanted to return power to the states. We knew of course that wasn't the real reason. Malcolm Baldridge, the secretary of commerce at the time, made it perfectly clear that the administration's hostility toward antitrust came down to one factor: they perceived it as being bad for business.

Toward the end of the Reagan years, I had a revealing conversation at a meeting of the National Association of Attorneys General in the Del Coronado Hotel near San Diego, California. President Reagan's attorney general Ed Meese was there.

"Bob," he said to me, "all that stuff about returning power to the states, that wasn't really what we wanted. We had a laissez-faire plan of non-enforcement. You guys outfoxed us. We won the battle but we lost the war! We never thought the states would have the competence to do this. We never imagined that you would be able to work together."

This view—that the states would not be able to cooperate with one another—harkened back to the early days of our nation's history when the colonies were governed by the Articles of Confederation, which failed because of rivalries. My colleagues and I discovered, however, that not only were we able to share information and cooperate with one another, but we were even willing to share resources. It was truly a historic accomplishment.

The Reagan administration had stopped enforcing antitrust laws against anticompetitive mergers. The attorneys general were united in wanting to enforce these laws, but the legal basis of our arguments varied according to the laws of each individual state. Many of the states had strong statutes, such as the Donnelly Act in New York, the Cartwright Act in California, and the Valentine Act in Ohio. But we couldn't go to court speaking fifty different dialects. We had to establish a common vocabulary and nomenclature, so we adopted a set of merger guidelines.

And in a similar way, to protect consumer interest with respect to vertical restraints, such as resale price maintenance and vertical mergers, forty-eight out of the fifty states agreed to enact Vertical Restraint Guidelines. The adoption of these guidelines was a huge triumph. Such action and the attention it garnered created a momentum by the attorneys general and people were realizing that the states were a force to be reckoned with.

My office tackled many more antitrust cases over the years, including one on behalf of American Express, which was facing a bank boycott issued by Visa and Mastercard. To the outside world, it seemed as if there was robust competition between credit card companies, but we soon found out that they were raising and fixing prices, standardizing procedures, and blocking competitors. We started to take a closer look.

There was a statute that said that under certain conditions—and we knew that in this particular case we met those conditions—a state could get the investigative files of the Justice Department and the Federal Trade Commission (FTC). We demanded the files of the Justice Department. In combing through them, it was obvious that the Reagan Justice Department lawyers who had prepared the files knew that in spite of all the evidence of collusion, the federal government was not going to take any action. The only thing that would get the federal government to act, one of the lawyers had concluded, would be if Visa and Mastercard were to merge.

It turned out that Visa and Mastercard were in fact already partially merging. At that point, credit cards were their primary business, with one tenth of one percent of their business being in debit cards. Visa and Mastercard recognized that debit cards were the wave of the future and would eventually replace cash and checks in the United States, so they were merging their debit card operations, which had been known as "Entrée."

Fifteen states, led by New York, filed a lawsuit not only to prevent that merger, but also to undo certain aspects which had already taken place. This was almost unheard of because courts are very reluctant to unscramble a merger, which is sometimes compared to unscrambling an egg. The best bet for a successful outcome was to go into court *before* the merger took place. But we went ahead and were successful in getting Visa and Mastercard to dissolve their new, jointly owned debit card network.

One of the theories that we utilized in this case is that monopolists always look forward to try to prevent competition from coming in. They

try to kill any emerging competition in its crib. It was clear that Visa and Mastercard were moving very aggressively and forcefully to eliminate future competition, especially in the market of debit cards.

The same thing was happening in telecommunications. Certain cable companies were taking very aggressive steps to not just continue their monopolization of the cable markets, but to prevent competition in the future. The competition on the horizon was known as the DBS market, the direct broadcast satellite operators, and there were a number of them. The cable companies were acting in a variety of ways to keep them from effectively competing. New York took the lead to put together forty states and announced an investigation challenging the practices of these companies.

By the time this was happening in the cable industry, we were close to the end of Reagan's second term. One of the very first things that President George H. W. Bush did was to appoint James Rill, a very seasoned Washington antitrust lawyer, as the head of the US Department of Justice Antitrust Division. Rill let the states know right away that he had come to make peace and wanted to work with us on the case involving the cable companies.

In a truly historic move, we then formed the Executive Working Group for Antitrust, a new structure in government. It was a triumvirate made up of representatives of the states (a small group of three to four states constituted the delegation headed by New York), the head of the Antitrust Division of the Department of Justice and the chair of the FTC, each of whom had significant antitrust enforcement authority. We met periodically to share information about investigations and potential actions and cooperated in the prosecution of cases. We also created training opportunities for federal and state prosecutors and a program of cross-deputization that would allow federal prosecutors to work on state cases and state prosecutors to work on federal cases.

This new group jointly pursued the investigation and prosecution of the cable industry, which resulted in a consent decree joined in by forty states that precluded the cable companies from preventing competition with direct broadcast satellite service providers.

This was the beginning of a new era. What we were doing in New York—vigorous enforcement and taking the lead in creating a coalition of attorneys general—would alter for the future the pattern of antitrust enforcement across the nation. The states became coequal enforcers along

with the federal government with equal respect eventually shown by practitioners for state as well as federal action. This movement eventually spread to other areas of consumer, environmental, and civil rights protection, as well.

We also worked on a series of airline cases which enabled us to protect competition for the shuttle route between Washington and New York and Boston. To this day, because of the action we took, instead of having only a single airline providing shuttle service between these cities, we have two airlines competing with each other. We also discovered that Piedmont and US Airways, as part of their merger, were going to eliminate routes. As a result, there would be no way to fly to and from various cities in New York—Syracuse, Rochester, and Buffalo—and Boston. Our intervention enabled us to preserve routes in upstate New York. We conditioned the merger on the maintenance of existing routes and a competitive fare structure that banned excessive fare increases for a period of time.

Our Antitrust Bureau also handled cases involving the concrete industry, road-paving, and garbage carting, which were dominated by organized crime. In pursuing one of these cases, we got a court to allow us to plant a recording device in a Jaguar that was driven by Salvatore Avellino, a capo of the Lucchese crime family. Those tapes not only made our cases, but they assisted in the big mob prosecutions that were handled by both the United States Attorney for the Southern District and the Manhattan District Attorney's Office in the major organized crime case that the media dubbed the "Pizza Connection" because of the frequent use of pizza parlors as fronts for heroin sales.

These cases had significant impact on the average citizen, which is why I was interested in them in the first place. It might not be readily apparent how a case involving the fixing of the price of concrete could affect the average consumer, but these collusive practices drive up the cost of construction for residential and commercial properties, which results in higher rents as well as costlier services and products.

Many believe that the threat of reduced competition, higher prices, and poor service is still with us today as a result of increased merger and acquisition activity. The recent merger between T-Mobile and Sprint created concern among consumer advocates and state attorneys general, as a number of them challenged the merger. They claimed that reducing wireless providers from four to three would give increased market power to

existing industry leaders and would inevitably drive up the cost of service for consumers.

* * *

The first antitrust statute passed in America was in Kansas on March 3, 1889. I thought it would be a great idea if all the state attorneys general could celebrate the hundredth anniversary of this milestone, and so I reached out to my friend Robert Stephan, the attorney general of Kansas, and he agreed to host the event in Lawrence, Kansas. We invited Ralph Nader, the biggest name in consumer protection, to address our anniversary gathering. It was an honor to have him participate. At one time, I was featured on the cover of *Advertising Age* with the caption "the most feared attorney general in America," but the big name in consumer protection was Ralph Nader. He had been on the scene for a long time and had tremendous stature and credibility. It was a wonderful event and it symbolically underscored the fact that antitrust enforcement began as a state activity one year before the Sherman Act of 1890. One hundred years later antitrust enforcement continued to play an important role in ensuring that our economy was based on free and open competition.

This story, with all its remarkable achievements, comes out of a bureau that is not huge by any means, with a mere seventeen lawyers during the years when we were aggressively pursuing cases of great magnitude and importance.

Those were the halcyon days for attorneys general in America. We liked one another, we respected each other, and we cooperated with one another. It didn't matter whether we were Democrats or Republicans, and our party affiliations never interfered with our work. Unfortunately, that nonpartisan era is gone. Today there is a Democratic Attorneys General Association and a Republican Attorneys General Association, with enormous fundraising being done by both organizations. Everything is politicized. The fundraising is particularly disturbing because millions of dollars in contributions are solicited from major corporations, which are subject to review and investigation by attorneys general. Even if there is no quid pro quo involved in those contributions, the appearance of soliciting and receiving these contributions is not good for the public perception of attorneys general.

* * *

The issue of antitrust surfaced during the confirmation hearing to fill the Supreme Court vacancy of Justice Lewis Powell. When Powell, a moderate on the US Supreme Court, announced his retirement in January 1987 during the second term of Ronald Reagan's presidency, Reagan assuaged his right-wing supporters by nominating Robert Bork. The potential confirmation of Bork, a staunch conservative and a highly controversial choice, created a firestorm.

Most notably, Bork had written a book, *The Antitrust Paradox*, which contained views outside the mainstream on issues relating to antitrust. Bork had a reputation as an originalist, believing that the US Constitution should be interpreted as the founding fathers had intended. He was a strong outspoken critic of what he called "judicial activism," believing that many judges by virtue of their personal philosophy were interpreting constitutional provisions and laws beyond their literal meaning and intent. He held himself out to be a "strict constructionist."

Senator Joseph Biden, chairman of the US Senate Judiciary Committee, was conducting hearings on Bork's nomination and asked that a panel appear before the committee to address Bork's views on antitrust. Having just finished serving for two years as chair of the National Association of Attorneys General Antitrust Committee and as president–elect of the association, I was asked to testify before the committee together with Robert Pitofsky, dean and professor of law at Georgetown University Law Center, and Attorney General Charlie Brown of West Virginia, the then-current chair of the Antitrust Committee of the National Association of Attorneys General.

The three of us testified that, ironically, Bork's radical views as reflected in his writings on antitrust were extraordinary examples of activism. We pointed out that he disregarded judicial precedent, the plain meaning of statutes, and the intention of members of Congress as drafters of legislation. We also demonstrated that Bork's record with regard to antitrust was contrary to law and precedent and his claim to adherence to judicial restraint was spurious. He actually said in *The Antitrust Paradox* that "Congress as a whole is institutionally incapable of the sustained rigor and consistent thought that the fashioning of a rational antitrust policy requires."

The Senate hearings were high drama and the panel's testimony came at a crucial moment. Lloyd Constantine, the chief of my Antitrust Bureau, helped draft my testimony, which indicated that Judge Bork, both in his scholarly writings and in the opinions he rendered as a judge, was a

renegade out of the mainstream in the area of antitrust. Bork unabashedly declared that Supreme Court precedents on antitrust were wrong and should not be followed. He was willing to contravene landmark legislation such as the Sherman and Clayton Acts, which had framed antitrust law for the past one hundred years. He was an unabashed judicial activist.

My testimony outlined that Bork explicitly declared that courts should *refuse* to enforce federal laws. He advocated legalizing vertical price fixing, notwithstanding federal law prohibiting it. In his opinions he displayed an eagerness to depart from the specific facts of the case and put forth his views which were not supported by court decisions. His antitrust views were anti-consumer and, if adhered to as law, would rob consumers of the opportunity to buy goods at lower prices. If he were allowed to be a member of the Supreme Court, he would take the court in the wrong direction. He viewed cartels, monopolies, and price-fixers as acceptable.

The extensive hearings and the intensity of the debate boiled over into partisan divisions. The Senate rejected Bork 58–42, with fifty-two out of fifty-four Democrats and six Republicans in the US Senate voting against his confirmation.

Following the defeat of the Bork nomination, President Reagan ultimately nominated Anthony Kennedy, who was confirmed 97–0 and served for more than thirty years. Justice Kennedy, perceived as a fair and balanced conservative, emerged as a crucial swing vote on many sensitive issues. He joined the liberal wing of the court in important decisions concerning gay rights, abortion, affirmative action, and the death penalty. It was Justice Kennedy's deciding vote and majority opinion that declared the Defense of Marriage Act, which defined marriage for federal purposes as the union of one man and one woman, to be unconstitutional and declared in *Obergefell v. Hodges* that same-sex marriage was constitutionally protected.

The battle over confirmation of Supreme Court nominees involving sensitive issues continues to this day, as we saw in the recent three Trump nominations. It's not yet clear what the appointments of Neil Gorsuch, Brett Kavanaugh and Amy Coney Barrett will mean in terms of the direction of antitrust enforcement.

Chapter 20

Reproductive Freedom

THE RADICAL ANTIABORTION GROUP OPERATION RESCUE announced in January 1992 that it intended to descend on Buffalo, New York, to shut down the city's two abortion clinics as part of its "Spring of Life" campaign. The organization had garnered national attention for the mayhem it created in Wichita, Kansas, the previous summer where, over a six-week period, 2,600 Operation Rescue protestors were arrested for a variety of illegal acts. Demonstrators created massive traffic jams and destroyed property, costing the city hundreds of thousands of dollars, and successfully shut down the city's abortion clinics for two full days.

Buffalo Mayor James Griffin told the press, in response to Operation Rescue's announcement, that he would welcome the antiabortion group "with open arms. If they can shut down even one abortion mill, they've done their job . . . I might even join them."

The mayor's position on this matter struck me as a dereliction of his responsibility and a disregard for the rule of law. I responded with a statement of my own: "I will not tolerate any complicity on the part of the mayor of Buffalo that will allow these self-appointed vigilantes to spread terror and trample on the rights of women." In an open letter to the mayor, I reminded him that federal courts ruled that Operation Rescue constituted a conspiracy in violation of federal law to deprive women of their rights. Mayor Griffin and I became embroiled in a very public dispute, which quickly became vituperative.

I had known Jimmy Griffin when he was in the state senate and I was in the state assembly. He was a very conservative Democrat and strongly anti-choice, but we had managed to remain on friendly terms and he

supported me when I ran for attorney general. But when the Operation Rescue issue in Buffalo began to percolate, I knew that the relationship was going to be put to a severe test because of my obligation to enforce the law protecting the rights of women under the Constitution of the United States and the laws of New York State. Engaging in a public scrap with an old ally wasn't easy, but the situation made it unavoidable, and it continued to escalate. At another point I said, "If the mayor does not assure the safety of the women who want to use the city's abortion clinics, if he doesn't do his job in making sure that they are granted access to the clinics—I will see him in court! It's as simple as that."

The mayor responded by disingenuously playing down the threat that Operation Rescue's activities posed. "Ah, it's just a little praying," he said. He obviously knew that Operation Rescue's plan to inflict its campaign of harassment and intimidation on the citizens of Buffalo was much more than that.

According to founder Randall Terry and other Operation Rescue spokespeople, the organization chose Buffalo as the site of its next major action because a majority of its 328,000 residents were either Roman Catholic or evangelical Christian and were thought to be against abortion. But it turned out there was no local consensus in favor of Operation Rescue and its agenda. The mayor may have wanted Operation Rescue to come to Buffalo, but the Buffalo City Council, the Buffalo branch of the League of Women Voters, and the Buffalo Council of Churches did not share his sentiments. All three organizations issued public statements indicating in the strongest possible terms that Operation Rescue was not welcome.

The antiabortion movement targeted the most vulnerable women in our society, poor women who were dependent on federally funded clinics for all of their health needs, including any decisions they might make regarding their reproductive capabilities. Antiabortion activists made repeated efforts to block federal funding to clinics where abortions were performed. They finally achieved their goal with the passage in 1976 of the Hyde Amendment, which banned the use of Medicaid and other federal funds for abortions. Encouraged by this victory, they went further, trying to create mandates imposing legal restrictions on what doctors could discuss with their patients in federally funded clinics. They demanded that funding be withdrawn from any clinic where a doctor discussed abortion. Some proposed legislation even went so far as to call for banning discussion of the use of any kind of contraception.

The Supreme Court, in its 1973 *Roe v. Wade* decision, declared that the state, especially in the first trimester of pregnancy, had no compelling right to intervene in discussions that might take place between a woman and her doctor where abortion was concerned. It ruled that a woman's decision to obtain an abortion was guaranteed by her constitutionally defined right to privacy. Such decisions take place within a zone of privacy where the State had no right to trespass. The antiabortion activists counted on—but in this they miscalculated—poor women's rights to privacy being a cause that no one would assiduously defend.

Poor women, particularly women of color, had always suffered in greater numbers under draconian abortion laws. The laws against abortion are a relatively recent development in American history. It wasn't until about 1880 that most states enacted laws making abortion illegal except to save the life of the mother, with some states allowing abortion in cases of rape or incest. The passage of these laws meant that countless women died as a result of botched abortions performed hurriedly and in secret. These often took place in unsanitary conditions, sometimes by doctors whose licenses had been revoked for reasons ranging from incompetence to chronic drunkenness to sexual abuse of their patients. Often, such doctors performed abortions with no ability to provide lifesaving antibiotics when infection set in, as it all too often did. Those who performed abortions charged a high fee for their services in consideration of the risk of arrest. Criminalization of abortion had given abortionists an advantage over desperate women who would do or pay just about anything to stop an unwanted pregnancy.

Affluent women who could afford to pay for better, less risky services took advantage of that opportunity, traveling to Puerto Rico or to certain European countries where abortion was legal to undergo the procedure. But the vast majority of women could barely come up with the necessary funds to pay for a third-rate abortionist's services. Countless women showed up at hospital emergency rooms when it was already too late, having hemorrhaged too much blood to stand a chance of survival. Sometimes they bled to death in bed at home, or they died, drenched in sweat, shivering and delirious as a result of preventable infections. Women who were unable to come up with the funds for a back-alley abortionist's services sometimes resorted to inserting knitting needles and other sharp objects into the vagina with equally tragic results. Year after year, thousands of women died.

By the early 1960s, it was becoming clear to increasing numbers of people in the United States that the abortion laws needed to be reformed. President Kennedy created the Presidential Advisory Council on Women, which called for the repeal of restrictive abortion laws. In 1970, three years before the *Roe v. Wade* ruling, Hawaii became the first state to allow abortions performed up to the fifth month, thereby repealing its criminal abortion law. In 1971, the Comstock Act, which prohibited the dissemination of information on abortion, was repealed by the US Congress.

There was a dramatic vote in New York in 1969 during my final year in the assembly when the abortion-rights bill was narrowly defeated. The next year, in 1970, abortion reform passed by a single vote in the Senate and then in the assembly after an emotional debate.

While the mayor of Buffalo apparently saw Operation Rescue founder Randall Terry as someone to admire, I saw him as someone who was capable of stirring powerful, base feelings in those who were susceptible to his message.

I felt that the tendencies exhibited by Operation Rescue and other extremist antiabortion groups—to pair incendiary language where doctors were "baby killers" and health-care facilities were "death clinics" with disregard for the rights of others—could eventually lead to acts of terrorism. Several of these groups, including Operation Rescue, had already perpetrated acts of violence against abortion clinics by breaking into offices, destroying property, and tampering with records. It was only a matter of time until they directed these acts of violence toward human beings.

Indeed, that was what eventually happened. In 1993, an antiabortion protestor by the name of Michael Griffin shot a federal clinic doctor, David Gunn, outside a health-care center in Pensacola, Florida, during an antiabortion demonstration. In August of the same year, another doctor, George Tiller, was shot in the arm by Rachelle "Shelley" Shannon, an antiabortion activist, while leaving the clinic where he practiced medicine in Wichita, Kansas. In July of the following year, Dr. John Bayard Britton and his bodyguard were shot dead outside the clinic where Dr. Britton's practice of medicine included providing abortions in Pensacola, Florida. The murderer in this case was former minister and antiabortion activist Paul J. Hill. In December of the same year, John Salvi, an antiabortion activist, burst into a Brookline, Massachusetts, abortion clinic brandishing a rifle and proceeded to open fire, killing two receptionists and wounding five others. In 1997, two bombs exploded outside an Atlanta, Georgia,

building containing an abortion clinic, leaving six people injured and the clinic itself in ruins. In 1998, off-duty police officer Robert Sanderson was killed in Birmingham, Alabama, in a bomb explosion at the New Women, All Women Clinic, where he worked as a security guard. Clinic nurse Emily Lyons was also maimed in the attack. In 1998, Dr. Barnett Slepian, an abortion provider in Buffalo, was shot and killed in his own home when a bullet that came through an open window shattered his spine and tore his aorta, barely missing his son's head. This occurred in the same city where, six years earlier, Mayor James Griffin had made light of the violent proclivities of antiabortion activists.

Between the years 1977 and 1999, 161 women's health-care facilities were the target of arson, forty were bombed, and an additional seventy-seven clinics were the targets of attempted bombings or arson. During this same time period, staff members and patients in clinics suffered hundreds of violent attacks by antiabortion extremists.

In preparation for Operation Rescue coming to Buffalo, I filed a federal lawsuit seeking to bar demonstrators from blockading either of Buffalo's two abortion clinics and to impose fines, beginning at ten thousand dollars a day and doubling every day, on those who violated the injunction. The lawsuit also called for federal marshals to help maintain order. I was concerned that local Buffalo police officers might take their cues from the mayor and allow women attempting to access the clinics to be intimidated by demonstrators.

Judge Arcara, who had served as district attorney of Erie County before his appointment, issued an injunction, establishing a fifteen-foot "free zone" around clinic doors, barring the intimidation of doctors at their homes, prohibiting Operation Rescue demonstrators from videotaping or photographing clinic clients, and calling for federal marshals to act immediately to quell disturbances and prohibit any kind of blockade.

Randall Terry's response was that he would not be deterred: "We have an injunction from heaven to follow through on these rescues." Displaying a twenty-three-week-old fetus, he said, "We're trying to stop two baby-killers. This is murder! We've had injunctions in every city we've gone to! I will *gladly* go to jail, *gladly* break the law to save her life." Terry and others lamented the fact that Arcara was "violating the laws of his own Catholic church" and threatened action to defy the junction.

But in fact, the organization had miscalculated on a number of fronts. By announcing his intentions so far in advance, Randall Terry had not

only given my office time to set into motion the legal proceedings that hobbled Operation Rescue's attempts to impose its will on others, but he had also given the opposition time to mobilize and organize well-attended counter-demonstrations.

Launching what was supposed to be the first day of several weeks of demonstrations intended to intimidate women by a show of overwhelming antiabortion sentiment, Operation Rescue activists found themselves facing hundreds of dedicated pro-choice activists from Buffalo United for Choice and the Pro-Choice Network of Western New York in front of the targeted clinic on Main Street.

Throughout that first week of protests in April 1992, in order to monitor police enforcement of the injunction, I visited the two Buffalo clinics Operation Rescue had threatened to shut down. Emotions were high on both sides. I remember the sound of shrill whistles constantly piercing the air, prayers being intoned through a bullhorn on one side and rowdy and raucous chants on the other. A group of pro-choice activists chanted "You're not in Kansas anymore! We'll defend the clinic door" as well as the provocative "Keep your rosaries off my ovaries!" On the other side, protestors shouted back: "It's not a fetus, it's a child!"

As the week wore on, the pro-choice groups often outnumbered the Operation Rescue contingents. Stopping by one of the clinics, I saw that there were far more pro-choice demonstrators than antiabortion protestors.

Perhaps because of such scenes and the consistently strong and energetic defense of the clinics, Operation Rescue decided to cut short its "Spring to Life" campaign. An Operation Rescue spokesman eventually announced that the group would be curtailing its Buffalo activities a week and a half ahead of schedule. While they tried to put the best possible spin on this decision—the group was going to go on to fight bigger and more important battles—it was not lost on anyone that Operation Rescue had failed to achieve its declared goal of shutting down Buffalo's clinics.

As it turned out, Operation Rescue's next stop was Manhattan. Once again, Randall Terry couldn't resist the propaganda opportunity of announcing his intentions ahead of time, and in this case, those intentions involved presenting presidential candidate Bill Clinton with a fetus to "jog his conscience."

Clinton was scheduled to appear at New York City's Madison Square Garden at the upcoming 1992 Democratic National Convention. Federal

District Court Judge Robert J. Ward issued a court order at my request prohibiting the group from following through on its threat. In addition to preventing members of Operation Rescue from approaching Clinton with the fetus, the injunction also established a safe zone around the convention and imposed fines and penalties comparable to those established by Judge Arcara's injunction.

A few days later, during the Democratic Convention, several members of Operation Rescue thrust an aborted fetus at Clinton as he was leaving his hotel. They were arrested and charged with violating the court order barring them from approaching Clinton with fetal remains, as was Randall Terry for his part in planning the action. In response to the Bush administration's refusal to enforce the injunction, I directed the Civil Rights Bureau in my office to prosecute the case.

Randall Terry's lawyers moved to dismiss the action, claiming that I had a personal animus toward their client. As evidence, Terry testified that at a women's march in Washington, DC, a couple of months earlier, while marching I had seen him standing in the crowd on the sidelines and had put my thumbs in my ears, waved my fingers, and stuck my tongue out at him. According to Terry, I then mouthed the words: "You're going to lose."

Sandy Cohen, the deputy bureau chief of the Attorney General's Civil Rights Bureau, was trying the case in court, and told the judge that Terry's assertion was preposterous and that I had never done or said that. Judge Ward asserted, "He's saying this is a question of fact. I want the attorney general in here to testify." The attorney general's office handles thousands of cases each year. I couldn't be personally involved in all of the trials and proceedings of those cases. This was the only case during my tenure where the opposition successfully drew me personally into the case.

I took the stand and testified that this had never happened. My wife, Diane, was also called to testify since she was marching next to me in Washington, DC, on the day in question. The judge was satisfied, concluded that Terry's claims were false, and the case proceeded. In the end, Randall Terry was convicted and sentenced to five months in federal prison and two months of house arrest. He was held at Allenwood Federal Prison in Pennsylvania from November 1994 to February 1995, at which point he was released but kept under house arrest through April 1995.

During this period of intense antiabortion activity by radical groups, my office brought a series of cases against abortion opponents on the basis

of alleged deception and false advertising in their telephone yellow page ads. These advertisements sought to lure pregnant women seeking abortion services to come to "clinics," but in reality the women encountered antiabortion staffers who would foist on them grotesque films and skewed information with the goal of convincing women to not proceed with abortion assistance. We successfully closed down these fraudulent operations.

Just as we were fighting off street-level and other attacks on a woman's right to choose, we also had to fight off attacks in the courts.

On April 22, 1992, the third day of Operation Rescue's assault on Buffalo's clinics, the Supreme Court began to hear arguments in the case of *Planned Parenthood v. Casey*, yet another attempt to weaken and ultimately overturn *Roe v. Wade*.

The case before the Supreme Court concerned the constitutionality of the Pennsylvania Abortion Control Act, which severely restricted the right of choice. The Pennsylvania law compelled physicians and counselors to make statements to their patients that were clearly designed to put extreme pressure on a woman *not* to seek an abortion. It imposed a twenty-four-hour waiting period before an abortion could be performed and mandated that minors obtain the consent of at least one parent before going through with the procedure. It also required a married woman to sign a statement that she had notified her husband before she could obtain an abortion.

The provisions of this act—as well as the provisions of statutes that had been passed by other states attempting to restrict choice—gave a pretty clear indication of what the patchwork of abortion laws might look like should *Roe v. Wade* be overturned.

After the Supreme Court announced it would review *Planned Parenthood v. Casey*, my office got involved.

There had never been a coalition as diverse, or as numerically significant, as the one that was put together for the Planned Parenthood case. Among those who gathered in my office to express unity were representatives of Planned Parenthood, the National Abortion Rights Action League, the National Organization for Women, the New York State Coalition for Choice, the National Women's Political Caucus, the New York Civil Rights League, the New York Civil Liberties Union, and the New York State Bar Association.

Attorney General Richard Blumenthal of Connecticut, Attorney General Robert J. Del Tufo of New Jersey, and I announced our intentions

to file a brief on behalf of sixteen states and more than a thousand elected officials, urging the court to adhere to the principle of *Roe v. Wade*.

This was the first case that provided an opportunity to overturn *Roe* since the appointment by President Bush of Justices David Souter and Clarence Thomas, both known to be socially conservative and thought to be opposed to abortion. They replaced liberal Justices William Brennan and Thurgood Marshall. Clearly, Thomas's rulings were steadfastly anti-choice, but I confess with hindsight that I erred in opposing the nomination of Souter. I thought he would be antiabortion, but he turned out to be a thoughtful and moderate force on the Court.

On June 29, 1992, the Court released a lengthy, multipart decision in the *Casey* case that upheld *Roe v. Wade*, but simultaneously declared the bulk of the Pennsylvania law constitutional. The twenty-four-hour waiting period was upheld, as was the requirement that a minor obtain parental consent for the procedure. The decision weakened the overall protection offered by *Roe v. Wade* by holding that the state could pass laws that protect the life and health of the fetus and the mother in far broader circumstances than previously allowed by *Roe v. Wade*. For instance, it allowed that the state could pass regulations affecting the first trimester of pregnancy, which under *Roe v. Wade* was entirely off limits. It also held that because of medical and technological advances, which would allow a fetus to be "viable"—that is, capable of surviving outside the womb of the mother—states could now constitutionally outlaw abortion before the third trimester. According to *Roe v. Wade*, it was only at the beginning of the third trimester that states could do this. Thus, the decision of the Supreme Court was a mixed bag. The basic core decision of *Roe v. Wade* was upheld, but significant incursions were made and it was clear that the battle going forward would be difficult.

During my tenure, I submitted more pro-choice briefs than any prior attorney general. To look back at those briefs is to be reminded of the unceasing efforts of opponents of abortion to gnaw away at *Roe v. Wade*. Some of these cases constituted victories or gains for those seeking to preserve a woman's right to choose, while others ended in only partial victories and still others resulted in unfortunate losses and setbacks. Sadly, at the time of the writing of this book, the effort to undermine *Roe* continues.

Each time there is a vacancy on the Supreme Court, the battle lines are drawn. The nation makes the determination about what might

happen to *Roe* when it makes a choice in the presidential election. Typically, the Democratic presidential nominees have been pro-choice and the Republican nominees have been anti-choice. The passion and potency of this issue was on full display when the Republican majority in the US Senate, in the last year of the Obama administration, shockingly refused to hold a hearing on the nomination of Merrick Garland, a highly experienced and qualified pro-choice judge on the Washington, DC, Court of Appeals. Mitch McConnell, the leader of the Republican controlled Senate, justified the inaction, saying it was too close to a presidential election (namely, eight months before) and the public should decide by voting for the president in the upcoming general election.

Roe v. Wade was at the center of the controversy surrounding the confirmation hearings of Neil Gorsuch, Brett Kavanaugh, and Amy Coney Barrett who were Supreme Court nominees of President Donald Trump. Amy Coney Barrett's nomination demonstrated the hypocrisy of Senator McConnell's position re Merrick Garland because after the death of Ruth Bader Ginsburg McConnell rushed to schedule a hearing on Barrett five weeks before the election and a vote on her confirmation took place seven days before the American populace would vote for a new president.

In 2020, in a 5–4 ruling, both Gorsuch and Kavanaugh sided with the antiabortion conservative Justices Thomas and Alito, in a case in which the Supreme Court struck down an antiabortion law in Louisiana which was virtually identical to a Texas statute which had been previously ruled unconstitutional. Chief Justice Roberts sided with the four liberal members of the Court not on the merits of the case, but on the basis that the concept of precedent compelled him to render such a decision. Chief Justice Roberts' ability to be the swing vote is now jeopardized by the presence of newly appointed Justice Barrett on the court.

It is my fervent hope that going forward, whoever is president and whatever is the makeup of the Supreme Court, *Roe v. Wade* continues to be respected as settled law, preserving a woman's most sensitive right to control her body.

Chapter 21

The Road to Marriage Equality

T HE STATUS OF LGBTQ PEOPLE HAD improved somewhat by the early 1980s, but there were still significant legal hurdles to overcome. The onset of the AIDS epidemic led some on the religious right to claim that the disease was God's punishment for homosexuality. AIDS was used as a new pretext for discrimination and the basis for increased anti-gay violence. As attorney general I was now in a position to do something unique and significant for gay rights.

Early in my term, I signed an executive order barring discrimination on the basis of sexual orientation. It protected only those who worked for the attorney general, but it was symbolically important because it was one of the first declarations by a public official to offer this protection. The executive order was kept in place by my immediate successor, Attorney General Oliver Koppel, but rescinded by Republican Dennis Vacco who followed him. Vacco was succeeded by a Democrat, Eliot Spitzer. One of Spitzer's first official acts as New York State attorney general was to reinstate the executive order banning discrimination that had been put in place in 1980.

I also hired openly gay lawyers and other staff members who eventually organized a gay caucus to discuss issues of mutual interest and to create a sense of solidarity among gay people in the office.

I instructed my staff to find cases of discrimination directed toward people with AIDS so that we in New York could intervene and be of help. In 1983, the office brought the first AIDS discrimination case to trial when a co-op board attempted to evict a respected AIDS researcher, Dr. Joseph Sonnabend, a long-term tenant on West Twelfth Street in Manhattan. Dr. Sonnabend's practice included forty patients with AIDS. Although the

transmission of HIV was through certain bodily fluids, some mistakenly believed it was airborne and members of the co-op board were unnerved by the sight of people with AIDS in the lobby of the building.

The chairman of the co-op's board of directors informed Dr. Sonnabend that board members were evicting him because they were frightened by his AIDS patients and worried that the presence of these patients would drive down the value of their property. In bringing the case, I stated: "This attempt to evict a distinguished researcher and clinician is symptomatic of the hysteria that has surrounded the AIDS crisis. Our lawsuit is a classic antidiscrimination case and is being filed to combat this irrational prejudice." We won the case and Dr. Sonnabend was allowed to remain.

As the state's chief legal officer, I joined lawsuits that would positively alter the relationship of gay people to the law, setting out to undermine the legal impediments which made it difficult for gay people to enjoy the rights of full citizenship. Much of that effort was focused on sodomy laws.

Sodomy was not just a crime but a felony in all fifty states, punishable in many places by a lengthy prison sentence. In Idaho, for instance, until 2003, a person convicted of sodomy could be given a life sentence. Sodomy laws were almost always applied to homosexual sodomy, while heterosexual sodomy went unpunished. Indeed, it was this double standard that served as the basis for the New York Court of Appeals to ultimately strike down the sodomy laws.

As long as those laws remained on the books, gay people could be prosecuted and persecuted. The criminalization of sodomy left them open to exploitation ranging from blackmail to robberies to violent attacks. Gay men were often preyed upon by predators who perceived them as weak and easy targets.

Over the years, my office would get involved in many important lesbian and gay rights cases, often in conjunction with other organizations—the Lambda Legal Defense and Education Fund (the first organization of lawyers dedicated to securing the rights of LGBTQ people), the American Civil Liberties Union, and the Center for Constitutional Rights—that shared the objective of challenging the legitimacy and constitutionality of the sodomy statutes. We were convinced that these laws should be entirely eliminated. The office developed strong ties with these organizations. In fact, the first executive director of Lambda, Barbara Levy, left to join the office soon after I became attorney general to work in the Civil Rights Bureau.

One of the most important cases I got involved with turned out to be the landmark case of *New York v. Onofre*. Ronald Onofre was arrested by the Syracuse police and accused of having had forcible sodomy with his younger lover, Russell Evans, in Onofre's home. Following his arrest, Onofre produced evidence establishing that the relationship with Evans was consensual. The district attorney, Richard Hennessey, proceeded to drop the forcible sodomy charge and instead charged Onofre with consensual sodomy.

Having acknowledged that he had participated in acts of sodomy, Onofre had a choice—he could either plead guilty or he could choose to challenge the validity of the law itself. He chose the latter, claiming that his rights of privacy and equal treatment under the Constitution had been violated. His conviction was sustained by the lower court and his case on appeal made its way to the state's highest court, the New York Court of Appeals.

My office was called on to defend the law. In a highly unusual and visible move, I chose not to back District Attorney Richard Hennessey in this case. As one legal scholar, writing about the case many years later, put it: "Most notable in his absence was Attorney General Robert Abrams." The appeal drew widespread attention among legal advocates. Amicus curiae briefs were filed by attorneys representing a Special Committee of the Association of the Bar of the City of New York, the National Committee for Sexual Liberties, the New York Civil Liberties Union, and the Lambda Legal Defense and Education Fund. The briefs asserted that the sodomy law under which Onofre had been convicted in Onondaga County Court violated the defendant's rights as defined by the US Constitution.

Pointing out that the conduct for which Onofre had been arrested was permitted for persons who were married, the Court of Appeals found that Onofre's right of equal protection under the law had indeed been violated. Further, since the consensual sodomy had taken place in the defendant's own home and did not involve the exchange of money for sexual services, the court also found that Onofre's right to privacy had been violated. The Court of Appeals judges quoted a giant of twentieth-century jurisprudence, US Supreme Court Justice Louis Brandeis:

The makers of our Constitution undertook to secure conditions favorable to the pursuit of happiness. They recognized in law the

significance of man's spiritual nature, of his feelings and of his intellect. They knew that only a part of the pain, pleasure and satisfactions of life are to be found in material things. They sought to protect Americans in their beliefs, their thoughts, their emotions and their sensations. They conferred, as against the Government, the right to be let alone—the most comprehensive of rights and the right most valued by civilized man.

In finding for the defendant, the Court of Appeals decision had a major impact. The sodomy law under which Onofre had been convicted was declared unconstitutional and sexual behavior between consenting adults in New York State was decriminalized.

District Attorney Hennessey challenged this by petitioning the US Supreme Court to review the Court of Appeals' decision. Once again, I made it clear that the district attorney did not have my support in his pursuit of this case. His petition was denied.

<p style="text-align:center">* * *</p>

New York v. Uplinger was another important case. Its facts are as follows:

On August 31, 1981, John Uplinger, a thirty-one-year-old gay man who lived in Buffalo, New York, was wandering through an area of the city frequented at night by gay men looking to establish a sexual connection. At around 3:00 a.m., when Uplinger noticed a young man seated on the steps of the Hotel Lenox, he approached him, introducing himself, and the two men struck up a casual conversation.

Eventually, Uplinger asked: "What do you like to do?"

"I don't know," answered the young man. "What do you like to do?"

"Do you want to just come over?" Uplinger asked.

"No, I'm scared what with the police," was the reply. "I'm just going to leave."

A few minutes earlier, a police car had pulled up in front of the hotel and the officer ordered Uplinger, the young man he was speaking to, and several others who were congregated on the steps of the hotel to move on. As the young man was about to leave, Uplinger made a sexual proposition. "If you drive me over to my place, I'll blow you."

The young man, who was working undercover for the Vice Unit of the Buffalo Police Department, pulled out a badge, identified himself as a

police officer, and informed Uplinger that he was under arrest. Uplinger was charged with violating section 240.25-3 of the New York Penal Law, which prohibited "loitering in a public place for the purpose of engaging in or soliciting another person to engage in deviate sexual intercourse or other sexual behavior of a deviate nature."

Uplinger's arrest was part of a Buffalo Police Department effort to "clean up" this area of the city. The Uplinger case followed a trajectory similar to that of Onofre. Once again, the defendant was convicted. He appealed his conviction and wound up before the New York Court of Appeals. The Court again found for the defendant. The basis of its decision was that the statute that criminalized "loitering for the purposes of soliciting deviate sex" was unconstitutional on the grounds that it violated Uplinger's right to free speech as defined by the US Constitution. The decision suggested that this statute was now, in light of Onofre, an arbitrary regulation and suppression of speech.

District Attorney Richard Arcara petitioned the Supreme Court to review the Uplinger case and the court granted certiorari, agreeing to consider it. I filed an amicus curiae ("friend of the court") brief in opposition. During the oral arguments, several justices referred to my opposing view and raised issues about the procedural posture of the case, questioning the authority of the district attorney to speak on behalf of the State when the attorney general has appeared and has taken a different view. The Court dismissed the writ of certiorari as "improvidently granted" and declined to address the merits of the case. Thus, the ruling of the Court of Appeals remained untouched, allowing consensual sodomy in New York State.

The office continued to file appellate briefs to chip away at the sodomy laws. In the 1986 US Supreme Court case of *Bowers v. Hardwick*, in which I filed an amicus brief, the struggle for gay rights suffered a major setback. The Hardwick case resembled Onofre in that Michael Hardwick was arrested for consensual homosexual sodomy in his own home. The Georgia State Court of Appeals found that Hardwick's constitutional right to privacy had been violated. As a result, sodomy was decriminalized in the state of Georgia. The State, in seeking to uphold its sodomy law, petitioned the Supreme Court to review the case and won a reversal.

The headline and article that the *New York Times* ran, reporting the decision the next day, read:

"HIGH COURT, 5-4, SAYS STATES HAVE RIGHT TO OUTLAW PRIVATE HOMOSEXUAL ACTS; DIVISION IS BITTER."

The paper wrote: "A bitterly divided Supreme Court ruled 5-4 that the Constitution does not protect homosexual relations between consenting adults, even in the privacy of their own homes."

What made this particularly disturbing was the contemptuous language of the majority opinion, which barely acknowledged the humanity of homosexuals and assumed that most people were in agreement with the moral judgments at the heart of this opinion. Justice Byron White, author of the majority opinion, stressed the "ancient roots" of the sodomy statute in English common law and noted that condemnation of homosexual practices "is firmly rooted in Judeo-Christian moral and ethical standards." He also summoned the authority of Sir William Blackstone, a famed English judge and scholar who described homosexuality as "the infamous crime against nature," a crime so heinous that it "cannot be named," a crime worse than rape. In light of the law's long-standing condemnation of homosexual conduct, Justice White said, it would be "at best, facetious"—a perverse joke—to suggest that homosexual conduct qualified as a "fundamental right."

Justice White, writing for the Court, dismissed the argument that homosexual activity when conducted in the privacy of one's home was somehow protected by the Constitution. He likened it to other crimes for which one could not expect a right of privacy to prevail: "Incest, adultery, possession of stolen goods, possession of narcotics."

My public response to the Hardwick decision: "The Court is allowing states to criminalize conduct engaged in by millions of Americans—married and unmarried, heterosexual and homosexual—even though these adults are engaging in consensual sexual intimacies in the privacy of their own bedroom."

The day after the decision came down, there were demonstrations in cities across the country. In New York City, demonstrators committed civil disobedience, shutting down traffic in Greenwich Village on two consecutive nights.

For gay rights advocates, however, this was only a temporary setback. People who took the long view went back to work, filing cases and filing briefs in an ongoing attempt to do away with the antiquated laws that made gay people second class citizens. Seventeen years after the Hardwick

decision, in 2003, in *Lawrence v. Texas*, the Supreme Court struck down that state's sodomy law on constitutional grounds. By extension, they invalidated the sodomy laws that remained on the books in thirteen other states, making same-sex sexual activity legal in every state and territory of the United States.

Once this occurred, other doors were, if not opened, at least unlocked. Marriage equality was now a realizable goal. On November 18, 2003, the Massachusetts State Supreme Court ruled that same-sex couples have the right to marry, paving the way for the 2015 Supreme Court decision that declared same-sex marriage legal in all fifty states. And in June 2020, the United States Supreme Court handed down another landmark decision protecting gay and transgender employees from discrimination in the workplace.

New York proudly played a leadership role in the evolving struggle for equal rights for members of the LGBTQ community.

When I look back and think of the time that I testified before the City Council in 1971 amidst the heckling in the City Council chamber and the sustained hostile reaction by my constituents for weeks thereafter, I never would have imagined that the country would make such a giant stride forward in a relatively short period of twenty-five years. It happened in part because it proved more difficult to deny the humanity of gay people once straight people realized there were gay people all around them—people who were members of their family, or people they had known, liked, and respected for a long time. This turned out to be true even among politically conservative families and friends, so the base of support began to broaden. Many parents were not going to turn away from their children who came out. Dick Cheney was not going to disown his daughter when she revealed she was gay. Good friends were likewise not going to turn their backs on each other when one of them unexpectedly came out. The explosion of acceptance began to expand and take hold.

I'll always appreciate that conversation on the City Hall park bench with Ethan Geto when he took me into his confidence and started me on this road. We have all come a long way.

Chapter 22

Safeguarding the Rights of New Yorkers

W HEN I TOOK OVER THE OFFICE from Louie Lefkowtiz, I discovered that it was widely perceived as the adversary of civil rights groups. Virtually all of the cases in the Civil Rights Bureau were defensive cases wherein the state was accused of civil rights violations. I felt these cases should be handled in a division of the office where other defensive work was done. It was my view that the Civil Rights Bureau should be the exclusive preserve for initiating important civil rights cases that could knock down barriers and win victories for those who were being prevented from enjoying their full civil rights. I reached out to civil rights organizations to determine what they deemed to be the most important issues. We joined hands and became partners.

The office was inundated with calls and complaints about civil rights violations, in part because we made it clear that we were serious about the enforcement of civil rights and also because of the Reagan Justice Department's retrenchment in civil rights enforcement, as well as federal budget cuts in legal services for the poor.

Housing segregation and racial steering were a prevalent practice. We sent undercover investigators to Long Island to look into claims that real estate agents were steering black and Hispanic potential homeowners to minority neighborhoods, refusing to show them homes in predominantly white communities. We obtained injunctions against offending real-estate brokers and imposed fines.

Discrimination in employment was also a pressing problem. In 1989, at the conclusion of an eighteen-month investigation, we filed suit against four employment agencies in New York City, alleging widespread discrimination in their placement of job applicants. The four companies were accused of classifying job seekers according to race and referring only whites to corporations which the agencies knew or believed would not accept minority applicants. It was also alleged that they refused to refer older applicants to certain firms.

Agency personnel, who interviewed and referred job applicants, used codes such as "front office appearance," "all American," and "corporate image" to indicate that the position should be offered only to whites. In addition, counselors would write "mature" or "too much mileage" on job applicants' cards to discriminate against older job-seekers. Codes such as "six" or a reversal of the counselor's initials were written on the applicants' cards to indicate that she or he was black. One counselor called an applicant and asked if she was black, explaining that if she was, he would not bother to send her to certain job interviews. This conversation was recorded and so we had ironclad proof of discrimination.

Another racial discrimination case was the Colony Club, one of several beach clubs lining New Rochelle's nine-mile waterfront. Rachel Rotenberg, a white woman, was about to sign up and pay for a year's membership when she thought to ask the manager of the club whether her babysitter, a young black woman who had accompanied her to the club that day, would be allowed to take the children to the pool on days when she was not able to be there. "As long as she wears a uniform," the manager had replied, adding: "Members like to be able to distinguish between members and helpers." He then added that if her babysitter were white, a uniform would not be necessary.

"I was quite shaken," she told our office, indicating, "After all, it's 1992 and this is New York."

The Civil Rights Bureau proceeded to launch an investigation, dispatching white and black undercover investigators to the club to inquire about membership. The white investigators were told that all they needed to do to secure membership was to pay the annual fee of $1,300, and then they could consider themselves members that very day. The black investigators were given the runaround. One was literally locked out of the club after she had requested to be taken on a tour of the grounds. Someone finally responded to her insistent ringing of the bell only to tell her that

the manager, with whom she had been talking ten minutes earlier, was suddenly busy and would be tied up for the rest of the day.

We sued the Colony Club, charging it with discriminatory practices. The club's lawyers claimed that as a private club the Colony was exempt from state and federal laws prohibiting discrimination in public accommodations. We asserted that the Colony was not exempt because it was not in fact a private club. The judge agreed, ruling the club's manager had said and done nothing to indicate that there were any criteria demonstrating the exclusivity of a private club; nothing beyond the ability to pay the cost of a year's membership would be taken into consideration for white applicants. The court compelled the club to take measures aimed at opening its doors to minority-group members, including an agreement to advertise in black newspapers and pay compensation to those who were discriminated against.

We filed a similar case against the Ocean Club, a beach and tennis club in Atlantic Beach on Long Island. The club's manager instructed two club members *not* to invite Jewish people to the club as their guests. He informed them that the club had a policy against granting membership to Jews. The couple filed a complaint that led to an investigation, a lawsuit, and a victory in federal court. The judge ruled that the club violated the rights of two of its members, and that it did not qualify as a private club. He noted that it advertised widely for new members, accepted members from the general public, and allowed non-members to pay for tennis court time. He regarded these efforts as the equivalent of "an invitation to a large segment of the public without any requirement that might indicate exclusivity."

The two cases had in common their use of the term "private" as being clearly disingenuous and opportunistic. They conveniently claimed that they were private clubs only *after* their illegal behavior had been uncovered.

As attorney general, it was my responsibility to safeguard the civil rights of *all* New Yorkers, including those with developmental disabilities. When a group of neighbors in Russell Gardens, Long Island, learned that the State Office of Mental Retardation and Developmental Disabilities (as it was then called), planned to buy a house and set it up as residence for twelve adults and support staff, they banded together to try to stop it. The angry neighbors sought to thwart acquisition of the property by causing summonses to be issued to the property owner and attempting to have the

property reassessed to increase its taxes. Neighbors also sued the owner to prevent the sale, claiming that operation of the home would violate certain restrictive covenants, despite a New York Court of Appeals ruling invalidating such covenants. They also persuaded the property's owner to void the contract of sale while they formed a corporation to purchase the property themselves.

Whether their actions were motivated out of fear of a decrease in property values, fear of the future occupants of the home, or something else was unclear. What *was* clear was that this represented a violation of the Human Rights Law, which prohibits housing discrimination against mentally disabled people. I filed suit against the various individuals involved in this conspiracy. A decision rendered after a three-day trial in federal court concluded that the group had indeed violated the Human Rights Law, and the home opened as planned. This case set an important precedent, enhancing the state's ability to aid thousands of developmentally challenged adults who had been relegated to large institutional settings.

On numerous occasions, we even had to sue the government for discriminatory practices. For example, the town of Huntington on Long Island had a longstanding policy against hiring blacks and Hispanics, and we successfully sued the town based on a pattern that was both shamefully and demonstrably clear. Damages were awarded to black and Hispanic workers who had applied repeatedly over a number of years for positions that were vacant and for which they were qualified.

By the time I became attorney general, women were beginning to enter occupations that had previously been dominated by men. Suddenly there were women carpenters, sanitation workers, taxi drivers, train and bus drivers, police officers, and firefighters. Women could be found in all professions in record numbers. In some cases, companies hired women begrudgingly and went out of their way to make the new hires feel uncomfortable and unwelcome. Instead of capitulating, many women contacted my office and we filed lawsuits, defending their right not only to work but also to work free of harassment and discrimination.

As a result of a series of women's forums that we held, I learned about women bus drivers being denied promotions. The Metropolitan Transportation Authority (MTA), the governmental agency that operated the subways and buses in the New York City metropolitan area, had only recently allowed women to become bus drivers. A promotion to the much coveted

position of dispatcher was open only to those with seniority. Women were unable to apply for the position since, as a result of the MTA's former discriminatory hiring policy, no women were in a position of seniority. This amounted to a clear illustration of ongoing discrimination against women by the MTA. We initiated an investigation and got the MTA to remove seniority as the basis for promotion, replacing it with a merit-based selection system. When a subsequent test was given to MTA employees seeking promotion, it was a woman who achieved the highest score and who was the first bus driver to be promoted to dispatcher based upon the examination.

I also learned of repeated abuses against women employees who complained that they were sexually harassed, both physically and verbally, during mandatory polygraph tests. Some told of being touched by the male who administered the test, others of sexually explicit suggestions being made. In two different polygraph lawsuits that we initiated, the court decided not only that the employer who had hired the polygraph company was also liable, but that in the future another female must be present during the polygraph test.

The Civil Rights Bureau secured disability benefits for women who were unable to immediately return to work after childbirth and achieved victories in cases where landlords discriminated against women or families with children. Many landlords were simply not renting apartments if children were going to be in the apartment.

Women were (and still are) paid at a lower rate than their male counterparts and systematically overlooked for raises or promotions. They were punished for becoming pregnant by losing their jobs. Whenever these fact patterns were provable, we brought enforcement actions to secure women's rights.

We also took an aggressive stance on the defensive side of the office, indicating that the attorney general's office should not continue to defend the state when it was clearly guilty of having violated someone's civil rights. The traditional route taken by my predecessors was to defend the state to the bitter and costly end. It was taken for granted that the attorney general as the state's lawyer was supposed to exhaust every avenue of defense and appeal. We took the position that the attorney general had no business wasting taxpayers' money defending the state's illegal actions.

This change in approach was not met with easy acceptance by the governmental bureaucracy. The state agencies that were being accused of

discrimination felt that the attorney general was *their* lawyer and should be appealing all of their cases routinely. We told the agencies that when there was merit to an appeal, it would be forcefully undertaken, but if the state's action or inaction was in violation of the law and there was no legitimate basis upon which to argue the constitutionality or correctness of an action, we would go no further. It took some jawboning with the counsel for the state agencies and with the Office of Counsel to the Governor, but we progressively moved forward.

The Civil Rights Act of 1964 addressed the problem of widespread discrimination. It was President Kennedy who first called for the passage of a federal law that would guarantee the civil rights of all Americans, but it was President Lyndon B. Johnson who signed this historic and high-minded piece of legislation into law. It signaled a step forward for the country, improving the lives of countless Americans in significant ways.

As president of the National Association of Attorneys General, I created a Civil Rights Committee for the first time in the one hundred-year history of the organization, encouraging state attorneys general to launch civil rights investigations. We shared information concerning what we in New York and a handful of other states were doing. The committee slowly became an effective vehicle in the fight to curb discriminatory conduct, which continued to pervade so many areas of our nation's activities.

The enforcement of civil rights is essential. It is inseparable from the definition of American democracy, which insists on the will of the majority but also protects the rights of minorities. We are a great country because of our commitment to civil rights and opportunities for all.

Chapter 23

The Tawana Brawley Investigation

O N A COLD SUNDAY MORNING IN late November 1987, I was flipping through the first few pages of the *Sunday Daily News* when I read the headline: "Racial Strife Floods the Valley." The first two paragraphs of the story were about a prison riot. I was taken aback by what I read next:

> The Dutchess County family of a 15-year-old black girl charges she was kidnapped, sexually abused and marked on her body with the letters "KKK."
>
> The victim of the alleged gang rape, Tawana Brawley . . . was dragged inside a car, knocked out, driven to a wooded area and forced to perform oral sex on at least six men. Tawana's long hair was chopped off and "N_ _ _ _ _r" and "KKK" were etched on her breasts and stomach in charcoal or marker.
>
> A sheriff's deputy found Tawana . . . in a dazed state behind an apartment complex. She was trembling inside a giant plastic garbage bag. Excrement was spread on her body . . . The "emotionally distraught" girl has provided few details other than to tell a black police officer that her assailants had included a white man with a badge.

My reaction to this news story, which I'm sure was no different from that of most people, black or white, who read it, was absolute shock and total disgust. My wife Diane was with me and I read the article to her. Our joint response was that it sounded like something out of the Deep South during the darkest days of Jim Crow.

At that point, I had no way of anticipating that the Tawana Brawley investigation would ultimately become the most widely covered and sensational case of my career.

On some level, this incident reminded me of what had happened in Howard Beach a year earlier when a pack of white teenagers had beaten and then chased three black men through the streets of that predominantly white neighborhood in Queens. The teenagers who waged the attack said blacks had no right or legitimate reason to be in Howard Beach. They chased one of the three men, Michael Griffith, onto the Belt Parkway, where he was struck by a car and killed.

Not surprisingly, the Tawana Brawley story soon started attracting major media attention. The information that was publicly available and in the hands of law enforcement was limited and sketchy. Tawana Brawley had disappeared for four full days over Thanksgiving and was found on Saturday of that weekend in the backyard of the Pavilion Apartments in Wappingers Falls, eighty miles north of New York City in the Hudson Valley. The local sheriff's office received a call from a resident of the complex about a girl lying on the ground in a plastic garbage bag. Shortly thereafter, an ambulance arrived on the scene, EMTs examined the girl, and she was then transported to St. Francis Hospital in Poughkeepsie where she was treated and released later that same day. Although she appeared dazed, the emergency room doctor who examined Tawana Brawley could not find anything demonstrably wrong with her.

While at the hospital, Tawana Brawley was interviewed at the family's request by a black police officer who asked the girl if she could identify any of her alleged attackers. She leaned forward and took hold of the silver badge on the police officer's uniform coat. He asked what she meant, and when she did not respond, he gave her his duty notebook on which she wrote the words "white cop."

Once Tawana Brawley was back home, her aunt, Juanita Brawley, contacted WCBS-TV, which sent a camera crew to the Brawley apartment in Newburgh. On-camera interviews with Tawana Brawley's mother, Glenda Brawley, her stepfather, Ralph King, and her aunt, Juanita Brawley, painted a graphic picture of what reporter Mary Murphy described as "an ordeal of sexual torture and racial abuse." Tawana Brawley managed to repeat in a weak and faltering voice her allegation that a white police officer had been among her alleged assailants. At the conclusion of the televised interview, the reporter said: "It is not clear what happened, but clearly *something* happened to this child."

Soon the Tawana Brawley case was all over the airwaves, signaling the start of a media feeding frenzy that would not die down for at least nine months.

Not long after the interview was aired, C. Vernon Mason, Alton Maddox Jr., and Rev. Al Sharpton contacted the Brawley family, claiming that the Brawleys would need their help since the alleged involvement of a police officer meant a cover-up was inevitable. The family named the three as their official advisers.

Mason and Maddox had previously represented the victims in the highly visible Howard Beach case, asserting that because their clients were black they were being treated like the perpetrators rather than the victims of a crime. They advised their clients to refuse to cooperate with the investigation unless a special prosecutor was appointed, which eventually happened. While Mason and Maddox were in the courtroom, Sharpton generated attention for the case by repeatedly leading hundreds of protestors through the streets of Howard Beach. The case concluded with multiple convictions and lengthy prison sentences for three of the defendants.

The advisers indicated that Tawana Brawley had described to them the following sequence of events. On the day of the abduction, she had skipped school, going instead to see her boyfriend, an inmate at the Orange County jail, and returned by bus to Wappingers Falls that evening. As soon as she got off the bus, she was abducted into the woods where, over the next four days, she was repeatedly raped, sodomized, degraded, and violated by a group of white men, one of whom wore a badge.

Four days after the Tawana Brawley story broke, a police officer and Dutchess County resident, Harry Crist Jr., committed suicide. Alton Maddox held a press conference following Crist's death at which he accused him of having participated in the attack on Tawana Brawley. Offering no evidence of Crist's guilt, Maddox asserted that Crist had committed suicide because his role in the attack was about to be revealed.

Once the accusations had been made against Crist, William Grady, the Dutchess County district attorney who had been in charge of investigating the case, withdrew, citing a conflict of interest because one of his assistant district attorneys was a close friend of Crist. An attempt to replace him with a local attorney did not pan out, so he asked Governor Mario Cuomo to appoint a special prosecutor to handle the case.

Around this time the three advisers had contacted the governor with the same request. The governor entered into protracted discussions with the advisers over the issue of a special prosecutor. During these

negotiations, a number of names emerged and many were rejected, but the advisers felt that mine was acceptable.

In late January, I heard from the governor. "Bob," he said, "I will be designating you as special prosecutor in the Tawana Brawley case."

So, this hot potato was going to be mine.

Following the instructions of her advisers, Tawana Brawley had refused to answer any questions or provide investigators with any further information. It was obvious that this was bound to be a daunting and difficult case.

The advisers wanted me to be the special prosecutor but only under certain conditions. They were demanding that I impanel a grand jury, commit to being involved in the case on a day-to-day basis, pledge to personally conduct any and all interviews with witnesses, and make opening and closing statements before the grand jury. They also wanted a voice in the composition, assignment, and role of my staff working on the case and how we would approach Tawana Brawley.

I conveyed to the advisers through the governor that while I would oversee the case, Jack Ryan, an able, experienced prosecutor with absolute integrity and the chief of the Criminal Prosecutions Bureau in the Attorney General's Office, would handle the investigation on a daily basis. I was, after all, still the attorney general of the state of New York and had a heavy load of responsibilities. This was an important case, I would assign it appropriate resources and give it my utmost attention, but I couldn't be involved to the degree that they were demanding. However, I assured them that the case would be my highest priority. The advisers said that this formulation involving Jack Ryan was unacceptable.

On January 26, it was announced that the governor had issued an order designating me to act as special prosecutor in the case. At a press conference that same day, I stated: "I'm determined to find out what happened and urge Tawana Brawley to cooperate with this investigation."

I invited Mason, Maddox, and Sharpton to meet with me and members of my staff at my office at 120 Broadway in New York City, so that we could ascertain the facts. For the first scheduled meeting, they were over an hour late, for which they offered no explanation or apology.

We assured the advisers that we were committed to handling the investigation with total integrity, independence, sensitivity, and discretion.

We let them know that the top-notch prosecutorial team of men and women that we had pulled together included African American women

assistant attorneys general Heather A. Williams, a Harvard Law School graduate, and Suzanne M. Lynn, chief of the Attorney General's Civil Rights Bureau, as well as Charles Sanders, an experienced litigator. We told them we had contacted Dr. Hilda Hutchinson of Columbia Presbyterian Medical Center, an African American woman who had created a clinic for rape victims. She was prepared to see Tawana Brawley and to guide us in our efforts to handle the interview with the teenager with appropriate sensitivity. But the advisers weren't having any of it. By the end of the first day, no progress had been made.

We spent six hours with the advisers the following day, providing them with a conference room where they could rest, make phone calls, and also discuss what progress had been made between sessions with us. We went out of our way to be accommodating, but as the day wore on I began to have a sinking feeling.

They continued to reject my decision to assign Jack Ryan a lead role in the day-to-day investigation. And they put forth additional demands which were ludicrous. They were now insisting that we must not work or cooperate with the US Attorney's Office and the FBI.

When the meeting ended, the advisers held a press conference at which they announced that Jack Ryan's involvement meant that they had been "double-crossed by the attorney general." They were soon calling for me to be replaced as special prosecutor.

Discussions broke off and we began working on the case. Jack Ryan went to the state police and got briefed by the deputy superintendent. He had decided to steer clear as much as possible from the early investigation conducted by the Dutchess County district attorney. It wasn't that we doubted its integrity, but we wanted to demonstrate that we were starting with a clean slate.

We established the headquarters for our investigation in the state armory in Poughkeepsie. The advisers released a statement, insisting that as the person in charge, I should be stationed in the armory and not down in New York City.

In early February, we got word that Bill Cosby and the publisher of *Essence* magazine, Edward Lewis, were planning to hold a press conference at which they would be offering a twenty-five-thousand-dollar reward to anyone coming forward to provide information that would lead to the capture of those involved in the rape and molestation of Tawana Brawley. Bill Cosby was the star of the most popular television program in

America, *The Cosby Show*, and a respected and widely admired figure in the white and black communities. This was many years before he was convicted and imprisoned for serious sex offenses.

When I heard about the scheduled press conference, I decided I owed it to Cosby to fill him in on what was happening. I wanted him to know directly from me that we were conducting a serious investigation and didn't want him to unwittingly lend credence to the advisers' claim that we were engaged in a cover-up. I was also concerned that any potential leads that might surface could be used for propaganda purposes by the advisers and wanted to be assured that any evidence would be promptly passed on to our team of investigators.

The advisers continued to lob new and explosive charges. On a Sunday afternoon in early March, standing before the press, Maddox announced that he was now prepared to reveal the identity of another of Tawana Brawley's alleged attackers. He named Dutchess County Assistant District Attorney Stephen A. Pagones, offering no evidence of Pagones's involvement, merely stating that Pagones had been a close friend of Harry Crist, the police officer who had committed suicide in December. He also said, as though this were an established fact, that Pagones "had his eye on Tawana for two years." He claimed: "What we have here is an officially sanctioned conspiracy."

Pagones was able to supply solid alibis for the time period in question. As for Harry Crist, Jack Ryan told me: "I talked to his parents. Crist did commit suicide, no question about that, but it was obviously the result of a break-up with his girlfriend." Jack had listened to the answering-machine message that Crist had left for his ex-girlfriend just before he killed himself, and Harry Crist's parents showed him their son's suicide note. "It was heart-wrenching," he said. "And it had nothing to do with the case. This is not someone who killed himself because he'd participated in the gang rape of a fifteen-year-old girl."

The advisers fed newly invented and sensationalistic details to the media at every turn. They claimed to have evidence of mafia involvement and of Pagones's secret ties to the mob. They also claimed to have proof that the Irish Republican Army was behind the alleged abduction and assault. No matter how extreme the accusations—and despite the complete lack of any tangible evidence—the Brawley advisers were able to generate headline after headline.

But eventually reporters for newspapers and television stations began to be skeptical of their outlandish claims and started competing with one

another to see who could find out "what really happened" to Tawana Brawley.

Throughout all the noise in the media, Jack Ryan and the investigatory team quietly, methodically, and professionally went about collecting witness statements so that he could piece together a coherent narrative that would account for Tawana Brawley's whereabouts over those four days in November.

Sharpton asserted that for Tawana Brawley to sit down and talk to special prosecutor Robert Abrams would be "like asking somebody who watched someone go into the gas chamber to sit down with Mr. Hitler." This is just one indication of how out of control the advisers were.

I impaneled a grand jury on February 29, 1988. Of the twenty-three men and women who made up the grand jury, two were African Americans, which roughly reflected the percentage of African Americans in Dutchess County.

In our daily briefings, Jack Ryan kept me informed of any new developments. One eyewitness, a resident of the Pavilion Apartments where Tawana Brawley had been discovered, remembered looking out the window on Thanksgiving Day. She saw a girl basically fitting Tawana Brawley's description creeping along the back of a building, then peering around the side, after which she had disappeared inside that building. Another eyewitness saw a young woman on that same day step inside a plastic bag, pull the bag about halfway up her body, and then hop along for a few feet before falling down. These witness statements raised serious questions for us.

Tawana Brawley and her family had lived at the Pavilion until earlier that fall, when they were evicted for non-payment of rent. Their former apartment, 19A, was still vacant. The landlord had not changed the lock on the door and the family still had keys. Upon arrival at the hospital, Tawana Brawley had appeared to be unconscious but the test administered by the emergency room doctor who treated her indicated that she wasn't. The doctor had held the teenager's arm up over her head and let it fall. "Had she been unconscious," he explained to Jack, "her hand would have fallen straight down and would have landed on her face. But she made a conscious decision not to let that happen." The doctor also remembered saying, "Tawana, I know you can hear me, open your eyes. Open your eyes if you can hear me." And Tawana opened her eyes.

More and more of the evidence that was emerging was at odds with the story that the advisers were telling the public. Jack called my attention

to the clothing she had been wearing when she was taken to the hospital. The jeans she wore were burnt in the crotch area. But there were no burn marks on any part of her body. One of her shoes had an obscenity carved into it—but there was no blood inside the shoe. Somebody had carved the word into the shoe, but it was also obvious that the shoe could not have been on her foot when that happened. It hardly seemed likely that one of her abductors would have gone to the trouble of removing the shoe before carving the obscenity into it.

Al Sharpton regularly bused people up from Brooklyn. On one particularly tense afternoon, demonstrators tried to enter the armory. When the state police attempted to stop that from happening, a scuffle ensued. Although there was videotape that showed otherwise, Al Sharpton later accused Jack Ryan of having kicked one of the demonstrators, a former boxer by the name of Coolidge Miller. From an upstairs window inside the armory, Jack had witnessed Coolidge Miller attempting to keep a state trooper from entering the building. Jack ran downstairs, opened the door, and pulled the state trooper inside. That night, Al Sharpton was back in New York City announcing on television that Jack Ryan, the man in charge of the Tawana Brawley investigation, had "kicked a blind man." It did turn out that Miller had less-than-perfect vision, but he was not blind. The same video that exonerated Jack also showed Coolidge Miller reading a flyer. The next day, Sharpton showed up in Poughkeepsie with a pair of handcuffs, which he dangled before many television cameras, announcing that he had come to make "a citizen's arrest—I'm here to arrest Jack Ryan, the man who kicks blind people."

Maddox would constantly attack our investigation in the press, claiming it was obvious that I aligned myself with "the culprits" in this case. Pretty soon, he took to calling the investigation "the Abrams cover-up," saying it was the embodiment of the racist system trying to destroy a teenage victim of a crime.

The outright hostility that the advisers showed toward the investigation increased over time. They continued to demand that I be removed from the case. At a certain point, Al Sharpton started waging a campaign for Alton Maddox to replace me. After a while, we found ourselves almost getting used to the outrageous statements regularly made by the advisers. Still, nothing could have prepared me for the vile report that was all over the news one day: Maddox had announced that "Attorney General Abrams masturbates to the crime scene pictures of Tawana Brawley."

In spite of all of this, I remained steadfast in my determination to carry on a dispassionate, thorough, professional investigation in the pursuit of justice, wherever that might lead us.

As the months passed and our calls for Tawana Brawley and her mother to provide us with needed information continued to go unheeded, the sympathy that the public had initially expressed for the teenager was now starting to be replaced by impatience.

The governor, sensing the change in the wind, began to worry about the outcome of the case and started to call my office on a regular basis to find out why we hadn't yet managed to compel Tawana Brawley to testify.

On the one hand, he tried to distance himself from this hugely controversial case. On the other hand, he wanted to control a situation that was inherently uncontrollable. He kept his eye on what was happening at all times, weighing in publicly from time to time because people expected the governor to be in charge of the situation. He was all over us, while at the same time trying to keep a safe distance from the case. This resulted in some tension between us.

Once it became clear that the public was getting fed up, I started receiving regular phone calls from the governor. He wanted me to have Tawana Brawley arrested, have her mother arrested, or at least give him some indication that progress had been made and that the whole thing would soon be over.

One of the consequences for the advisers having generated so much publicity was that the case was being tried in the media. Eyewitnesses were regularly interviewed by reporters who had staked out the armory to be on the lookout for potential witnesses. Whenever a witness statement contradicted the story that the advisers were telling, they would attempt to discredit the witness. For example, Perry McKinnon, someone from Sharpton's own camp, went on television to tell the world that Sharpton had early on confided in him that he himself did not believe Tawana Brawley's story, and that "the only Tawana Brawley story is that there is no Tawana Brawley story . . . This is not about Tawana Brawley—it's about Mason, Maddox, and Sharpton." Sharpton held a press conference the next night to refute these allegations, claiming that McKinnon was "a mental case and a pathological liar."

More and more people were questioning whether the abduction and the violation had ever occurred. Reporters were tracking down leads all

over the mid-Hudson Valley, interviewing friends of Tawana Brawley and her family, as well as neighbors at the Pavilion Apartments, and reporting that there was no corroboration of her story. It seemed that the attitude of the public by June had become: Enough of this nonsense, she should be forced to appear before the grand jury to testify. But I was not about to compel a sixteen-year-old, let alone one who claimed to have been sexually violated, to testify.

The governor would sometimes seem to remember that he had put me in charge of this case and on other occasions it seemed as though he was, or should be, in charge. At one point—in mid-June—when the public's impatience with Tawana Brawley's refusal to cooperate with the investigation was becoming hard to ignore, the governor sent me a letter. The purpose seemed to be to distance himself from and, to some extent, raise concerns over my handling of the case. He showed the letter to me and my staff about fifteen minutes before he sent it out as a press release.

Letter from Governor Cuomo to Attorney General Abrams:

You have asked for my advice with respect to the Brawley matter.

Before I offer you my personal view, let me repeat what I have already said a number of times, publicly and privately: I believe you have done everything you could reasonably be expected to do in a difficult assignment and in the face of extraordinary obstacles. I'm grateful.

Despite that, it appears that this investigation may end leaving us with nothing but victims. Tawana and members of the Dutchess County community whom the Brawleys and their advisers have accused, but refuse to confront, are victims. And in a real sense, the people of the entire state are victims as well, because our law has been mocked and trifled with.

I am—as I know you and many others are—especially concerned about the blatant refusal by the Brawleys and their advisers not only to offer their cooperation but to respect the mandate of the law when it has been properly and legally applied to them.

Whatever else happens here, we cannot allow the legal process of our courts and law-enforcement system to be deliberately and contemptuously violated. To permit that would be to weaken the force that has tied this democracy together for 200 years and

protects especially the most vulnerable of us from oppression. Given the emotionalism and the tension that has been created among our people, we may be tempted to let pass the current fla-grant repudiation of the court's process, for fear that enforcement would be more troublesome than productive. That would be a mistake. At the end of this investigation, I believe we must be able to say to ourselves and to the rest of this state, that the law was applied in this case, as we believe it should be applied every-where, honestly, fairly and evenly. Not to apply it here, will make it more difficult to apply it everywhere else.

Of course the ultimate judgments are up to you, the courts and the enforcing authorities. But since you regard my opinion as useful, and have requested it, let me tell you that I agree with your conclusion that the process of the court, already outstanding, should be enforced. The details of how and when should be left to appropriate law enforcement discretion.

Then you should continue to pursue this investigation as long as there is the slightest hope for producing evidence that will, finally, tell us what happened, with or without the help of the Brawleys. Only when you and the grand jury believe all leads have been exhausted and there is no further realistic hope that the truth will be uncovered, should the investigation be terminated. When it is, then, provided in my Executive Order, I would ask you to prepare for me and the people of the state a report on all that has occurred, from the event in November of 1987 until the con-clusion of the investigation. I understand that the report will have to respect the confidentiality of the grand jury testimony.

These are not easy decisions, and we may never know with certainty if we have made the right ones, but I think it would be wrong to allow the present situation to continue as it is, every day further discrediting and weakening our system of law.

Mario Cuomo

I remember the day when I decided to make an important call to the governor. I said to myself, *If he's going to second-guess everything in connec-tion with the case, then I might as well get his opinion on a sensitive issue.*

"Governor," I said when he came to the phone, "here's what I'm think-ing—I am not going to subpoena Tawana Brawley, but I might subpoena her mother, Glenda Brawley."

With indifference, the governor said: "That's up to you."

* * *

We decided to subpoena Glenda Brawley. We presumed that she had asked her daughter what had happened and therefore had the essential informa-tion. It was a last-ditch effort to get closer to Tawana Brawley's story and the truth.

Glenda Brawley ignored the subpoena. We eventually sought to hold her in contempt in order to put additional pressure on her to provide us with some details of what had happened. There was a court hearing in Poughkeepsie on the contempt issue. Maddox never made any arguments that the subpoena was invalid. The judge, Justice Joseph Ingrassia, ordered Glenda Brawley held in contempt and sentenced her to thirty days in prison. This was not at all the outcome that we anticipated. We counted on her being held in contempt but without a jail sentence. Now, we had to find her, arrest her, and have her incarcerated.

As soon as the proceedings ended, I was surrounded by reporters all of whom were asking variations on the same three or four questions. Above all, they wanted to know how the attorney general was going to respond to this act of defiance on the part of Tawana Brawley's mother.

I made the following statement:

> This is a truly sad and unfortunate day. Glenda Brawley received disastrous and irresponsible advice from her attorneys and from her representatives. They utterly failed to protect her interest. They utterly failed to offer a defense. They offered no defense whatever for her. They made no attempt to produce her so that she could make an informed decision to hear from the judge what faces her by not coming before the grand jury. I'm urging her now to try to purge this contempt rather than face a sentence in jail. This has all been an effort not to punish the mother of a possible alleged victim. It has been an effort to get information. I'm urging her to cooperate with the grand jury so that we can find out exactly what happened and bring justice, so that we can find out if indeed there were

attackers and what information we can have to go and charge those attackers. So I'm urging Glenda Brawley to take the steps to purge this contempt that the judge has found here today.

The questions kept coming, even after I had said that I had no further comments. I then walked away, with several die-hard reporters pursing me down the hall.

Glenda Brawley was given sanctuary at the Ebenezer Missionary Baptist Church, the oldest black church in Queens. A few days later she was moved to the Bethany Baptist Church in the Bedford Stuyvesant section of Brooklyn. The sanctuary question posed a dilemma for us, as the advisers had known it would. We were not about to have the doors of a church broken down in our attempt to arrest Glenda Brawley. It would have been perfectly legal to do so—you can get a search warrant for a church the same way you can get one for a private apartment—but we knew this was exactly what the advisers wanted us to do.

We found out that Glenda Brawley, accompanied by Al Sharpton, would be traveling by bus to Atlanta for the 1988 Democratic Convention, where Sharpton was going to level more charges and create explosive headlines.

On the day of their departure for Atlanta, hundreds of supporters gathered to see the Brawleys and Al Sharpton off. Glenda Brawley emerged from the church handcuffed to Tawana Brawley, who was handcuffed to Al Sharpton. At Sharpton's cue, the three of them lifted their fists in defiance. Addressing the hundreds of demonstrators who had shown up in support of Glenda Brawley, Sharpton said, "We are challenging Bob Abrams to show further disrespect to the Black community to come into the church and arrest her." The crowd cheered as he declared that Glenda Brawley would be "protected by a Black Army. Yes, we challenge Bob Abrams to come into this church and do what he has to do. We will turn this town upside down!"

A plan the State Police developed to stop the bus to effectuate the arrest was thwarted and Glenda Brawley managed to evade arrest by traveling around the country for several months and eventually settling in Virginia Beach, Virginia.

* * *

On September 26, 1988, we received a phone call from a *New York Times* reporter to tell us that he had copies of summaries of evidence that had so far been presented to the grand jury. We were shocked to hear that somehow this material had gotten into a reporter's hands. The next day the *Times* published a massive story. The very aggressive team of reporters for the *Times* had gotten hold of this privileged document and spread it over several pages. This was very distressing and embarrassing because anything related to a grand jury investigation should not be publicly revealed.

The summaries showed that the detailed and methodical digging that had been undertaken by our investigation had raised extremely serious doubts about the validity of the Tawana Brawley allegations. The Brooklyn district attorney and former special prosecutor, Joe Hynes, was asked to conduct an investigation about how the summaries had gotten leaked. My staff and I cooperated fully with the Hynes probe, but notwithstanding a thorough investigation, he was not able to figure out how it had happened.

At the conclusion of the grand jury's work, we were faced with a significant dilemma.

The grand jury had produced an impressive report—thorough, detailed, and powerfully persuasive. I felt the public was entitled to see the work that was done and the conclusions drawn. It would put to rest for any fair-minded person the doubts that were floating around due to the assertions of the Brawley advisers. But under New York State law, grand jury evidence cannot be released to the public. Fortunately, we found two exceptions. If in the course of a grand jury investigation, a public official is accused of "misconduct, nonfeasance or neglect in office," New York State law provides that he has a right to make a request to clear his name. Stephen Pagones made that request and after due consideration, the grand jury voted to release its findings to the public.

The grand jury also identified a deficiency in existing law which it concluded was an important subject for legislative action. This served as another basis for allowing public release of the report.

The recommendation for legislative action stemmed from the accusations made against Harry Crist by Tawana Brawley's advisers. The grand jury reached the conclusion that Harry Crist's suicide was unrelated to the case because there was no evidence to support the accusations that had been made publicly against him. Since the family of a deceased person was not able to bring a lawsuit for defamation of the person who died, not even

if the allegations were knowingly false and maliciously made, the grand jury concluded that legislative action should be taken in order to correct this.

Over a period of eight months, the grand jury heard in excess of six thousand pages of testimony from more than 180 witnesses and received more than 250 exhibits into evidence. With the cooperation of the FBI and its lab in Quantico, Virginia, we were able to piece together information that filled in gaps and told a story that was inconsistent with the one the advisers had been conveying.

I'll never forget the day that we released the grand jury report to the public at a press conference held in the armory in Poughkeepsie.

I was seated at a table with a vast array of microphones in front of me. There were dozens of reporters and photographers representing newspapers, magazines, wire services, and radio and television stations, some of which were broadcasting live, their stations having interrupted their normal broadcast schedule to provide their viewers moment-by-moment coverage of the disclosure of the grand jury report. I made a definitive statement that was in its own way nearly as explosive as the original story. I stated: "We have the facts. We have solved the case. The allegations Tawana Brawley made are false."

Emphasizing the glaring absence of any physical evidence to back up the story of the alleged abduction and assault, I reviewed for the assembled reporters some of the more salient points that had led the grand jury to reach its conclusion.

If a fifteen-year-old girl had been forcibly raped or sodomized by multiple assailants over a four-day period, there is a high probability that medical or forensic evidence would have been found. None was.

There was in fact no semen or urine found in Tawana Brawley's mouth or on her body, which contradicted the advisers' repeated claims that tests had demonstrated conclusively the presence of five different types of semen as well as urine in her mouth. Microscopic examination of vaginal slides prepared at St. Francis Hospital found no motile sperm. Lab tests found no blood or sperm cells on the materials gathered from her fingernails or from the specimens taken from her mouth, rectum, or vagina. There were no semen stains or blood found on any of her clothes and no foreign pubic hair on her body.

There were in fact no signs of physical or sexual abuse found by the doctors who examined Tawana Brawley at St. Francis Hospital. There were no bruises or lacerations, broken bones, discolorations, or contusions

184 / The Luckiest Guy in the World

other than a slight scratch on her left breast and a quarter-sized bruise behind her left ear. There was no tenderness or blood in the rectal area or trauma to the mouth or back of the throat. There were no cuts, dried blood, bruising, swelling, or other injuries to her vaginal or pelvic areas or the surrounding skin.

Had Tawana Brawley been outdoors continuously from Tuesday evening, November 24, to Saturday afternoon, November 28, when the temperature several times dropped to the freezing point, there was a high probability she would have suffered from exposure, but doctors found no evidence of exposure. Had she been deprived of food for four days, Tawana Brawley would have shown signs of malnourishment, but this wasn't the case.

The mountain of evidence left behind in Apartment 19A suggested to the grand jurors that Tawana Brawley had used the apartment in order to plant on her own body what was supposed to be evidence of the assault. All of the items necessary to account for the state of her appearance when she was found in the garbage bag on November 28 could be found in or in the immediate vicinity of Apartment 19A. A razor blade found inside Apartment 19A turned out to be consistent with the instrument used to cut the racial epithet into the side of one of her pink shoes. Pieces of charred cotton found in the apartment may have been used by Tawana Brawley to write racial slurs on her body and on the pink shirt that she was wearing the day she was discovered. The writing on her body was visually consistent with writing produced using moistened charred cotton residue, and moistened charred cotton residue was found in the apartment and under Tawana Brawley's fingernails. Pieces of charred cotton were found by the sink. It was also noted that the obscenities scrawled on Tawana Brawley's body were written upside down, suggesting that she may have written them herself. Carpet fibers consistent with those from Apartment 19A were found on the jeans, on the blouse, and on one of the shoes Tawana Brawley was wearing when discovered on November 28.

Other evidence found inside the apartment included dog feces consistent with the feces smeared on her body, as well as hair from Tawana Brawley's head. Clumps of Tawana Brawley's hair were missing the day she was discovered. Evidence left behind in the apartment suggested that she had cut her own hair before smearing it with feces. A pair of latex gloves smeared with dog feces had also been found near the plastic bag in which Tawana Brawley was first discovered.

Among the witnesses cited in the report were experts in forensic serology, hair and fiber analysis, fingerprints, handwriting analysis, forensic chemistry, psychiatry, medicine, and other fields, as well as people with direct knowledge of the Brawley case.

Besides failing the consciousness test that the physician at St. Francis Hospital administered, the report also pointed out other signs that Tawana Brawley was feigning unconsciousness. She had opened her eyes twice, according to witnesses, prior to the arrival of EMTs. She resisted the efforts by an EMT to open her eyes and grabbed with both of her hands the arms of one of the EMTs examining her. She also resisted an EMT's attempts to straighten her legs on the stretcher upon which she was placed and resisted the emergency room physician's efforts to open her eyelids.

The report highlighted the significance of the testimony of an eyewitness who claimed that at approximately 1:30 p.m., on Saturday, November 28, she had looked up while vacuuming and had observed through her sliding glass back door Tawana Brawley in a squatting position in the area behind Apartment 19A. According to this witness, Brawley, after looking around for a couple of seconds, stepped into a large plastic garbage bag and pulled it up to her neck. She remained stationary for another couple of seconds and continued to look around. She then hopped two times and lay down on the swampy ground beneath an air conditioner on the back wall of an apartment at 17 Carnaby Drive.

Based on photographic evidence that backed up Steve Pagones's alibis for the time period in question and testimony regarding the contents of Harry Crist's suicide letter, the grand jury dismissed allegations that Steven Pagones and Harry Crist had participated in the alleged abduction of and attack on Tawana Brawley.

Members of the grand jury also dismissed accusations of a cover-up on the part of law enforcement, noting that the sheriff's office had promptly notified the FBI of the case. The sheer number of coconspirators who would have had to participate in this cover-up seemed to point out just how implausible these allegations were.

The advisers were quick to denounce the findings of the report in a four-hour broadcast over radio station WLIB, a major radio station serving the black community in New York. Sharpton claimed that plans were in the works for Tawana Brawley to give public testimony about what had happened to her. But in fact this never occurred.

The grand jury report was credible enough that the bulk of the community believed what it said. Newspaper editorial boards felt that the job that we did in handling the Brawley case was professional, serious, and ultimately uncovered the truth. It was stated that I had done a public service by exposing the lies that were told in relation to what had allegedly occurred. The *New York Times* pointed out the "avalanche of evidence" contained in the 170-page grand jury report included "minutely detailed medical, scientific and eyewitness testimony." Many other major newspapers published editorials that praised our handling of the case.

The *Poughkeepsie Journal* asserted that it was "obvious from the grand jury's report that every possible lead in the case was followed, and that despite the lack of eyewitnesses and the testimony of the victim, the state investigators were able to develop significant evidence to prove unequivocally what did *not* happen to Tawana Brawley."

The *Chicago Tribune* was equally unambiguous: "The grand jury deserves thanks for producing a report so thorough that no doubts can remain about Tawana's story." Editorial after editorial noted that the investigation had been handled correctly from the start in spite of the considerable pressure exerted on my office from all sides.

News organizations and individual reporters greeted the report with respect for its thoroughness and professionalism, but they wanted more—the "who, what, when, where, and how" were not enough. They also wanted to know "why." And eventually, the "why" was disclosed twice—in a major article by Les Payne, a reporter and columnist at *Newsday*, and in the book *Outrage: The Story Behind the Tawana Brawley Hoax* by a team of six reporters at the *New York Times*. According to these accounts, several of Tawana Brawley's friends stated that she was terrified of her mother's live-in boyfriend, Ralph King, a man with a violent past who had spent time in prison for shooting and killing his wife. In a previous incident, he stabbed his wife fourteen times. It was revealed to the grand jury that a few weeks before her disappearance, Tawana Brawley had attended a Sweet Sixteen party in Fishkill, New York. The party ended between 1:00 and 2:00 a.m., but Tawana did not return home until 5:00 a.m. When she walked in, Ralph King was waiting for her. She was grounded and lost her phone privileges.

According to the authors of *Outrage*, Tawana Brawley eventually confided in her former boyfriend, Daryl Rodriguez, that she had in fact concocted the story of the abduction and assault. Her mother, Glenda Brawley,

helped her stage the scene in a desperate attempt to spare Tawana Brawley from having to endure yet another encounter with Ralph King's violent temper. The plan quickly spiraled out of control.

At the time the grand jury report was released, I publicly expressed my strong view that the advisers had engaged in an utterly reckless, disgraceful, and destructive course of conduct increasing "the atmosphere of tension between the races throughout this nation."

I filed disciplinary charges against Maddox and Mason with the appropriate grievance committees, outlining repeated instances where I believed the lawyers had violated disciplinary rules governing the conduct of attorneys. They had deliberately made false statements, accused innocent people, and counseled their clients to engage in illegal conduct.

At the outset of the case, C. Vernon Mason had a good reputation. He had run a credible race in the Democratic primary for district attorney of New York County against Robert Morgenthau. However, it seemed that part of his agenda in the Brawley case was to make himself well known, and indeed he did. People in the community came to him with their legal matters, enabling him to enhance his law practice. This turned out to backfire because he generated so much business from the community that he ultimately neglected his clients, some of whom filed grievances against him, which resulted in his being disbarred.

As a result of the charges I filed against Alton Maddox, his license was suspended because he never cooperated. He said, "I can't get justice—in America, in New York, from the bar association, from the organized bar, it's a racist group, it's a racist society." His license remains suspended to this day and he continues to make outrageous statements online regarding the case and me.

It became clear that Sharpton wanted to use this case to launch himself into public view and be seen as a fierce advocate for African American interests. He wanted to have his name in headlines, to be able to advance his personal agenda. Even though he was greatly discredited for his conduct with regard to this case, he has in fact been able to position himself politically as a power broker and host of an MSNBC cable television show. To his credit, in years subsequent to the Tawana Brawley case, he has effectively spoken out about racism in genuine and legitimate cases of police abuse and helped focus attention on problems in the criminal justice system.

Sharpton is not a lawyer, so no charges could be filed against him. However, Steve Pagones sued him for defamation and won $65,000 in damages. Sharpton stated that he was penniless and others in the black community came forward and raised money for him to help pay that judgment. Tawana Brawley was also sued for false accusations made against Pagones and was ordered to pay $190,000.

I'd always had a very strong record politically in the African American community. I was grateful that many important African American political leaders and pillars of the community such as Percy Sutton, Basil Paterson, David Dinkins, and the Reverend Calvin Butts of the Abyssinian Baptist Church let it be known that they did not question my motives or my integrity. Reverend Herbert Daughtry's comments were carefully stated and sensitive to the integrity of the investigation.

For a long time afterward, both at the office and at home, I received hate mail and threats.

The Brawley case raised and brought to the surface the issue of racial prejudice in the criminal justice system. It became the lightning rod for the yet unfulfilled promise of racial justice and tapped into the psyche of African Americans whoever they were and wherever they lived, and it caused many white Americans to reflect deeply about their own attitudes toward race. It is important for us to remember that while the allegations that a black teenager's charges would not be investigated fairly were misplaced in this particular case, there is validity to the charge that the criminal justice system has failed to operate with fairness on far too many occasions.

From slavery to emancipation, to the ending of school segregation, to the civil rights movement in the 1960s, to this present day, our country has been struggling with the issue of racial tension and inequality since its birth 245 years ago. Discrimination based on race is still prevalent and we must redouble our efforts to fight for its eradication. It is unacceptable that members of the African American community continue to be subjected to the routine use of excessive force by police and that unjustified police shootings have led to the tragic deaths of so many African Americans. While significant progress has been made, it is imperative that we keep striving to come closer to that long sought after, elusive goal of equality.

Chapter 24

Museum of the American Indian

E D COSTIKYAN, A BRILLIANT AND ARTICULATE lawyer, came to my office at Two World Trade Center in February 1985. I can still see him standing there with his Ben Franklin glasses, his three-button suit, and his bow tie. As he made himself comfortable in a chair across from me, he said, "Bob, I'm here representing the Museum of the American Indian. As I'm sure you've been told by your staff, we've received an offer from Ross Perot to build a world-class facility in Dallas, Texas. We plan to accept that offer and move the collection to Dallas."

I was reminded of my conversation with Robert Moses years earlier when I was Bronx Borough president and he told me he was going to move the Hall of Fame of Great Americans out of the Bronx. My reaction was the same: *Hell no!* I said, "Eddie, you know you can't do that because the trust indenture that created the museum won't allow it. It says, 'There shall be a Museum of the American Indian in the City of New York.'"

He said, "We are filing a petition in court seeking approval to do it."

I responded, "As attorney general, I'll strenuously oppose it."

Thus began a fascinating, hard-fought, multiyear battle for control of a unique collection—the world's largest gathering of two million artifacts of Native American cultures from the North Pole to the South Pole.

Costikyan went out of his way to paint Perot, the Texas business tycoon, as the museum's white knight who had come along to save the collection. As evidence of the museum's need for the move, he mentioned the run-down warehouse where the museum stored the bulk of its collection.

At the invitation of Roland Force, the museum's director, Pamela Mann, the head of our Charities Bureau, and I went to see the museum's warehouse storage facility. The tour was meant to impress upon us its deteriorated condition and the fact that it housed 96 percent of the museum's holdings because of the museum's shortage of display space. He also reiterated his complaint about the deterioration of the Washington Heights neighborhood in which the museum was situated, gravely compromising its ability to attract visitors.

The first thing I noticed when we entered the building was an enormous canoe, the sides of which were painted with Native American designs, and an immense number of masks stacked up in pell-mell fashion against a wall.

As we made our way through the large room, Force pointed out some of the museum's treasures. I remember wampum belts, buckskin dresses, beaded and feathered headdresses, shields, tomahawks, papoose carriers, sacred weavings, dust-covered bearskin rugs, and elk and buffalo heads which had been preserved by Native American tribes. There were Aztec drums, artifacts made of gold, and feathered objects from Brazilian Amazonian tribes. The museum's collection included material from tribes of all parts of North, Central, and South America.

It was disturbing to note the fact that such a huge proportion of its vast holdings had been stored for decades in a damp and deteriorating building with a dangerously leaking roof. Until recently no reliable inventory of the museum's holdings had been undertaken.

The museum had been weighing a number of relocation options since 1977. Members of the board had tried but so far failed to secure the US Custom House overlooking Battery Park as the museum's new headquarters. To some on the board, the Custom House, a landmark seven-story Beaux Arts building designed by Cass Gilbert, seemed ideal. Board members had also become weary of protracted negotiations with the American Museum of Natural History for some sort of joint operation. We learned that the museum had received proposals to relocate to Las Vegas and Oklahoma City, but those offers had ultimately been rejected in favor of the one made by Perot.

The museum was founded in 1916 by George Gustav Heye, a mining engineer. His trust said that he was creating a museum in New York to honor and showcase his extensive collection of Indian artifacts and to educate the public about Native American culture. When the museum

first opened its doors in 1922, it was one of several cultural institutions located in what was at the time a wealthy upper Manhattan neighborhood.

During the tenure of Attorney General Lefkowitz, Edward Carpenter, a member of the board, had brought to his attention questionable practices and evidence of neglect. Lefkowitz launched an investigation, which ultimately found that the board had systematically falsified its records, had illegally and unethically sold off important artifacts, and had engaged in sloppy bookkeeping and improper maintenance of its collection. The museum became the subject of scandal, the latest example being the controversial issue of deaccessioning, the process by which a museum sells or trades its possessions. The museum had no established deaccessioning policy, which resulted in parts of the collection ending up in the hands of friends of board members, including television personality Dick Cavett. Others had been sold to private collectors. Lefkowitz had ordered the dissolution of the board of trustees, with the exception of the whistleblower, Edward Carpenter. The new board was charged with conducting an inventory of its holdings and of establishing a proper deaccessioning policy. Roland Force came on as director as part of the reorganization.

With its plan to leave New York, the museum once again found itself the subject of public criticism. The opening lines of editorials in the *New York Times*, *USA Today*, and the *Daily News* reflected the sense of betrayal and anger incited by the board's readiness to give away this collection: "A Treasure Not for Trading," "Dallas Tries to Lure Indian Museum," and "The Indian Museum Must Stay in New York."

As attorney general, I had authority over all charities created in New York and all charitable activities based in the state. I was essentially the lawyer to fulfill the intent of George Heye's indenture specifying that there shall be a Museum of the American Indian in the City of New York. The attorney general was responsible for seeing to it that his wishes were carried out, which is how the office became embroiled in the case.

We made a motion to dismiss the museum's petition. The judge denied our motion but ruled that if the museum wanted to get out from under the trust's restriction of staying in New York, it would have to demonstrate it was "impossible or impracticable" to remain in New York.

We subpoenaed the museum's chairwoman of the board, Mrs. Wilmot H. Kidd III, to appear and explain the museum's reasons for rejecting a long list of alternate locations in New York. Our position was that while

the museum had pursued the American Museum of Natural History and the Custom House, it had yet to exhaust other viable alternatives in New York City, including the architecturally beautiful old police headquarters in lower Manhattan, the Federal Archives building in Greenwich Village, and the former Gimbels building on East Eighty-sixth Street.

We also informed the lawyers for the museum of our intention to take the depositions of certain key players, including Ross Perot. Costikyan opposed this. We won that motion but by that time Perot had withdrawn his offer.

Meanwhile, the case had begun to take on a life of its own. Governor Mario Cuomo, New York's senators, businessman and philanthropist David Rockefeller, and even President Reagan eventually added their voices to the impassioned discussions that followed.

Mayor Ed Koch was now pushing for the museum to enter into an arrangement with the American Museum of Natural History. Museum directors ultimately rejected that option out of what appeared to be a well-placed concern that the collection would be swallowed up and would cease to exist as a separate entity with its own unique identity.

The museum continued to fight for its relocation to the US Custom House in lower Manhattan, but its tenancy was opposed by those who were arguing for the Custom House as the site of a New York Holocaust Museum. Senator Moynihan, cochairman of the Senate Committee on Environment and Public Works, which was responsible for the preservation of historical and architecturally important public buildings, supported the move of the museum to the Custom House. Senator D'Amato strongly opposed it. Others argued for the involvement of the Smithsonian Institution, essentially reinforcing the museum's argument that its responsibility was toward preserving a national—not only a local—treasure.

I went to Washington, DC, three times to testify before Congress and make the fundamental point that the museum could not be removed from New York.

After years of discussions, we ultimately wound up with a Solomonic resolution: the Smithsonian Institution, a highly respected, government-run cluster of museums in Washington, DC, would acquire the assets of the museum and take responsibility for operating and maintaining the collection; fifteen members of the twenty-five-member new board of the National Museum of the American Indian would be nominated by the Heye Foundation; the museum would retain its historic quarters at

155th Street in Washington Heights; and a new twenty-five-million-dollar facility would be created in the Custom House at Bowling Green, thereby doubling New York City exhibition footage. The collection of two million artifacts would be preserved as a result of the construction of tempera-ture-controlled pods at a cost of $44 million; thus the collection was no longer in danger of rotting and molding away in an inadequate warehouse. Finally, the Museum was awarded the last available site on the Mall in Washington, DC, where a new National Museum of the American Indian budgeted at $106 million was to be built.

The Smithsonian got a federal appropriation for its support of the collection. New York City, as well as New York State, also contributed money, which would be earmarked exclusively for the New York facility at Bowling Green. It would be called the George Gustav Heye Center.

Since our agreement, the new facilities have been built and opened to the public. In recent years there have been more than a million annual visitors to the Washington, DC, museum who have had the opportunity to view the unique collection in a sensitively designed building. More than 350,000 people annually visit the Heye Center at Bowling Green.

This was an extraordinary menu of achievements to preserve and expand the museum, reminding the public of the extraordinary richness of the cultures of US Native Americans and the indigenous peoples of the Western Hemisphere.

Chapter 25

Rare Hebrew Books

"**B**OB, ARE YOU AWARE OF THE Judaica auction that Sotheby's is having?" Ludwig Jesselson was saying on the other end of the phone in June 1984. "It's *very* suspicious. They have these rare books for sale that were last in a Jewish seminary in Berlin before World War II. They may have been stolen by the Nazis. You should look into this."

I said, "Okay, Luddy, thanks for alerting me. Let me find out what's going on."

Ludwig Jesselson, a world-class collector of Judaica, was one of the most respected and significant philanthropists in the Jewish community. He was also a trustee and later chairman of the board of Yeshiva University. He escaped Germany prior to the Nazi takeover, came to America, went to work for Philipp Brothers, the world's largest marketers of raw materials, and worked his way up to the position of chief executive officer.

I called Pamela Mann, the head of the Charities Bureau in the attorney general's office. "Pamela," I said, "I just got this call. Let's investigate and see what's going on with respect to this auction."

Indeed, after a preliminary review we were convinced that there were problems surrounding the potential sale of these books. We needed to know who the rightful owner was. The catalogue did not divulge this information, listing the consigner as an anonymous person, which only heightened the mystery. We discovered that many people shared Jesselson's concern that these extraordinary books had perhaps been stolen by officers of Hitler's SS or possibly a rank-and-file soldier who had sacked a Jewish institution, allowing a Nazi to wrongfully get the benefit of the sale.

There were sixty-one books up for auction. Among the most spectacular and precious was a Bible penned by a scribe in 1487 in Prague, with commentaries by Rashi, one of the most prominent commentators in Jewish life. The other uniquely valuable book was a fourteenth-century *Machzor*, a special prayer book for the high holidays of Rosh Hashanah and Yom Kippur.

We tried to get information about the seller but the consignment agreement required the auction house to keep the seller's identity confidential. We learned that the books and manuscripts had come from the Hochschule, a Jewish seminary in Berlin that had been shut down by the Nazis in 1942.

Arguing that this was a suspicious sale, we brought a motion for a temporary restraining order to stop the auction. It was our position that the consigner's right to sell these works needed to be established. Furthermore, we contended that they had come from a public institution and should not go into private hands. As part of the Jewish patrimony, the books should be available to scholars and members of the public. The motion was denied and the sale went forward.

There was now a risk that the books and manuscripts would be resold by the successful bidders and irretrievably dispersed. We immediately filed a motion for a preliminary injunction.

Suddenly we received blockbuster news. The alleged owner of the books and manuscripts was discovered to be Alexander Guttmann, an eighty-year-old professor at Hebrew Union College, the Reform movement's seminary in Cincinnati, Ohio. His identity came as a stunning surprise to everyone. Guttmann claimed that he had brought the books and manuscripts to the United States from Germany. On the advice of his lawyer, a few years before the sale, Guttmann had transferred ownership of the books and manuscripts to his wife, Manya Guttman, who had put them up for sale. Pamela's sense was that "Manya Guttman probably thought that she should get them sold while her husband was still alive because he was the only person who could substantiate her claim to them."

Pamela and Assistant Attorney General Noel Dennis flew to Cincinnati to take the deposition of Alexander Guttmann, who told the following story.

He was living in Germany during Kristallnacht, in 1938, when the Nazis stormed into synagogues, set them on fire, burned religious books, rounded up and arrested thirty thousand members of the Jewish

community, and killed at least a hundred Jews. The effort to annihilate European Jewry was beginning.

At that time, Guttmann was a young professor at the *Hochschule fur die Wissenschaft des Judentums* (the College for the Scientific Study for Jewish Culture), where he was in charge of ordaining rabbis. He saw the handwriting on the wall and, in 1940, accepted an invitation from Julian Morgenstern to become a visiting Talmud professor at Hebrew Union College in the United States. With the war in Europe already in progress, it was extremely difficult to obtain a visa but Guttmann applied for and was granted one.

Guttmann claimed that Heinrich Veit Simon, the head of the Hochschule, called him into his office and said, "I hear that you have a visa. I'd like you to help us preserve the most valuable and unique books in our library." The Hochschule library had approximately fifty thousand books. According to Guttmann, Veit Simon told him that if he did in fact manage to get the books to America, given the grave risk attached to trying to get them out of the country, they would be his. Guttmann stated that while the Nazis allowed a handful of Jews to leave, they could not take any valuable possessions with them. Anyone who tried to do that risked being arrested and sent to prison.

The Nazis sent soldiers to watch Guttmann pack his suitcases, to make sure that no unauthorized materials were being taken out of Germany. He packed ordinary books together with clothes. Later that night, at great personal risk, using an open window, he slipped back into the room where the suitcases were stored, and he replaced the ordinary books with the priceless volumes.

He kept the books for forty years on a shelf in his closet and now—because he was getting old and infirm—he had given them to his wife and she had put them up for auction.

Pamela reported that Guttmann seemed nervous throughout his testimony. She said that it had been hard to get him to talk at first. She indicated when he was originally asked to recount the story of how the books had come to be in his possession, he made no mention of the fact that Veit Simon had told him that the books would be his if he managed to get them out. He merely stated that Veit Simon had asked him to take the books out of the country. "Guttmann's lawyer kept prompting him throughout the deposition: 'What did he say would happen if you got them out of the country? That they would be yours, right?' 'Oh yes, right.'"

Pamela said, "At that moment it was obvious that he had constructed this scenario as the rationale and justification for his assertion of proper ownership of the books." She felt he had never been told, "If you take them out of the country they belong to you."

Guttmann's behavior did not demonstrate that he was the rightful owner of these books. He had other manuscripts that he shared with students but he never shared the books from the Hochschule. He never disclosed to anyone that he had them. His behavior was inconsistent with the idea that the books legitimately belonged to him.

The president of Hebrew Union College, Alfred Gottschalk, was upset with Guttman because he felt that he was lying. If he had been forthright earlier in conveying to the world the story he was now telling, those books could have been studied at Hebrew Union College and served as the basis of seminars and discussions with other scholars. Gottschalk had asked Guttmann directly, when it was revealed that the books contained the stamp of the Hochschule, whether the books in question were his—and Guttmann had denied that they were. Gottschalk stated, "This is very painful. He denied it. This I don't understand. This is the part that bothers me most."

Pamela said, "My guess is that it was not his idea to sell the books. The idea probably came from his wife because she wanted them sold so they could have some money to pass on to their children."

After the deposition, Guttmann's lawyers appeared open to settlement discussions.

We felt the public was not provided with the facts relating to the provenance of the books. This case had the potential to establish significant precedents but it was also a case of first impression and was not an easy one to prove if it ever went to trial. Guttmann's attorneys were also raising issues about the attorney general's authority and standing to bring the case. Because of these uncertainties as well as the time it would take to try the case and to exhaust appeals, we entered into settlement negotiations.

Prior to the auction, the handwritten Prague bible and the fourteenth-century *Machzor* had been withdrawn from the catalogue and sold for $900,000 in a private sale. The anonymous purchaser gave those two books to the Jewish Theological Seminary (JTS), an institution affiliated with the Conservative movement.

We came to a global resolution that I thought took into account the strengths and weaknesses of the case as well as the equities involved. People could pick it apart, but it accomplished many of our major goals.

We felt that the books were part of the history and legacy of the Jewish people and belonged in the public domain. At the same time, we needed to acknowledge the competing claims among the three streams of Judaism: Orthodox, Conservative, and Reform. We sought the guidance of the Jewish Restitution Services Organization (JRSO), which had been dealing with restitution issues since World War II. At the end of the war, a set of laws was created by the Allies to deal with the issue of property the Nazis had confiscated which now had no owners. Ordinarily, unclaimed properly would go to the state, but given the fact that the state in this case was the perpetrator of the theft, another solution had to be found.

We could not have reached the settlement without the generosity of another anonymous donor. The first anonymous donor who had bought the books for the JTS was thought to be Ivan Boesky. There was a second anonymous donation of $900,000 which was put in the pot to help us effectuate the settlement. We think the donor was Ludwig Jesselson.

The details of the settlement were as follows: the two books from the JTS were returned. The JTS paid $900,000 for the books and so the $900,000 from the second anonymous donor would go back to JTS.

The Prague Bible and the *Machzor* would ultimately remain in two libraries affiliated with the Orthodox branch of Judaism, Yeshiva University in New York and the Hebrew University Library in Jerusalem. The public would have additional access to them because we worked out an arrangement whereby they would be placed on display for a designated period of time at the New York Public Library, at the JTS, and at the Hebrew Union College.

Guttman was given $900,000. Some people felt that since it appeared that he lied, why should he get any money? The auction sale produced $2,000,000. He was not getting the full benefit of the sale. But he did risk his life to successfully take those books out of Germany. If he was caught, he, his wife, and his child would have been killed. He in fact protected the books. His conduct was not admirable from our point of view, but there were positives and there were negatives. It was our opinion that the reason he was selling the books at that point was that he was getting old and was under pressure from his wife, saying, *what are you doing with these books? They're just lying here. No one knows that they're here! We're not getting the benefit of them. You should pass on something to your children and your grandchildren.*

The court ordered the return of all of the unique books bought at the auction that could not be found in other libraries. Proceeds from the sale

would be used to reimburse purchasers of the returned books. Those returned books would be distributed to Hebrew University Library in Jerusalem, Yeshiva University, JTS, Hebrew Union College, and the Leo Baeck Institute in London, which were institutions affiliated with each of the streams of Judaism. Those institutions would also receive the remaining balance of money in the pot, including any profit that Sotheby's was to gain, to be used to purchase other important works. The settlement also included a commitment on the part of Sotheby's concerning how it would make disclosures to the public related to provenance in any future auctions.

This interesting set of facts has been the subject of commentary and analysis in law review articles. It was for me a reminder of how the attorney general's office is called upon to play a myriad of roles, which are at times esoteric, and often involve matters of significant public interest.

Chapter 26

Mario Cuomo

OVER THE YEARS, MY RELATIONSHIP WITH Mario Cuomo was, at its core, one of mutual respect, but there were occasional ups and downs. The Brawley case was an example of how tension could arise between us. Some of this was institutional—the result of a governor and an attorney general doing their jobs. But I had many different kinds of interactions with Mario Cuomo.

In early 1977, prior to the mayoral primary in New York City, Governor Hugh Carey, who played an important role during New York City's fiscal crisis to help save it from going into bankruptcy, reached out to me. He did not have confidence in Abe Beame to do what was necessary to keep the city afloat. He urged me to support Mario Cuomo for mayor. I had a good feeling about Cuomo. I would never have endorsed Beame because he was supported by the party bosses and he had proved to be a poor fiscal manager, but I had strong, positive relationships with Herman Badillo, Percy Sutton, and Bella Abzug, who were also running. I did not have a meaningful alliance with Ed Koch, the remaining candidate. I ultimately supported Mario, incurring pain and cost with the other candidates, who were upset and disappointed. My endorsement was important for Mario because he did not have support from other significant elected officials. In the course of actively campaigning with him, we established a strong bond. Koch and Cuomo scored the highest of the five on primary night but since neither candidate received more than forty percent of the vote, there was a runoff. Koch beat Cuomo, but Mario decided to stay in the race and run actively in the general election as the Liberal Party candidate. Carey and I, along with other Democratic officeholders,

took the position that since Koch was a mainstream candidate, we would be supporting him in the November election on the Democratic line. I had a conversation with Mario about this and he was gracious and understanding. Mario ran a strong race but lost to Koch by almost ten points.

The following year, 1978, as the statewide races began to come into focus, Mario started telling insiders that he was interested in running for attorney general. This was three years after my first run for attorney general, when I won the primary for the Democratic nomination and lost the general election to Attorney General Louie Lefkowitz. Having used the intervening years to further cultivate and strengthen my statewide base, I was gearing up for another run, hopefully this time a successful one, because perhaps Lefkowitz would retire. Most people were telling Mario he would have a tough time winning if he ran against me. He approached David Garth, the political media guru, and attempted to get him to run his media campaign, but David told him that he had already signed on to run Governor Carey's reelection effort. He also told Mario I would be difficult to beat. David called me to tell me of his conversation with Cuomo.

Then suddenly a political thunderbolt hit. Lieutenant Governor Mary Anne Krupsak, who was not getting along well with Carey, decided to challenge him in the primary for the Democratic nomination. Carey's poll numbers weren't strong. He then asked Mario to run with him on the ticket in the lieutenant governor slot. Although Mario had certain doubts about whether he would work well with Carey as his lieutenant governor, I think he saw that being in that post was a strong and natural platform for him to run for governor down the road and so he told Carey he would do it. This was also good news for me because I wouldn't have to confront the prospect of running against Mario, who obviously would have been a difficult opponent. Carey easily defeated Krupsak for the Democratic nomination for governor and so Mario ran with him for lieutenant governor. In the fall general election, Carey, Cuomo, and I won our races.

Mario and I had a cordial relationship as he began serving as lieutenant governor and I began my service as attorney general. Our duties did not overlap in any way, but we would see each other at Democratic Party events and at governmental receptions. Our respective offices played each other in softball on Governor's Island, which was very competitive and a lot of fun. We also were seated together at the rostrum when the governor delivered his annual State of the State address.

In 1980, two years into my term as attorney general, Mario and I found ourselves in leadership roles on different sides of the Democratic presidential primary sweepstakes. When Senator Ted Kennedy indicated he was ready to challenge Jimmy Carter for the Democratic nomination, I stepped into the fray and became the leader of the Kennedy for President campaign in New York State.

Mario became the statewide spokesman for the Carter campaign. At times we were on radio programs, speaking on behalf of our respective candidates. We had friendly dueling quotes in the newspapers about the campaign or policy positions of our candidates. Kennedy won big in New York, beating Carter by capturing 59 percent of the vote to Carter's 41 percent. Carter scored victories in subsequent state primaries and ultimately won the nomination.

In 1982, Carey announced that he would not run for a third term. Mario, who had a contentious relationship with Carey while serving as his lieutenant governor, had been thinking of challenging him in a primary. Carey's announcement that he would not run again created a clear path for Mario to go forward. This situation, however, created in Mario's mind a political problem between the two of us. He felt that I had my sights on running for governor and was going to enter the race. Staffers and others were, in fact, encouraging me to consider running for governor, but I promptly concluded that the timing wasn't right. I was completing my first term as attorney general, loved the job, and had put in place a great team who were producing important results for the people of New York. I relished the idea of continuing to implement and actually expand my agenda as attorney general. I had no interest in shifting course. Diane completely agreed with my thinking.

Mario wound up having a rematch with Ed Koch in the primary, this time in a statewide race. Koch was a popular incumbent New York City mayor. Mario, an underdog with strong union support, came from behind to defeat Koch in the primary and was elected governor, beating Lew Lehrman, the Republican candidate, in the general election.

As governor and attorney general, Mario and I got along pretty well. From time to time there were some skirmishes, such as disagreements about appealing certain court decisions. My staff correctly took the position with the governor's staff that under the statutory framework and case law in New York it is the attorney general's role and responsibility to make decisions about when and where judicial rulings should be appealed.

I had been alerted to the institutional tension that exists between governors and attorneys general throughout the country at a seminar organized by the National Association of Attorneys General in December 1978 for the twenty-two newly elected attorneys general. The governor of Arizona, Bruce Babbitt, who had previously served as Arizona state attorney general, spoke at one of the sessions outlining the potential friction between a governor and an attorney general even if both were members of the same party, indicating that the structural roles of both inherently laid the groundwork for conflict. This prepared me for the conflicts that arose with Governor Carey and Governor Cuomo, the two governors with whom I served.

A big flare-up occurred in February 1984 concerning a proposal that Mario put forward to adopt sports betting in New York State. This could raise $500 million to help close the budget deficit that the state was confronting. I read about the proposal in the newspaper and as soon as I saw it, I said to myself: *This is a problem.* New York State has a constitutional prohibition concerning gambling and so in order to institute gambling, you must amend the state constitution. There had been two constitutional amendments in the last fifty years relating to gambling: in 1938, to allow for betting at horse-racing tracks, and in 1961, to allow the state to operate a lottery. The newspaper stories I read said nothing about changing the constitution, only that the governor was seeking to add these funds to the state budget. I immediately called my staff to ask whether they had heard from the governor's office about the proposal. They had the same reaction as I did about the problematic nature of the idea. No one had heard from the governor's office.

When my chief deputy contacted the counsel to the governor, he was met with tremendous pushback and hostility. The response was that what the governor was proposing was perfectly appropriate. We acknowledged that there was a desperate need to raise revenue, but insisted that since this was a sports betting proposal it would have to be done in a legal and constitutional manner. The governor's office responded that illegal sports betting was already taking place in the state, and since that revenue was not being taxed, it was lost to the treasury of New York. This proposal was aimed at capturing those dollars and putting them to public use. We took no position on the policy merits of the proposal. We reiterated that the only way a gambling proposal could proceed was to have the Constitution amended, namely to have two separately elected legislatures approve it and then have it submitted for a vote of the people.

The governor's office felt we were wrong and said they were going to proceed to work with the legislature to have this proposal incorporated into the budget.

My staff and I agreed I would be violating my oath of office if I allowed this to take place. Because the governor's office continued to move forward, we decided to issue an opinion with carefully restated statutory and constitutional authority as well as case law precedent and analysis. Jim Conroy, on my executive staff, had the responsibility of drafting the twenty-eight-page opinion which we forwarded to the governor and released to the public.

When the governor continued to press for inclusion of the $500 million to the budget, Warren Anderson, the majority leader of the Senate, pointed out that the attorney general issued an opinion that the proposal was not constitutionally sound, and so it never got adopted. Mario was furious and took great umbrage at what I did. He was a sophisticated man and a great lawyer and I never understood why he didn't realize that I had no choice but to reject this proposal. It was patently impermissible.

The next skirmish I had with Governor Cuomo occurred a year later and involved the appointment of a special prosecutor. This time he outmaneuvered me, including withholding the payment of my proposed appointee's salary, resulting in my candidate withdrawing.

There was another incident which occurred between us in 1986 which further reflected the complicated nature of our relationship. There was considerable speculation about who was going to be Mario's running mate for lieutenant governor when he ran for reelection later that year because Al DelBello had resigned midway in his term.

I briefly thought about whether it made sense for me to pursue that opportunity. I rejected the idea even though it was widely thought that Mario was going to run for president in 1988. If he did that and won, the lieutenant governor would become governor and serve out the remaining two years of his term and be positioned to run for a full term in 1990. I felt there was no real responsibility attached to the lieutenant governor's role, which was totally dependent on what the governor wanted to assign to the occupant of that post. For a fleeting moment, the thought crossed my mind that if the governor formally offered me, while serving as lieutenant governor, the responsibility of simultaneously serving as the commissioner of Environmental Conservation, this might provide real substantive challenges and responsibilities. I enjoyed what I was doing as attorney general

in the area of environmental enforcement and thought that was high-priority work. This concept was unprecedented and so I asked my staff to check whether it would be legally feasible and to touch base with the governor's staff to see if that would be in the realm of possibility. The response was positive on both fronts but with further thought I dismissed the idea because I did not want to lose my independence and become reliant on the governor's will to keep me in that position. My staff conveyed to the governor's office that upon reflection I would not be interested in pursuing that course.

Some weeks later, on a Sunday evening while Diane and I were watching 60 Minutes, the telephone rang. It was the governor's son, Andrew Cuomo, on the line. After some small talk, he said, "The governor wanted me to call you to say he'd be interested in having you run with him on the ticket as lieutenant governor." By now my campaign for reelection as attorney general was already in place and so I was surprised by this call. I responded by saying, "Andrew, please tell the governor I am greatly flattered by his offer. I very much appreciate this outreach but it's not in the cards. I love my job as attorney general and I'm going to seek another term."

"But, Bob," Andrew said, "do you understand what I'm saying? Do you realize what might happen down the road?" He was, of course, alluding to the fact that the governor might run for president and that the lieutenant governor might wind up as governor.

I said, "Andrew, please tell the governor how much I really, really appreciate his offer and obviously the confidence it implies. But I love being attorney general and I'm slated to be president of the National Association of Attorneys General next year, which will allow me to have some national influence on issues that I feel deeply about, and so the timing's not right."

Cuomo ultimately selected Stan Lundine, an upstate congressman, to be his running mate, and Stan served ably in that post for the following eight years.

It was always interesting to be in Mario Cuomo's company. He was a fascinating man. There were many dimensions to him. He was brilliant. He was a physically strong man and had an extraordinary work ethic. He would work around the clock and forgo vacations. His life was guided by his origins. His parents emigrated from Italy and worked very hard to raise and provide for the family. He remembered his roots, told public stories

about them, and lived his life by those basic precepts. He lived and dressed modestly without being tempted by the pecuniary glitter of life. He was the most gifted orator of our time. His soaring words and phrases would not only lift the spirits but also lift people from their seats to standing, roaring ovations.

While our relationship over the course of many years was uneven, Mario was extremely gracious to me when I announced that I was going to leave the office of attorney general. He told the press that I was "the nation's leading state attorney general for years, a political leader of total integrity, complete commitment and high principle" and that I would "be missed for a long time." I shall always be deeply appreciative for his generous comments.

Campaigning for Herman Badillo (Center) in his 1973 primary campaign for mayor of New York with Congresswoman Shirley Chisholm.

That's me (center with shirt and tie) marching at a rally in Washington, D.C. in solidarity with leaders of the American labor movement, including: Lane Kirkland, President of the National AFL-CIO, Lenore Miller, President, Retail, Wholesale and Department Store Union, Jack Sheinkman, President, Amalgamated Clothing and Textile Workers Union, Lynn Williams, President, United Steel Workers of America, United States Senator Harris Wofford.

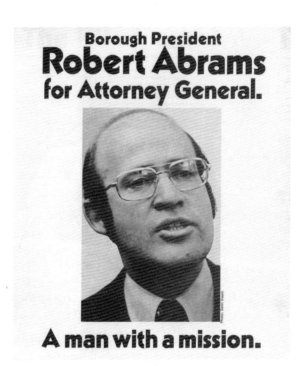

Cover of campaign brochure in 1978 race for attorney general.

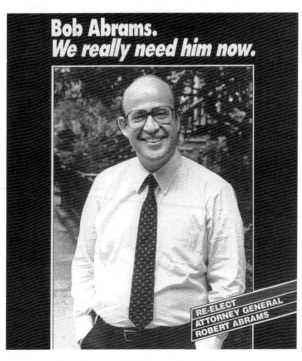

Cover of campaign brochure in 1982 race for reelection as attorney general.

Mayor David Dinkins introducing me to Nelson Mandela when he visited New York City in 1990. Elizaabeth Holtzman is at center and Joyce Dinkins is to the right.

Campaigning with Hugh Carey running for governor in the Democratic Party primary on July 4, 1974 at Nathan's Famous Hot Dogs in Coney Island, Brooklyn. Diane is shaking Congressman Carey's hand.

At press conference in support of Anatoly Scharansky, Jewish refusenik activist arrested by Soviets, with Senator Patrick Moynihan and Prime Minister Golda Meir.

After making a successful plea for ballet dancers Valery and Galina Panov to be allowed to emigrate from the Soviet Union to Israel, I was able to greet them at JFK Airport when they visited the United States for the first time.

Presenting Cardinal John O'Connor with a $1 million check for use in parochial schools resulting from milk antitrust price fixing investigation.

With Diane, Mom, Rachel and Senator Ted Kennedy at a fundraising dinner for me.

With members of the Brawley team heading toward the N.Y.S. Armory in Poughkeepsie, Assistant Attorneys General, Christine Duisin, Heather Williams, Jack Ryan, and Tim Giles, Director of Communications.

At press conference releasing Grand Jury report in the Tawana Brawley case.

With Governor Mario Cuomo at a NYS Law Enforcement Council press conference.

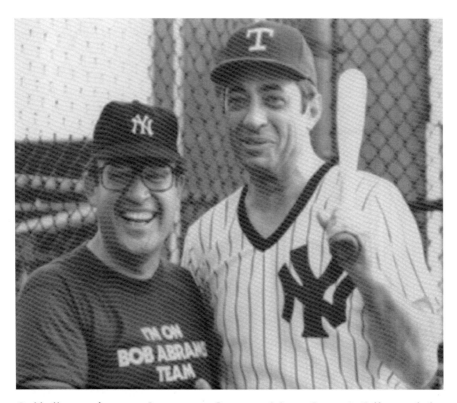

Softball game between Lieutenant Governor Mario Cuomo's Office and the Attorney General's Office.

Announcement by attorneys general of major states – John Van de Kamp - California, Neil Hartigan - Illinois, Jim Mattox - Texas. I'm at podium while serving as President of National Association of Attorneys General, 1988-89.

Delegation of state attorneys general visiting Israel, on the Golan Heights, overlooking Syria and Lebanon.

On the steps of the U.S. Supreme Court with my colleagues state attorneys general from throughout the United States during my tenure as president of National Association of Attorneys General.

I'm having a hearty laugh with President George H. W. Bush at the White House after presenting him with a copy of the recently published book *Powers and Duties of State Attorneys General.* I just told him that as President of the United States, he had many burdens and if he ever had a problem falling asleep he should begin to read this book and he'd be sound asleep in seconds.

Campaigning for the U.S. Senate with Bill Clinton in 1992.

Candlelight vigil for crime victims at the Cathedral of St. John the Divine in New York City.

On behalf of the president of Italy, the Italian Consul General of New York is presenting me with the Cavalieri Award, the highest honor the government of Italy can bestow on a foreigner.

Hosting my weekly Sunday two-hour radio call-in program, "Ask the Attorney General".

U.S. Senator Birch Bayh discussing his presidential campaign with me and assemblyman Jerry Kremer.

Greeting Jacqueline Kennedy Onassis at voting place, Upper East Side, Manhattan.

Diane's parents and my parents going with us to the 1982 State Democratic Convention in Syracuse.

Dad loved to meet voters with me on the campaign trail.

Campaigning with David Dinkins in his race for mayor of New York City.

Senator Joseph Lieberman campaigning with me and Diane in front of famous Ratner's Restaurant on Manhattan's Lower East Side.

Providing testimony and support with women activists concerning legislation allowing women the right to choose.

My family and I celebrate my reelection as attorney general on election night 1982.

Vice President Walter Mondale making an appearance in New York as the Democratic nominee for president in 1984.

Ten state attorneys general (left side) at meeting with the Procurator General of the USSR (center right) in the Kremlin, 1988.

Traditional Jewish dancing at our wedding, with bride and groom being lifted on chairs, Bronx Botanical Garden, September 14, 1974.

Family photo in Central Park.

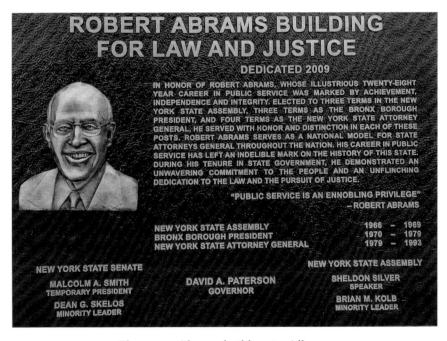

Plaque on Abrams building in Albany.

The family at the dedication of the Abrams Building for Law and Justice in Albany, August 2009.

Family photo for our annual holiday card, 2019. (Photo taken in Jerusalem.)

Chapter 27

The 1992 Senate Race

B EING ATTORNEY GENERAL OF NEW YORK provided me enormous grati-
fication. But after more than a decade in office, I started to ask myself
whether I should pursue another position that would provide even more
meaningful service. I began to look at the 1992 US Senate race.

The potential opportunity to serve in the United States Senate, to be
in a chamber of a hundred votes and voices, which not only made policy
for the country but also had a significant impact around the globe, would
be a great challenge and an incredible honor.

The incumbent, Senator Alfonse D'Amato, a conservative Republi-
can, had held the office since 1980 after serving several years as a local
elected official in Nassau County. He was a machine politician but more
than that, he and I had significant policy differences. He favored cutting
important social programs for the poor, the elderly, and the environment.
He was also opposed to a woman's right to choose.

Almost from his earliest days in office, D'Amato was dogged by accu-
sations of misconduct. As senator, investigative journalists uncovered and
reported on allegations that he improperly used his office to help family,
friends, and campaign contributors. In the summer of 1991, the year before
his reelection campaign, the Senate Ethics Committee concluded an
investigation and found that he had conducted his office in an "improper
and inappropriate manner" and was "negligent in failing to establish
appropriate standards for the operation of his office." The Committee fur-
ther cited the "misuse" of his office by his brother for personal gain on
behalf of a client.

I knew that D'Amato was a rough customer. I saw the kind of primary
fight he waged against Jacob Javits and his general election campaigns

against Elizabeth Holtzman and Mark Green. I knew it would be a tough and nasty fight. I announced my candidacy early, more than eighteen months before the primary, hoping to take advantage of my recent landslide reelection victory, the support of elected officials, and my expected Liberal Party endorsement. It turned out, however, I was not the only Democrat who was ready to challenge D'Amato.

Two prominent women—Geraldine Ferraro and Elizabeth Holtzman—subsequently announced their candidacies, as well as Al Sharpton and Congressman Bob Mrazek, who withdrew a few months after he entered the race.

Geraldine Ferraro was a former three-term member of Congress and the first woman to be on a major party national ticket as Walter Mondale's vice presidential running mate in 1984. At the time of the Senate race, she was an icon with an enthusiastic following. Elizabeth Holtzman was a former member of the House who, as an insurgent reformer, won an upset victory over longtime member of Congress Emanuel Celler, then chairman of the House Judiciary Committee. She was subsequently elected Brooklyn district attorney and at the time of the Senate race was serving as New York City comptroller. Holtzman and Ferraro were two of the best known and most respected female officeholders of that period.

It was a daunting prospect to run against these two women, but I hoped that my record as an advocate for women would shine through and carry me to victory. Diane worked diligently with me on the campaign, particularly on women's issues, mobilizing women around the state. I was fortunate to have her assistance in organizing women party and elected officials, and feminist leaders.

Al Sharpton, who was constantly seeking to position himself as the leading national figure on issues involving the African American community, was the other contender.

Elizabeth Holtzman ran a lot of negative ads attacking Geraldine Ferraro, accusing Ferarro's husband of being close to organized crime. My campaign ran some tough ads too, but they were not nearly as negative as Holtzman's. Ferarro hadn't released her tax returns and we kept stating that she should do so.

The result in the end was extremely close. I won the primary, narrowly edging out Ferarro. Sharpton came in third, and Holtzman placed fourth.

Ferraro, the heralded frontrunner right from the get-go, was convinced that she was going to win, and let it be known that her loss was because she had been unfairly attacked. She refused at first to concede after it

became clear on primary night that I had won. Ferraro further refused to offer her support during the general election campaign and we spent an inordinate amount of time trying to obtain it. It wasn't until three days before the general election that she publicly endorsed me. Historically, at the end of a primary, even if it was bruising and hard-fought, the opposing candidate supports the winner.

At the start of the general election campaign, I was reeling. Our cash register was empty. And there was D'Amato sitting and waiting like a Cheshire cat—with a full treasury. At that point he had four million dollars to spend on TV and radio commercials and before long he would have twelve million dollars to spend on the campaign. He had avoided a pesky primary fight against Larry Rockefeller Jr., who was a young, idealistic, progressive Republican with a strong record of seeking to protect the environment. D'Amato challenged his petitions and successfully got him thrown off the ballot. This saved D'Amato millions of dollars of expenditures and allowed him to avoid a tough primary campaign, which would have included a discussion of his ethical and substantive record, exposing his vulnerabilities. D'Amato came bursting out of the gate immediately at 12:01 a.m. the morning after the primary with a barrage of ads attacking me.

He claimed, falsely, that my wife and I avoided meeting our property tax responsibility and that I wanted to raise everyone else's taxes. "Bob Abrams wants to raise taxes on everyone who makes over $35,000 a year," one of the early ads claimed. The *New York Times* called D'Amato's ads characterizing my support for tax increases "misleading." In one ad, he used a vote from my first year in the assembly, twenty-six years earlier, distorting it to say that I supported a bill that was lenient toward drug dealers, when in fact the bill made no mention of drug dealers. Virtually all of his ads were filled with mischaracterizations and innuendoes. It didn't take long for D'Amato's campaign to raise doubts among some voters about my record and character.

In retrospect, I made a mistake in not fighting back against the distortions and malicious undermining attacks on me. I had been the attorney general for fourteen years, with a known record of fighting for the people of New York. I thought the electorate knew who I was and what I stood for. I had not only a strong record among Democrats, but an equally strong record among Republicans throughout the state. I thought: *the voters won't believe this garbage, and so I can just brush this off.* I was wrong.

I also had to quickly raise money to get commercials on the air, which required me to spend most of my time making fundraising phone calls. At the same time, I had to be visible on the campaign trail. So, I tried to do both—make phone calls and make selected appearances that would be covered by the press. D'Amato's ability to get on the air while I struggled to gather funds really set my campaign back. He was on the air alone, negatively defining me without my message being broadcast.

We put out policy papers on housing for the homeless, a woman's right to choose, social security, and health insurance, saying that health care should be a fundamental right in America. But I had a difficult time getting the press to focus on any of the substantive issues that I raised. Reporters at press conferences would focus almost exclusively on the politics of the race and not the substance.

D'Amato mastered the dubious skill of playing one group off against another. He specialized in preying on fear: fear of being taken advantage of, middle-class voters' fear of being separated from their hard-earned money, and anxiety over job security and the economy. He painted me and other Democrats who sought to do something for segments of the population that desperately needed assistance as "hopelessly liberal"—taking from the hard-working middle class and giving to the poor.

At one point I made an unfortunate mistake when I was campaigning upstate, which was probably a turning point in the campaign. We made two or three stops—and it turned out that wherever we went, D'Amato's henchmen had gotten there first. They would interfere with our press conferences, thrusting their D'Amato signs up and down in front of me, shouting me down and heckling.

On the evening of that long and tiring day, in Binghamton, I was on my way up to the lectern, at the front of a large room filled with students, when one of them next to me made a negative comment about D'Amato's campaign. Thinking about the scuffles that had taken place and the tactics used all day, I blurted out, "Yeah, the guy's a fascist." A reporter for the local Binghamton paper quoted me in a story that appeared in the paper the next morning.

As luck would have it, the day after my comment was Columbus Day and D'Amato was interviewed at the New York City Columbus Day Parade, with tears rolling down his cheeks, saying how he was emotionally hurt and how all Italian Americans were defamed by my comment. It was absurd to see tough Al D'Amato crying and playing this to the hilt. But it soon became clear that it was registering with Italian-American voters.

My reference to fascists had no ethnic intent. I had in mind how the tactics employed by D'Amato and his henchmen were reminiscent of tactics employed by fascists throughout Europe in the 1930s. I obviously had no underlying negative feelings about Italians. To criticize any racial or ethnic group was totally foreign to my thinking. There is a large Italian population in the Bronx, and I had always had a great relationship with that community. The president of Italy had presented me with the Cavalieri Award, the highest honor the government of Italy can bestow on a foreigner. I had also been presented with the B'nai Brith Sons of Italy award. I was the guy who got the money for the first Italian-American library and cultural center in the nation, built with public dollars in the Belmont section of the Bronx. I'd spent a lifetime being very inclusive, embracing *all* people.

But the fallout from this remark quickly began to take on a life of its own. D'Amato's media guy, Arthur Finkelstein, immediately created a commercial featuring Benito Mussolini with a voiceover inferring that I was anti-Italian, and D'Amato began demanding that I apologize, a call that others joined, including Governor Mario Cuomo.

I felt an apology would be tantamount to an admission that it had been a biased comment, and so I initially resisted, but after several days of being on the defensive, I apologized to get this false and phony issue off the front page and behind me. I was really annoyed with myself for letting my frustration get the better of me in an unguarded moment.

A very key factor in the Senate race was also the timetable. The campaign for the general election was very short, a little more than six weeks after the conclusion of the primary.

Another important factor was former Mayor Ed Koch. He made a powerful TV commercial for D'Amato. It was payback time. I had supported David Dinkins in the Democratic primary against Koch when Koch was seeking a fourth term—and Koch lost. Koch had been in office for twelve years and was constantly making confrontational and divisive remarks about minorities, which I thought was not healthy for the city. I felt that it was time for a change and that it would be an important development if New York City elected a black mayor for the first time. Koch carried that grudge for years and this was a great moment for him to get even. D'Amato poured huge amounts of money into playing the Koch commercial on television. Koch also campaigned extensively in the streets with D'Amato, generating 6:00 p.m. and 11:00 p.m. television news coverage.

There was also a larger dynamic—a bit of a turning point in American politics. In the new politically conservative atmosphere that had begun with Ronald Reagan's election in 1980, Republicans had been successful at convincing many Americans that "tax and spend liberals" were to blame for many of the country's problems. The term "liberal," which many Democrats had until then applied to themselves with pride—pride in the political and philosophical roots of liberalism and its long history of tolerance—began to take on a whole new set of associations and in the process became a term of opprobrium. D'Amato's "hopelessly liberal" tagline took advantage of this trend.

Into that mix stepped the Australian publisher Rupert Murdoch, who took over the New York Post in 1985 and turned the venerable liberal newspaper, the oldest in the nation, into a leader of sensationalist journalism and staunch right-wing politics. The Post's amplification of D'Amato's talking points in its news coverage and its multiple endorsements in editorials and opinion columns were very helpful to him.

In both the primary and the general election, I had no idea whether or not I was going to win. On primary night I had a feeling that I was going to pull it off—that was my own gut feeling but I had no idea how it would actually turn out. On the day of the general election, I had a sense we were not doing well, especially upstate and in the suburbs, but I didn't know how it would end. The campaign did not do daily tracking polls in the closing two weeks of the campaign.

Election night was exciting and nerve-racking. A big crowd of my supporters filled the ballroom at the Sheraton Hotel and my family and campaign team gathered in a suite upstairs. As soon as the polls closed, the early returns had us behind by seven or eight points. Some TV stations declared D'Amato the winner early on but then the gap started closing. The wire services and TV stations pulled back their projections that D'Amato would be the winner. D'Amato's lead was down to six points, then five, then four, then three, then two, then one, and there was excitement building that perhaps I could pull it off. But the momentum stopped and, in the end, close to midnight, we saw we weren't going to make it.

Ultimately, I lost it by a hair. It was very close, with more than six million votes cast and a 1 percent margin. It was a difficult, frustrating, and disheartening race, but I was determined to move forward and meet the challenges ahead.

PART THREE

LIFE AFTER ATTORNEY GENERAL

Chapter 28

At a Crossroad

I ENTERED THE SENATE RACE TO WIN but it didn't turn out that way. It was obviously very disappointing, but I wasn't about to dwell on it. If a disappointment hits, you've got to put it behind you and move on. Life is short. One of Frank Sinatra's great songs "That's Life" says it all: if you fall on your face, you have to pick yourself up, dust yourself off and start over again.

After a short post-election vacation, I went back to the office and threw myself into my work. I still had two years left to my term in one of the great public offices in America. I got briefed and caught up on the pending investigations and met with my key staff about charting new directions.

I began to prepare for another reelection run for attorney general. Despite the fact that I had lost the Senate race, I felt I could still win overwhelmingly when presenting myself to the voters of New York. This would require traveling the state to reconnect and be reunited with the voters on the issues that enabled me to build a reputation as a strong independent attorney general. I knew I couldn't take the reelection campaign for granted. I would have to work hard, continue to launch investigations, and bring actions that were cutting-edge and relevant to the lives of people throughout the state.

However, there were a couple of other matters on my mind. First, my daughter, Rachel, was graduating from high school and applying to college. She had outstanding grades and was likely to get into Columbia, her first choice for college. When I went to Columbia, the tuition was $750 a year, so I was shocked that her tuition, room, and board would cost

upwards of $50,000. Since I was just about able to cover existing expenses, how was I going to deal with this new economic burden?

I was also not enamored at having to raise at least $2.5 million for the new attorney general campaign. Going back to fundraising and asking my supporters to help me again was not something I relished. I'd have to begin to do that quickly in order to scare away any potential competitors in the primary who might have a misplaced idea that because I'd lost the Senate race I would be vulnerable. A big campaign kitty would also discourage a potential strong Republican competitor in the general election.

But was running for reelection the right path? Some of my friends over the years would say to me, "Bob, you've admirably, over the course of your life, devoted yourself to the public but there will come a time when you will have to think of yourself. You don't come from a wealthy background and you will face the financial issues of providing for your retirement, for your wife, your children, and grandchildren when you are gone." Those thoughts also permeated my thinking.

And so, I started asking myself the question, *If I don't run again, what will I do?* I could seek a job in the not-for-profit world, heading a foundation perhaps, or I could join a law firm. As the attorney general, I knew I could virtually pick any firm in New York City and be welcomed as a partner.

However, I worried that it might be a mistake to give up my post. Every day for months I would challenge myself: *Are you sure you won't regret giving up this great job of protecting people, this job that provided such independence in decision-making where I could establish an important public interest agenda, where I could hire who I wanted, where I could use the bully pulpit, where I could undertake actions without asking permission of a governor or mayor?* All the attorney general has to do is check his conscience and his soul. Should I launch this investigation? Should I file this lawsuit? Should I impanel a grand jury and seek criminal charges? If you make this announcement that you're retiring, how are you going to feel the next day? The next week? Are you going to be miserable? Are you sure you are ready to make this transition? Every day, fifteen times a day, I would ask myself these questions.

Then there were additional issues. If I chose the law firm route, would I be successful in the role of partner in a major law firm? Could I meet expectations and bring in business? I had been out of the private sector for

decades. Would my pattern of success continue, and would my reputation remain intact? I told myself to brush aside the doubts and forge ahead.

Finally I made up my mind. I had to be adventurous and try something new. I had to have the courage to chart a new path and the humility to understand that someone else could come into the job of attorney general and establish a record that was as good as mine, if not better.

I reached out to two long-term friends, Len Boxer and Chuck Moerdler, who were partners at Stroock & Stroock & Lavan. We had a couple of breakfast meetings at which they extolled the virtues of their firm, including the quality of the lawyers, the decency of the partners, and the firm's culture and strong social conscience expressed through pro bono service provided to not-for-profit organizations and people who could not afford the high legal fees charged by private New York City law firms.

After many helpful conversations with Diane, I decided over Labor Day weekend in 1993 that I was going to approach Stroock about joining the firm.

I also decided to leave office at the end of the year, thus creating a vacancy that would allow the Democrats to keep control of the attorney general's office. I knew that the state constitution provided that any vacancy in statewide office would be filled by the legislature sitting in joint session. Since the Democrats held a huge majority in the assembly, that majority would outnumber the slight majority that the Republicans held in the state senate and thus the Democrats would control the vote. I wanted the progressive efforts that I had initiated to be continued by the next attorney general. This period of a one-year incumbency would allow the interim attorney general to gain some recognition and give him or her a leg up in the general election against the Republican challenger. At a press conference held in the attorney general's office, packed with members of my staff and the press, I informed New Yorkers of my somewhat unconventional decision to leave the office one year before my four-year term ended. It was an emotional and bittersweet moment for me. I was excited by this new chapter in my life that I was about to undertake but also apprehensive about ending my role in public office.

My announcement was an unexpected thunderbolt in the political world and the story wound up on the front page of the *New York Times*. I received dozens of phone calls and letters wishing me well from throughout the state and from attorneys general across the country. I was gratified

by the many tributes from editorial boards of newspapers about my performance in the job over the years.

Assemblyman Oliver Koppell from the Bronx, who was chairman of the Judiciary Committee in the assembly, was selected to fill the vacancy for attorney general for the one-year balance of the term. I knew Ollie, who was a graduate of Harvard College and Harvard Law School and had been a liberal Reform Democrat leading the Benjamin Franklin Reform Democratic club in Riverdale. Koppel lost to Karen Burstein in a hotly contested Democratic primary among four candidates, and Burstein ultimately lost to the Republican candidate Dennis Vacco in a close race. So one of the goals of my plan didn't work out and the Republicans again had control of the attorney general's office.

But my plan of establishing myself at Stroock worked out even better than I'd hoped.

Chapter 29

Private Life

THE ARRANGEMENT I ESTABLISHED WITH STROOCK allowed me to be an active partner working on matters for private clients while also pursuing pro bono activities servicing public needs and involving public issues. I've been fortunate that these twenty-five years of private life have blended the public and the private in such a way as to continue to make my life interesting and meaningful.

During my tenure as a partner at the firm, many individuals and companies came to me for assistance with various problems and legal issues they were confronting. In a number of instances, former attorneys general from across the country with whom I worked when we served together referred matters to me. I provided my clients with vigorous representation and attempted to resolve the issues at hand with creative solutions.

I worked very closely with Jamie Bernard, a brilliant lawyer who is low-key and self-effacing. I benefited enormously from his efforts and he has become a wonderful friend.

I was very gratified that Stroock stood by the understanding we agreed to, allowing me to provide service on a pro bono basis. Public service was the cornerstone of my life and just because I was leaving elected office and entering private life, I did not want to cut out public activity altogether because of the personal satisfaction I derived from that work.

While I was at Stroock, the firm increased its historic commitment to pro bono work by adopting a new Public Service Project. Over a ten-year period, the firm contributed more than 150,000 hours of free legal services to those who could not afford expensive legal fees. It is also one of the few firms in New York to have established a pro bono partner position leading the effort.

In addition, I proposed to the firm—and they allowed me to organize—thirty Leadership Forums featuring prominent speakers addressing topics of public importance. These forums brought together elected officials, key policymakers, our clients, and members of the public pursuing insights into important subjects and potential solutions to difficult problems.

During my time at the firm, I worked on a number of interesting public service matters.

The New York City Bar Association asked me to be a member of a delegation that went on a mission to Moldova, the poorest nation in Europe, a landlocked country between Ukraine and Romania, and one of the former republics of the USSR. Moldova is deemed by foreign policy experts to be one of the "frozen conflicts" in the world, ready at any moment to boil over and become an open conflagration. After the fall of the Soviet Union, a portion of the country broke away with the help of the Russian Army and succeeded in taking over the industrial portion of the country. The rebels declared themselves a new nation, Transnistria, which no country in the world recognizes aside from Russia. It created its own currency, its own government, and its own supreme court and legislature. It has corruption problems and uncontrolled borders that encourage human trafficking. The five members of the delegation spent a week in Moldova and met with the president of Moldova and the president of the breakaway country, Transnistria, with the Russian ambassador and the Romanian ambassador and met twice with the American ambassador. Upon our return, we issued a voluminous report, which was viewed as meaningful and constructive, moving the conversation in the right direction.

I spent time as a member of the board of the American Jewish Joint Distribution Committee—more familiarly known as "The Joint." It has an illustrious one-hundred-year history of aiding Jewish communities all over the world—from assisting families in Europe after World Wars I and II to providing medical and nutritional assistance to hundreds of thousands of poverty-stricken elderly Jews living in the former Soviet Union. I traveled to remote places like Uzbekistan, Crimea in Ukraine, and Khabarovsk and Birobidzhan in Siberia to monitor the impact and effectiveness of their programs. My trip to Siberia was in the month of January when temperatures were as low as twenty-five degrees below zero and I had to wear thermal underwear and five layers of clothing. It was certainly frigid, but

it was exciting and very meaningful to extend a hand to those who could easily be abandoned. I even found time to sit on a three-legged stool on a frozen lake and do a little ice fishing.

Each year during my tenure at Stroock I led a delegation of state attorneys general to Israel under the auspices of the America-Israel Friendship League and the Ministry of Foreign Affairs of the government of Israel, which has been very successful in promoting greater understanding of the special relationship and shared values between Israel and the United States. We met with and were briefed by government officials and we toured the country to see the historic and religious sights. As chairman of the Delegations Committee, I supervised visits by other groups as well, including superintendents of schools from throughout the United States, speakers and majority leaders of legislatures, presidents of colleges and universities, student editors of law reviews from law schools, African American leaders, women leaders, Hispanic leaders, and high school students, including a significant number of minority students from the New York City school system. The value of these missions is that participants get to see firsthand what is going on in this sensitive and important area of the world and not through an interpretive lens or reporting by the media.

As attorney general, I was in the vanguard of seeking governmental and ethics reform. When the 125-year-old Citizens Union, with its distinguished history as a governmental watchdog fighting for reform, reached out to me to serve on its board of directors, I agreed. I worked on many issues with Citizens Union—including campaign finance reform, merit selection of judges, strong ethics laws for statewide officials and members of the legislature, reform of the Board of Elections with effective recruitment and training for election poll workers, and an amendment to the New York State Constitution dealing with gerrymandering. For many years, I moderated *Citizens Union Searchlight*, a weekly public affairs TV show on cable station NY1. I also served for more than twenty years as president of its educational arm, the Citizens Union Foundation.

When Jonathan Lippman was chief judge of New York State, he had a terrific idea of harnessing the talent and expertise of lawyers who had entered retirement by getting them to commit to spending time volunteering for those who could not afford to hire a lawyer. I was asked to be a member of that committee, part of a diverse group of lawyers from across New York State to come up with ideas to implement the program. By the

time Lippman stepped down as chief judge, we had recruited over two thousand lawyers who were contributing over twenty thousand hours of pro bono service a year to individuals and community organizations.

In an historic effort, 113 former attorneys general, Democrats and Republicans, came together from virtually every state in the union to support a beleaguered colleague, Don Siegelman, who, after serving as attorney general, was elected governor of Alabama. I undertook a leadership role in creating this coalition that spoke out against a politically inspired and unfair investigation and prosecution of Siegelman.

In fulfilling a campaign promise to provide a free college education to every child in Alabama, Siegelman proposed establishing a statewide lottery to pay for that program, subject to a vote by the people of Alabama via a referendum. In the course of the campaign for the lottery, the casino interests opposing the referendum spent a huge amount of money to defeat it. Siegelman had to raise money to fund the pro-education lottery campaign and accepted a large contribution. That contribution was characterized as a bribe and was the key basis of an indictment filed against him. The reality was that no money went into Siegelman's pocket; the funds were used to help support an issue-oriented campaign, namely support of the referendum to fund the free college program. The Republican establishment wanted to cut down Siegelman, who was a rising Democratic star and a true force in Alabama politics. It was uncovered that there was duplicity engaged in by the local Republican-dominated US Attorney's office and even by the federal judge before whom the case was tried. Siegelman, who served five years in prison, with stretches in solitary confinement, deserved to have a bipartisan outcry due to the great injustice he suffered and the overwhelming evidence of wrongdoing in the handling of his case. I flew to Birmingham, Alabama, to testify as a character witness at his trial.

Shortly after leaving the attorney general's office, I visited John Sexton, the dean of the New York University School of Law, and told him of my concern that many law school students might not be pursuing the path of politics and public service. Many were of the belief that it was a dirty and grimy profession. The press too often focused on the few who betrayed the public trust and did not tell the stories of the kind of able, noble men and women I had met in my twenty-eight-year career in public life. I believed that law schools had to do more to encourage their students to at least consider entering politics and/or doing some stint of public

service. What emerged from the conversation was the idea that the NYU School of Law would establish an annual Public Service Lecture in my name whereby a prominent public servant would come to the school each year to discuss his or her life and career. I felt that if students saw these men and women in the flesh, up close, and could ask them questions about their lives or about current controversial issues, they might come away from the session thinking, *Wow, I really liked and admired that person and I want to lead a life like that.*

Joe Lieberman, a close personal friend, was the first speaker to kick off the series. A man of sterling character and total integrity, Joe served with me when he was the attorney general of Connecticut. He went on to serve four terms in the United States Senate and was the vice presidential candidate on the ticket with Al Gore, which won a plurality of votes but wound up on the losing end of a 5–4 Supreme Court decision that designated the Bush-Cheney ticket as the winner of the 2000 election.

The following is a small sample of the terrific speakers who have participated in the program. Ted Kulongoski, who served as state labor commissioner, attorney general, governor, and Supreme Court judge in the state of Oregon inspired students with his life story, which included a childhood in an orphanage run by nuns, a stint in the army, and a pre-college career as a truck driver. The governor of Wisconsin, Jim Doyle, who also served as attorney general and attended Stanford and Harvard Law School, spent three years with his wife on a Native American reservation helping residents, and then spent three years assisting people on the island of Djerba, off the coast of Tunisia. Another inspiring speaker was Janet Napolitano, who served as US attorney in Arizona, attorney general and governor of Arizona, and then was appointed by President Obama as Homeland Security secretary. Mike Turpen, former attorney general of Oklahoma, also spoke; his charismatic persona and eloquent presentation was enthusiastically received by the students.

Governor David Paterson appointed me to serve on the United Nations Development Corporation, which assists the United Nations with its physical and structural needs. George Klein, the long-term devoted chairman of the board, asked me on several occasions to join him at meetings with the deputy secretary general of the United Nations to discuss a plan to construct a new billion-dollar building as part of the United Nations campus. Unfortunately, the ponderous bureaucracy of the United Nations delayed approving the plan and ultimately placed it on hold.

In 2004, Mayor Mike Bloomberg asked me to be a member of the New York City Charter Revision Commission to conduct hearings and study potential amendments to the New York City Charter. As a result of our work, we formulated some propositions which were placed on the ballot and approved by the voters of New York City. The mayor of New York and the chief administrative law judge would now be required to establish an ethics code governing the conduct of administrative law judges and hearing officers. In addition, going forward the City would be required to impose fiscal constraints in relation to balancing its annual budget, prepare a four-year financial plan, establish a reserve fund of $100 million, and impose conditions relating to short-term debt and the City's annual audit.

After Superstorm Sandy, the devastating storm that hit New York in 2012, Governor Andrew Cuomo created a Moreland Commission to investigate the adequacy of the response of the utilities of New York State. He asked me to serve as cochair of the commission with Benjamin Lawsky, superintendent of financial services in New York. We conducted public hearings throughout the state and studied various proposals for improving the way utilities prepared for future storms. Many of the recommendations for strengthening resiliency going forward were adopted by the legislature, as well as structural changes in the regulatory system.

While attorney general, I worked on the abortion issue with the Center for Reproductive Rights, a national clearinghouse for important litigation relating to a woman's right to choose. I brought the Center to the firm as a pro bono client. Stroock represented the Center in many litigations, including two amicus curiae briefs we filed in the last two years in the United States Supreme Court. In those cases, we represented the members of the House and the United States Senate who are pro-choice, opposing changes in Texas and Louisiana law which restricted the opportunity for women to have access to abortion services.

I've served for several terms on the board of the Fund for the City of New York, which helps fledgling community programs and struggling arts and cultural organizations obtain bridge loans, which enable them to continue their important work serving diverse groups in New York City.

I was also asked by my successor attorneys general to play a role in their transitions after their successful election to the office. And so I provided advice and counsel to attorneys general Eliot Spitzer, Andrew Cuomo, Eric Schneiderman, and Letitia James concerning the staffing

and agenda for the office they were about to inherit. I was honored to offer whatever insight I had gleaned over the years to assist them in taking charge and shaping the office.

One of the most unexpected and unusual developments during this period for me was my involvement with the Church of Jesus Christ of Latter-day Saints. Together with Ernie Michel, a Holocaust survivor and a former head of the UJA-Federation in New York, I was able to resolve a controversy concerning the Church's use of the names of Jews who were murdered during the Holocaust in its practice of proxy baptism. The good will that emerged from the resolution of this issue enabled the Latter-day Saints and Jewish communities to come together in unity and mutual support. My involvement enabled me to develop a close relationship with the elders of the Church, who were members of the Quorum of the Twelve Apostles. One of the significant outgrowths was a Jewish–Latter-day Saints delegation that I organized to visit Israel in 2016 on the 175th anniversary of Latter-day Saints leader Orson Hyde's 1841 visit to the Mount of Olives proclaiming that Israel was the land of the Jewish people with a rebuilt Jerusalem as its capital. The delegation commemorated the event at the Brigham Young University Jerusalem Center overlooking the Old City and visited the mayor of Jerusalem and the prime minister of Israel and placed a wreath at the Eternal Flame commemorating the six million who perished in the Holocaust.

The current warm relationships with leaders of the Church have enabled the establishment of joint symposia conducted by Yeshiva University and Brigham Young University and visits by Jewish leaders to church headquarters in Salt Lake City, as well as ongoing dialogue between the two communities. Nothing could be more gratifying than an opportunity to forge the bonds of increased understanding among people.

A treasured moment of my life took place in August 2009 when, pursuant to an executive order by Governor David Paterson, the name of the Justice Building on the Albany Mall was changed to the Robert Abrams Building for Law and Justice. The dedication ceremony attended by several hundred people included judges, friends, colleagues, a number of former attorneys general from around the country, and members of my family, and featured remarks by Governor David Paterson, Hubert H. Humphrey III, the former attorney general of Minnesota, and my son-in-law Rabbi Ian Pear, who delivered the invocation.

During the past twenty-five years, I was able to attend meetings of the National Association of Attorneys General and the Conference of Western Attorneys General, enabling me to connect with current attorneys general and the issues in which they were engaged. It also allowed me to continue relationships with former attorneys general who attended these meetings, guaranteeing the continued bond and, in many cases, lifelong friendships. We formed an organization called SAGE, the Society of Attorneys General Emeritus, to continue the special collegiality that we enjoyed during our years of service together, also recognizing that it was an historic period when the role and function of the office was reshaped to provide meaningful protection for the citizens of our respective states.

Chapter 30

Assorted Career Anecdotes

M Y LIFE HAS BEEN FILLED WITH episodes, adventures, and people. And I share a few of those moments with you now.

* * *

My mother called me at the Borough president's office at 6:40 p.m. and in an excited voice, said: "Bobby, are you okay?"

"Yes, Mom, what's the matter? Why do you ask?"

"Dad and I are having dinner and the evening news is on and we heard the broadcaster say the name Abrams and that he died and we looked up at the TV screen and there was your picture."

It turned out that General Creighton Abrams, who succeeded William Westmoreland as commander of US forces in Vietnam, had died. The news program mistakenly showed my photo on the screen when they made the announcement. It put a scare in the lives of my parents.

In addition to telling my mom that I was alive and well, I quoted for her Mark Twain's quip on learning that a newspaper had mistakenly printed his obituary: "The reports of my death are greatly exaggerated."

* * *

I was at a party at Steve and Peggy Kumble's Fifth Avenue apartment in early 1983, shortly after Hugh Carey left the governor's office. Carey had become affiliated with the Finley, Kumble law firm. The firm had previously attracted former New York City mayor Robert Wagner, a good friend of

Governor Carey. The party was called for 6:30 p.m. and it was already close to 8:00 p.m. with Carey having yet to show up. Steve, who was a friend and supporter of mine, told me that the governor was expected and Steve didn't know where he was. It was the pre-cell phone era and so there was no easy way to track him down. Carey had a reputation for being late so there was no real worry on Kumble's face. Close to 8:30, Carey came in flustered, saying, "I've been driving around this area for more than a half hour."

Carey said, "I left my apartment and hailed a cab. When I got in, I said, 'Steve Kumble's apartment.' The cab driver said, 'What?' The driver turned around and said, 'Where are you going, buddy? What address?' I said, 'How the hell do I know? It's on Fifth Avenue." The driver asked, 'At what street?' I told him, 'I don't know exactly. I know the general area!'"

For the past eight years Carey had had a car and driver and staffers who doted over him. He had not yet readjusted to the vicissitudes of private life, like knowing the address of where you're going.

* * *

The first few years after I left public life, people might recognize me while I was sitting in my seat on a plane or a train. I remember one time I was on a plane coming back from Washington, DC. I was sitting on the aisle and this woman on her way back to her seat stopped, looked at me, and asked, "Are you—? Are you—?" It was obvious that she recognized me but she couldn't remember who I was. Finally, she said, "Did you used to be somebody?"

I chuckled and in a friendly, smiling way, I identified myself.

* * *

Win or lose, Diane said we should have a short vacation after the Senate race. She made a reservation at a nice hotel in Jamaica. The afternoon when we arrived, we went down to the relatively deserted beach and sat in chairs under an umbrella at the water's edge. We brought books and newspapers to read. After about ten minutes, I looked up and suddenly saw this thin, well-tanned, gray-haired man. I thought I recognized him. As he got closer, I said to Diane, "Look, that's Ralph Lauren." He was splashing his feet in the water about fifteen feet away from us. As he approached, I said, "Ralph!"

He looked toward me and gave me a warm, "Bob! What are you doing here?"

I said Diane and I were there for a few days' vacation. "How about you? What brings you to this beautiful island?"

He responded, "We have a house here. How about coming over for lunch?" We enthusiastically accepted.

We had met Ralph and his wife, Ricky, at some public charity events and at a few dinner parties. They were always very friendly and down to earth.

We took a taxi from our hotel to the address Ralph gave me. Ricky greeted us warmly at the door and welcomed us into their beautiful home. It was a villa in Round Hill, elegantly but tastefully furnished in island décor. Ralph and Ricky were gracious hosts, providing tall, cool drinks and introducing us to their children. While enjoying our lunch on the veranda, our conversation ranged from my recent campaign to the state of the world to their love of the island, its people, and the spectacular natural beauty of its flowers, magnificent trees, and crystal blue waters of the Caribbean Sea.

At one point, Ralph and I were recalling for all assembled our memories of growing up in the Bronx. He was from Mosholu Parkway which was not far from Pelham Parkway where I grew up. We talked about our parents, our schools, and the games we played. We were describing stick ball when Ralph suddenly decided he and I had to demonstrate how the game was played. He unscrewed the handle from a broom, brought out a dozen tennis balls, and we stepped out onto the manicured grass lawn, a picturesque bluff overlooking the water. There we were, two boys from the Bronx belting out tennis balls into the majestic blue Caribbean Sea.

* * *

As attorney general, I was invited to speak to many different organizations in the course of any given year. After accepting an invitation and agreeing to speak, the organization would ask for my bio that would provide basic information for the person who was going to introduce me.

My office had prepared different bios tailored to the various kinds of events I might attend. If the group was an environmental organization, the bio would focus on the leadership efforts I had undertaken in that area. There were specific bios geared toward civil rights, women's issues, gay rights, organized labor, African American community, Hispanic community, Jewish community, and senior citizens.

One time I was being introduced by the pastor of an African American church in Brooklyn. I was seated on the platform behind the pastor and in front of us was a church packed with hundreds of parishioners.

The pastor got up and said how honored he was to introduce the guest speaker, the attorney general of the State of New York. He then went on to say that Robert Abrams was "a towering leader in the Jewish community. He was a frequent visitor to Israel. He was responsible for establishing Jewish Heritage Week in the New York City school system." Upon hearing that, I said to myself, *Oh no! My secretary sent the wrong bio. She sent him the Jewish bio instead of the black bio.* Knowing what was included in the Jewish bio, I was terrified that for the next five minutes the audience was going to be bombarded with material about my Jewish exploits which of course would have been totally inappropriate. Fortunately for me, the pastor was a savvy guy and did not go on at length about all I had done for the Jewish community and sprinkled in what he knew about my efforts on behalf of the black community. It could have been an embarrassing situation but I was saved by an alert pastor, God bless him.

* * *

Another anxious moment occurred in Buffalo when I was scheduled to do an on-camera live TV interview. In preparation for the interview, I took my glasses off and started cleaning them with my handkerchief when the bridge suddenly broke. I said, "Oh no! I need my glasses. I won't see very well without my glasses."

Tim Gilles, my press person, was there. I turned to him and said, "Tim, scotch tape! Let's get some scotch tape. It's not visible, we can pull it together. We've gotta get some scotch tape."

Tim ran around and found a roll of scotch tape. He applied it. The bridge was resting on my nose and it felt pretty solid and I sat down to do the live interview. As I was being introduced on camera by the person who was doing the interview, I suddenly felt that the heat of the lights was having an impact on the tape and it was giving way. I realized it wouldn't be long before my glasses were going to literally fall apart. It was obviously very disconcerting. I was trying to answer the questions, I was on live television, I felt this thing happening. So I put my two hands on both ends of the frame, trying to keep the glasses together. I didn't know if I should explain to the audience what was going on. I struggled. At first I was

trying not to explain, but then it got to the point where I was holding them together and so I said, looking into the camera, "If you're wondering why I'm sitting like this, my glasses broke. I hope you don't mind."

* * *

At the time of the rioting in Crown Heights and the murder of Yankel Rosenbaum in 1991, as attorney general, I sought to have calm restored to the community and to have adequate police presence to ensure public safety for all concerned. I spoke directly with the police commissioner and visited with the leadership of the Lubavitch community.

I also spoke with the US attorney requesting a federal investigation, and with the district attorney, who said he would welcome such a probe. I reiterated my request for an aggressive federal investigation in a second letter to then-Attorney General William Barr in August 1992 on the anniversary of Rosenbaum's slaying, and once again in October when the prosecution of Lemrick Nelson, who was accused of attacking and killing Rosenbaum, ended in an acquittal.

During that same period, the prosecution of police officers in Los Angeles in the case of Rodney King, an African American who was brutally beaten by local police officers, ended in an acquittal at the local level, but the federal authorities successfully pursued and prosecuted the police officers responsible for the attack. Within hours of the verdict, I placed a call to United States Attorney General Janet Reno, at home. Some months before, I along with other attorneys general had been in a meeting with Janet Reno and she gave us her home phone number indicating she would be accessible to us if we ever needed her. Reno picked up the phone and I explained why I was calling. I said, "Just as the federal government intervened in the Rodney King case after the police officers were acquitted at the local level, I believe that the facts warrant a more aggressive involvement by the federal authorities here in the Yankel Rosenbaum case." She said she was glad I called and that she would discuss the matter with her staff. The Department of Justice indeed stepped up its efforts and after protracted proceedings, Nelson was convicted of violating Yankel Rosenbaum's civil rights and was sentenced to nineteen and a half years in prison.

Thankfully, as a result of a great deal of hard work and good-faith efforts on the part of local leaders in the African American community and the

Jewish community, a long period of calm and the rebuilding of effective working relations has taken place. This was an important conclusion to this tragic episode because a great deal of friction and dangerous tension had developed between the African American and Lubavitch communities living in Crown Heights. Both sides voiced strongly felt grievances but labored at reaching closure and an ability to work together going forward.

* * *

It was late one night in April 2017 while I was in Jerusalem with my family about to celebrate the Passover holiday that I received an email from New York Supreme Court Justice Robert Reed, one of the former assistant attorneys general in my office, who asked if I'd heard the tragic news about Judge Sheila Abdus-Salaam. I was jolted by those words and feared what I was about to learn. I quickly jumped onto the internet to get more information. The horrific news reports indicated that the body of Judge Abdus-Salaam was found in the Hudson River near 125th Street. I was truly shaken to the core.

Sheila was a great success story. I had hired her as a young lawyer. She worked in the attorney general's office for six years in two bureaus, the Civil Rights Bureau and the Real Estate Finance Bureau. When she left my office she received a position as general counsel for the New York City Office of Labor Services. After serving there for a number of years, Sheila called me and said some of her friends were urging her to seek a judgeship. She wanted to know what I thought.

I was immediately supportive, saying, "That's a great idea!"

She then asked, "Would you be willing to serve as a reference for me?"

"Of course!" I said. "I'd be so happy and proud to do that."

Sheila initially became a civil court judge, then a Supreme Court Justice, then was promoted to the Appellate Division, the intermediate appellate court in New York State. I was called by members of judicial screening panels, which were evaluating various candidates for these positions, and gave Sheila high marks. In addition to her keen mind and total integrity, she brought a calm fairness and extraordinary temperament to her responsibilities. As she served in each of these positions, she received praise for the quality of her work.

While serving on the Appellate Division, Sheila called me and told me that she wanted to submit her name for consideration for appointment

to the Court of Appeals. The highest court in New York State, the Court of Appeals is widely respected and considered one of the most important tribunals in the United States. It consists of the chief judge and six associate judges. Sheila asked if I would once again serve as a reference for her and I said I would be honored. If she received this appointment, it would be historic because never before had there been an African American woman serving on the Court of Appeals.

There was a vacancy on the court due to the death of Theodore T. Jones and then a second one was going to have to be filled due to the upcoming retirement on December 31 of Judge Carmen Beauchamp Ciparick.

New York's constitution provides that a judicial nominating committee solicit names of potential candidates to fill a vacancy on the Court of Appeals. After interviewing and evaluating all of the candidates, the committee submits seven names to the governor, who selects one to be a member of the Court of Appeals.

I was in Albany during the selection process for the Ciparick slot because the Moreland Commission on Superstorm Sandy, which I cochaired, was giving a report to Governor Andrew Cuomo and his cabinet. Sheila's name had been one of the seven sent to the governor by the nominating committee. When the report was concluded, I took the opportunity to go over to the governor to say, "Governor, I just want you to know that Sheila Abdus-Salaam is a terrific person. She worked for me for six years. She's an outstanding judge. She's got great credentials, having graduated Barnard College and Columbia Law School. She's a person of integrity and good character and has an outstanding judicial temperament."

The governor said, "I know. She's first-rate. You realize there's another appointment down the road."

At that point, one of the governor's staffers came by reminding him that he had to move on to his next meeting and so our conversation was cut short. What the governor said was a bit enigmatic and subject to interpretation, but I came away from it feeling very positive. I had known the governor for many years and knew that at times he would intentionally say and do things that were draped in mystery. I immediately called Sheila and shared the conversation with her, telling her that it was my interpretation that the governor was giving me a signal that she was not going to be selected for this current opening but when it came time to fill the

vacancy due to the death of Judge Theodore Jones, he would select her for that slot. I told her that the governor often did not like to be direct, particularly with regard to sensitive matters such as this, and that he was discreetly signaling to me that she would eventually be appointed. Sheila thanked me for my support. "Let's hope it works out the way you outlined," she said.

Sure enough, the governor selected Jenny Rivera from the list to replace Judge Ciparick. Soon thereafter, the nominating process to fill the vacancy left by the passing of Judge Jones began. Sheila submitted her name, and the committee in due course announced the seven names that it had selected and sent them to the governor. Sheila's name was on that list and she was ultimately picked to fill that spot.

Sheila's appointment was universally heralded. I remember calling her to congratulate her. In her quiet, modest way she was so happy and pleased.

I invited Sheila to come to my firm to speak to the young lawyers a few months after her elevation to the Court of Appeals. She gave an inspiring talk about how thrilling it was for a person from her humble background to be able to serve in such an exalted position.

I saw Sheila a few times while she was serving on the Court of Appeals. She always appeared happy and fulfilled. A few months before her death, she married Gregory A. Jacobs, a canon within the Episcopal Diocese of Newark.

The news of Sheila's death was painfully shocking. No one expected it. No one could fully understand what happened. The New York City Police Department and the New York City Medical Examiner's Office investigated and found no criminal involvement and ultimately ruled it a suicide.

I spoke at two memorial services held for Sheila, one at the New York City Bar Association, hosted by a group of minority bar organizations, and one organized by her alma mater, Columbia Law School. The speakers at both services made clear how much Sheila gave back to everyone and how her life continued to be an inspiration for lawyers in the minority community.

Chapter 31

Israel and Soviet Jewry

ALTHOUGH I'M NOT A RITUALLY RELIGIOUS person, I am immensely proud of my Jewish heritage. Throughout my life, both during the period I was in public office and during the time I've been in private life, I have devoted myself to a number of Jewish causes. I will discuss two here—my love of Israel and my efforts during the struggle to win freedom for Jews living in the Soviet Union.

My first trip to Israel was in 1968, a year after Israel's miraculous victory in the Six-Day War when the Israeli military vanquished the much larger and better-equipped armies and air forces of Egypt, Jordan, and Syria. The swift and dramatically decisive victory provided important territorial gains, which had the potential for making Israel more secure with broader borders. Jews all over the world took pride in the heroism of the frontline fighters and the brilliance of the strategic moves by Israel's military commanders.

I joined millions of tourists who traveled to Israel in the years after the Six-Day War to visit, once again in Jewish control, the Jewish Quarter and the holy Western Wall in the Old City of Jerusalem, as well as the newly won areas of the West Bank and the Golan Heights. On that first visit, I was blown away by the vibrancy of this country. It had built impressive institutions in a short period of time: universities, hospitals, and social welfare networks that were available not only to its Jewish citizens but to its one and a half million Arab citizens, which at that time represented almost 25 percent of its population.

Beyond the admirable infrastructure, I saw the vibrant democracy that is at the core of a flourishing Israeli society. I saw the openness and

vitality of public debate with an unparalleled diversity of opinion publicly displayed. I saw its many newspapers with widely varying points of view engaging in open discussion of governmental policies. I saw the respect the government gave all houses of worship, Christian, Muslim, and Jewish, which were open to all people. I saw the economy being built so that jobs and the potential benefits for a full life were available to all. I visited Yad Vashem, the memorial museum dedicated to the six million Jews who were murdered by the Nazis during the Holocaust with the message that never again shall our people be marched into gas chambers to be slaughtered for no reason other than they were born Jewish. I saw the rich display of song and dance in the theaters and kibbutzim, exhibiting the pride of a people with thousands of years of history and their daily joy in rebuilding the Jewish homeland. I saw what had been a forbidding, arid desert and rocky wasteland transformed into a beautiful land with thick green forests, verdant vineyards, and orchards of fruit trees. It was a memorable first visit to Israel.

On my next trip, I was able to have a private meeting with Prime Minister Golda Meir. Being with her was one of the great thrills of my life. She was an iconic world figure. Born in Kiev, in Ukraine, she came to the United States as a child with her family in the early 1900s to live in Milwaukee, where she went to school and later became a public school teacher. A member of the Labor Zionist Youth Movement, married at the age of twenty-three, she and her husband moved to Palestine. They lived on a kibbutz where she picked almonds, planted trees, and worked in the kitchen. She became a leader of the kibbutz and active in the Labor Federation, which led her into politics. Ultimately, she was elected Israel's prime minister in 1969, one of the first women in world history to lead a nation.

After going through security, I was led into the prime minister's office and was astonished by how sparse and unpretentious it was. She greeted me with a warm smile. In that perfect English with the Midwestern twang, she said, "How nice to meet you, Mr. Abrams" and guided me over to the chair in front of her desk. Usually the desk of every country's leader is an imposing piece of furniture made of a beautiful hard wood, but in this case my eyes cast on a simple and ordinary industrial metal desk that clerks sit at in the United States.

I told her how excited I was to be in Israel and how much I respected and appreciated what she and her fellow Israelis were doing to build the Jewish homeland, including risking their lives to secure its survival.

She responded, "You know, Mr. Abrams, we are very few in number and each life here is precious and valuable. When one of our soldiers dies in battle, it is a severe loss that not only the family suffers, but the nation suffers as well."

She took a volume from the bookcase behind her desk, saying, "We remember each member of the military who gives his or her life for our country." She told me that when a solider perishes in the line of duty, the story of that person, with photographs, was retained for posterity. Opening the book, she pointed to a photo of a young man, showing him playing a musical instrument. As she turned the pages, she showed me a poem that one of the young fallen heroes had written about trees and nature and the beauty that God had created in the world.

I then told her that I had been on a recent trip to West Africa visiting several countries and that, while I was in Monrovia, Liberia, I went on a tour of a rubber tree plantation. We stopped at a house perched on a hill and as I stepped inside I was greeted by the farmer who lived in that house and given a cold drink. I looked around the room and saw some framed photos on the wall. From where I was seated, I thought I saw Hebrew writing adjacent to the headshots of people. I got up from my chair, walked to the wall, and confirmed that indeed it was Hebrew writing. I asked my host what this was and he proceeded to tell me that Israel had sent some agricultural experts to assist with the cultivation of their crops and trees. The framed montage was photographs of the Israelis who participated in the project. He then explained how Israel designed this program to help underdeveloped nations and how fortunate the people in Liberia felt to be able to benefit from this generous initiative. He was gushing in his praise and appreciation for Israel's support that had so much benefited his country.

Golda Meir, with a slight smile, said, "They may be very appreciative and offer thanks for our humanitarian efforts but they still vote against us at the United Nations General Assembly," making reference to the bias against Israel expressed in so many ways at the United Nations by the majority of nations in the world, a situation which exists to this very day.

Over the years I have been fortunate to meet with eight of Israel's prime ministers.

I have visited Israel dozens of times since my daughter Rachel and her family moved to Jerusalem twenty years ago. My other daughter Becky

followed her lead last year. Those visits have taught me how important it is for people to come to see the country for themselves with their own eyes and not only through the lens of the press. I believe that the media does not provide the public with the reality of what Israel is all about. Newspapers and television usually cover Israel when there is conflict—in the wake of a suicide bombing or when acts of hostility occur between Israelis and Palestinians. So many people are fearful of visiting Israel because they believe that it is not safe. The press coverage, for the most part, conveys the notion that Jews and Arabs hate each other and will never be able to live together. My experience has shown me something very different. The country is safe, and there is a sense of normalcy that currently exists in Israel whereby Jews and Arabs work together, go to school together, and respectfully coexist.

When my daughter Rachel gave birth in Jerusalem three years ago, in Hadassah Hospital, there were Jewish and Arab patients, Jewish and Arab doctors, and Jewish and Arab nurses. After her delivery, Rachel was assigned to a double room, and in the next bed was an Arab woman who had also just given birth. Her family and our family shared the room as visitors, exchanging warm wishes and congratulations, as we all reveled in the new additions to our families. When I take my grandchildren to the zoo in Jerusalem, I'm there with Arab families and Jewish families. On a recent visit, Rachel asked if Diane and I could take the kids to their dentist's office for their scheduled appointments. We went to a building in the heart of Jerusalem where the dentist's office is located. As we waited in chairs for our grandkids' names to be called, we sat amid Arab families who were also waiting. The three dentists would come out of rooms calling the name of the next patient to be seen. I can still hear those names: Mohammed, Omar, and Fatima interspersed with our grandkids Eliyahu, Gavriella, Michaella, and Darya. Not exactly the image portrayed to the outside world.

When Rachel needed a repair to her patio in her apartment due to a leak, she interviewed several contractors; one was an Arab contractor and that's the one she chose to do the work. He worked with his Arab colleagues in the apartment while Rachel and her family were there and he did an excellent job. When I stroll the Mamilla Mall, looking at the shops in the heart of Jerusalem, there are many Arab women shopping there with their children or their friends. Some of my daughter's neighbors have told me how bookings are being made in a popular catering hall in the

Arab village of Abu Goush a few kilometers from Jerusalem for bar and bat mitzvah celebrations.

When I traveled a few years ago with a delegation of attorneys general to Israel, we visited the Galilee Medical Center in the northern part of the country, servicing a population of 600,000. The CEO of the hospital, Dr. Masad Barhoum, a Muslim Arab, told our group, "I don't like this country—I love this country because it gave me the opportunity to become a doctor and encouraged my promotion to run this hospital." Last year, with a different delegation of attorneys general, we met with lawyers who were the leaders of the bar association in the Nazareth district, who told us they were Jewish, Christian Arab, and Muslim Arab and worked together in mutual respect and harmony. People have to see Israel for themselves without the media telling them what to think or believe.

Obviously, dealing with the complex issues of four million people living in Gaza and the West Bank is an imperative that has remained unresolved for far too long. It won't be easy, but I am hopeful that a peace accord will one day be signed by the Israeli government and the Palestinians and that two internationally recognized sovereign states will exist side by side, living in peace.

* * *

In the late 1960s and throughout the '70s and '80s, the plight of Soviet Jewry was a major issue for the Jewish community. In the United States, London, and Paris, an organized effort to assist Soviet Jews was picking up steam and I became deeply involved. The movement was an international human rights campaign for Jews living in the Soviet Union who, at the time, represented 25 percent of the world's Jewish population. Jews who applied to emigrate to Israel or elsewhere were routinely denied or refused, labeled "refuseniks" and thereby effectively trapped within the borders of the Soviet Union. As a result, their entire lives were thrust into turmoil. They couldn't get into the school of their choice, promotion at their place of employment was blocked, and they might even be fired from their jobs. They were subjected to surveillance and became pariahs to their neighbors and friends.

The anti-Semitism of the Soviet system was both current as well as a legacy. Deep-seated, state-sanctioned anti-Semitism existed in czarist

Russia, which had periodically exploded into violent pogroms. That anti-Semitic violence eventually served as the impetus for successive waves of Russian Jews, my own family members among them, to leave Russia and to establish themselves in the United States at the end of the nineteenth and first part of the twentieth centuries. The old scourge of anti-Semitism gained new modes of expression following the revolution of 1917. The Bolsheviks promised freedom for Jews from the ghetto, and ironically, many Jews supported the Revolution, becoming Communists and leaders of the party. They forfeited their religion for a new faith that betrayed them in a devil's bargain in which the Soviets soon reverted to their traditional anti-Semitism and turned on their Jewish citizens.

In the decades following the establishment of the Soviet Union, there was a systematic effort on the part of the Soviets to culturally annihilate the Jewish population. It nearly succeeded. Jews were effectively prevented from attending synagogue and from observing any holiday traditions or following any rituals, including bar/bat mitzvahs, marriages, circumcision, and burials. The Jewish population became acculturated and divorced from its heritage. Vast numbers of Jews were no longer tied to the Jewish past.

The Soviets tried to keep out information from the West but didn't succeed. The 1967 Six-Day War in Israel was a monumental event for Jews in the Soviet Union because they heard that the tiny nation of Israel had stood up against huge, overwhelming might and prevailed. A sense of pride enveloped Jews throughout the Soviet Union. It turned out that in spite of decades of efforts by the government to deny Jews their religious and cultural existence, Jews *knew* they were Jewish. Somehow there continued to be a Jewish yearning, a Jewish spirit, and a Jewish soul. The spark was rekindled. All of this fed into a whole movement as people applied for permission to emigrate.

In mid-1974, I asked my colleague in the Borough president's office, Ed Perlmutter, to join me on a trip to the Soviet Union to meet with the minister of the interior who exercised jurisdiction over the granting of visas. I had spoken to the Soviet ambassador to the United Nations, Yakov Malik, who indicated that such a meeting would be arranged. Ed and I were part of an ordinary touring group and were hoping to break away for this appointment but we were frustrated by not yet being contacted by the Soviet authorities. Then one day in Moscow at lunch, our guide came over to me and in a quivering voice said, "Mr. Ah-brams, there are some gentlemen here to see you."

I turned around and saw two men wearing trench coats and fedoras, watching me from a distance.

I looked at Ed and said, "Ed, this is it. Come with me, something's going on."

We walked over to the two guys. One of them stepped forward and said, "Mr. Ah-brams, we're here to take you to the Interior Ministry." It was a scene out of a movie. These two men were the Hollywood prototype of secretive KGB agents.

We were then led outside and told to get into a parked black sedan. We drove for about ten minutes and pulled up in front of an imposing government building. We got out of the car and were ushered up the steps toward a huge wooden, hand-carved door, and from there across a lobby to another set of steps covered by red carpet, at the top of which we were led into a huge room. There was nothing in the room except a long table with chairs on each side. We were told to sit. There were chocolates and bottles of soda and glasses on the table. I remember as we sat down, Ed and I looked at each other as if to say: *Are we going to get out of here alive?*

In walked two men, one of whom sat down opposite me on the other side of the table, and the other sat next to him.

I extended my hand to the man seated opposite me. "Minister Tchelikov?" As we shook hands, he shook his head and informed me, "I am Deputy Minister Viktorov. Minister Tchelikov is at his dacha in the country." It was summertime.

"Oh, I see," I said, making no attempt to hide my disappointment. "As you may know, I'm the Borough president of the Bronx in New York City. The reason I asked to see Mr. Tchelikov is I wanted to discuss some sensitive topics about Soviet Jewish emigration."

He said, in pretty good but heavily accented English, "By all means, please let me know what is on your mind."

I said, "There are many Jews in the Soviet Union who have applied to go to Israel—and they're being prevented. Under the Universal Declaration of Human Rights and the Helsinki Accords, to which Russia is a signatory, they're allowed to be reunited with their families. They have all the proper papers, they have affidavits signed by their relatives—"

He quickly interrupted, saying, "No, no, no! This is Western propaganda. Jews can go, whenever they want. They apply and we have many who leave."

"This is not propaganda. There are lists. Look, I have a list!" I said, taking out of my pocket a list with the names of "refuseniks." "There are hundreds of names on this list."

"No, no, no. If any name is on the list, it's because the person has security secrets. We can't let people go with secrets of the state. Those are the only people who can't leave."

"Really?" I said. "Well, what about Valery Panov, he's a well-known ballet dancer with the Kirov Ballet." I said, "Here's a man who's been denied and he has no security secrets—he's a ballet dancer!"

Viktorov leaned over and had a quick exchange in Russian hushed tones with his colleague.

The deputy minister nodded, then turned to me again and said, "Well, my colleague tells me that Panov was denied because his wife is not Jewish and therefore is not eligible."

I said, "Well, that's ridiculous, you guys have answers for everything. He's Jewish and he and his wife have filed the appropriate papers. They should be able to leave."

He frowned, turned to the other man again, and after a few minutes of back and forth between the two, Minister Viktorov said, "The Panovs will be able to leave."

I said, "You're telling me that they are going to be able to leave?"

"They will be allowed to leave."

While in Leningrad, we visited Valery Panov and his wife Galina, who were dubious about the good news we conveyed because they had heard commitments like this before. But indeed several weeks later after we returned to the United States, we heard from Clive Barnes, the drama critic of the New York Times, and his wife Trish, who were actively involved in the Panovs' case, that they were granted permission to emigrate. A few months later, I presented the Panovs with a bouquet of roses when they arrived from Israel at JFK Airport for a visit to the United States.

In 1977, I was elected chair of the Greater New York Conference on Soviet Jewry, which served as an umbrella for eighty-five member organizations. The Conference assumed an important role in monitoring Soviet compliance with the Helsinki Accords, signed in 1975 by thirty-three countries including the Soviet Union, guaranteeing the right of family members to be reunited. This became the basis for Jews to demand that they be allowed to leave and go to Israel.

I attended important international conferences in Paris where delegates met to plan strategy for the movement, in Brussels where we heard presentations by Golda Meir, US Senator Frank Church, Nobel laureate Elie Wiesel, and civil rights leader Bayard Rustin, and in Jerusalem, at a world plenum organized by the Jewish Agency which addressed Soviet Jewish absorption issues in Israel.

As chair, each year I helped organize and lead the largest march and demonstration in the world, Solidarity Sunday, which attracted between 150,000 and 250,000 people to Dag Hammarskjold Plaza, adjacent to the United Nations. Marchers displayed banners and placards, some of which said: LET US LIVE AS JEWS OR LEAVE AS JEWS. The demonstrators would march down Fifth Avenue and as they filed into Hammarskjold Plaza, there would be chants: "Two, four, six, eight, let our people emigrate!" We always had inspiring prominent speakers, including United States senators, leading cabinet ministers from Israel, and "refuseniks" who had recently won their freedom. It was thrilling to be the master of ceremonies introducing the speakers and addressing such a huge crowd. I'd ask, "What do we want for our brothers and sisters?"

The crowd would roar in response: "Freedom!"

I'd ask, "When do we want it?"

The crowd would respond: "Now!"

It was an endless sea of faces. There were hundreds of placards with the names and photographs of "refuseniks." It was always a huge event and the story and photos would make the front page of New York City's newspapers the following day and would be carried as news around the world.

Over two decades, I also helped mobilize support for Soviet Jews by participating in press conferences and rallies and addressing audiences large and small.

In 1987, the United States Information Agency organized a delegation of attorneys general to visit the Soviet Union during the period when Mikhail Gorbachev began instituting his liberalizing policies of "glasnost" and "perestroika." I was part of that delegation and asked the attorneys general if they would be willing to focus on the issue of Soviet Jewry while we were there. "Of course!" they said. No one hesitated—they were all for it. I furnished them with the latest immigration numbers and a list of "refuseniks."

The attorney general delegation put a lot of pressure on the Soviets. Whenever we had a meeting with government officials, the group always

raised the issue of Soviet Jewry in a forceful manner. Steve Clark, the attorney general of Arkansas, was the leader of the delegation and in his strong southern drawl, he would say, "Our group is very concerned about the plight of the Jews living in the Soviet Union. We know there are large numbers of Jews who have applied to emigrate, which is their right under international law, and your government has refused to allow them to leave. I have a list of three hundred such cases and I would like you to review each one and provide us with a status report." After defensive responses by the Soviet officials with whom we were meeting, the other AGs would jump in and ask pointed questions with a persistent edge.

We arranged for the attorney general delegation to visit with Vladimir and Maria Slepak, two prominent "refuseniks" on whose behalf I had worked back in the United States for many years. They were heroic figures who endured great travail during the seventeen years that they waited for approval of their application for a visa. Vladimir had been exiled to Siberia for five years for posting a sign on his apartment balcony on Gorky Street in Moscow that said LET OUR PEOPLE GO. They were courageous in defying the KGB effort to squelch their activities and voices. Their situation was especially punishing for them because the Soviets had allowed their two sons to leave for Israel but steadfastly refused to grant them their own visas. They displayed that same courage to our attorney general delegation when they gathered prominent "refuseniks" to come to their apartment which was under surveillance by the KGB. Each "refusenik" at that session was able to provide us firsthand, powerfully poignant descriptions of the brutality of the Soviet regime. A few days later, a jubilant Vladmir Slepak told me his dream had been fulfilled because he and his wife had received permission to leave for Israel.

The movement was an effort involving thousands of people throughout the world, Jews and Gentiles working seamlessly together, and the most extraordinary thing about it was the fact that it was successful. Protest movements often are flashes in the pan that accomplish little. This effort succeeded—more than one million Jews emigrated from the Soviet Union to Israel and 250,000 went to live in the United States. Those who remained began to live openly Jewish lives under a liberalized policy.

This development was not only an historic victory for the Jewish people, but it also gave encouragement to others in the world who were engaged in battles against powerful forces.

Chapter 32

The Operation

THIS EPISODE HAPPENED ELEVEN YEARS AGO and it helped put my life in proper perspective, so it seemed a natural way to conclude this memoir.

"You have a large mass in your abdomen—it's cancer. It's malignant."

Those were the words of Dr. Samuel Singer as he told me the results of my CAT scan in October 2009.

I responded, "What does that mean? Is it life-threatening? How much time do I have left?"

He said it was a "well-differentiated liposarcoma" and that I would need immediate surgery. He said, "It's hard to precisely answer your question," adding that in "20 percent of the cases we can cut the tumor out and you can go on with your life. We would have to monitor you for several years to see if the tumor grows back. In 60 percent of the cases tumor regrowth recurs within the first five years after surgery." So it sounded like the odds were stacked against me.

I wanted the best possible news but was prepared for the worst. It had been a great run, a good life with lots of excitement and fulfillment and family bonds.

My personal physician, Dr. Richard Cohen, had recommended Dr. Singer at Memorial Sloan Kettering.

Dr. Singer scheduled me for surgery three days after our consultation. My wife and daughter Becky drove me to the hospital for a 6:00 a.m. sign-in. I was pretty calm, being very fatalistic. I'd know by the end of the day what my fate would be. As they rolled me away on the gurney to the operating room, I said to my daughter who was standing nervously next to Diane, "Don't worry, Becky, I'll dance at your wedding."

The operation lasted six hours. The first thing I remember was Dr. Singer saying, "How are you feeling? Do you hear me?" I later learned this was the morning after the operation.

I was very woozy, still sedated from the anesthesia, but I nodded to him that I heard him. He then said, "Mr. Abrams, unfortunately you are still bleeding and we will have to take you back into the operating room to open you up again so that we can see what's going on. We want to know if we have your permission to do that."

I said, "Doctor, do what you have to do—but be sure you tell my wife what's going on."

I later learned that I had been given ten pints of blood during the night and that Dr. Singer had removed the cancerous tumor. The tumor measured thirty centimeters and weighed twenty-five pounds. I was astounded upon learning that. Over the years, I had heard stories about people being operated on for malignant tumors. Sometimes the removal involved a tumor the size of a pea or even a golf ball. I remember one time talking to the attorney general of Illinois, Jim Ryan, who had cancer, and he told me he had a tumor removed which he and his family were told was the size of a grapefruit. That story was supposed to be a shocking show-stopper because of the size and magnitude of the tumor. And now I was hearing about a tumor that was fifteen inches long and weighed twenty-five pounds.

Dr. Singer told me that there was no telling exactly how long that tumor had been growing inside my body. It could have been years. What was astonishing to me was that up to the very moment of diagnosis I had been feeling okay. There was no overt indication that this dangerous thing was growing inside of me.

They had me up and walking within a day of the operation, but I spent seven days in the hospital before going home. The recovery was a long and slow process. I gave Diane a strict order that I didn't want people to visit me or call me at the hospital or at home. It was very draining to talk. Friends and family meant well by trying to reach out to me, but the reality was that any phone call was difficult and a setback. It would take a tremendous amount of effort and energy to talk. The thing I needed most was to rest and to try to regain my strength and to get my bodily functions going again.

I had always been a high-energy person who could work sixteen-hour days. It was alien to me how weak I was and how tired I could get if I went

for a short walk around the apartment or around the block with the help of an aide.

I was unbelievably fortunate. I was in the hands of a great doctor who specialized in this area and knew what he was doing. I was unbelievably fortunate to be in the small percentage of those situations where the surgeon could cut out the tumor without it growing back and to avoid chemotherapy or radiation treatment as part of my recovery plan. It has now been more than eleven years and there has not been any sign of a reappearance.

I had CAT scans done every three months for the first two or three years to determine whether there was any growth or return of the tumor. I now have an annual CAT scan for Dr. Singer to review.

As I was recovering, I was wondering how I could ever repay Dr. Singer. How could I adequately show my appreciation to him for saving my life? I found out that he was a Yankees fan and so I came up with the idea of taking him to see a Yankee game in the owner's box. I called Hal Steinbrenner and he arranged for us to sit in his box and watch a game. Randy Levine, president of the Yankees, came by during the game, chatted with us, and gave us Yankee caps. Dr. Singer was thrilled beyond belief. I continue this tradition of annually taking Dr. Singer to a Yankee game. We've become friends and I look forward to our yearly outing watching the team with the greatest record and tradition in baseball.

Within a year and a half of that operation that saved my life, I was able to dance at my daughter's wedding. To those in attendance I retold my pledge to Becky, the one I made when they began wheeling me out on the gurney to the operating room.

I truly feel that I have been given a second life. Things could have ended very differently. I feel so grateful that I have continued to have the opportunity of sharing time and life's pleasures with my family: being with my wife, watching my children and their spouses grow in their professional stature, playing and talking with my grandchildren, and watching them grow up. I am so grateful that I have been able to continue to work at my profession and to undertake pro bono initiatives and to continue the friendships with people I admire and with whom I have fun. I literally get up each morning and say, "Thank you, God for another day." Indeed, I feel so fortunate that my life has been filled with such good things. Every day for me is a blessing. I'm the luckiest guy in the world.

Afterword

WE ARE LIVING IN TUMULTUOUS TIMES. Our nation has undergone an unparalleled health crisis resulting from the coronavirus pandemic, a corresponding serious economic downturn, and an introspective review of the role of racism in our society. We are in a state of uncertainty, where division is rampant. With a civil war and the Great Depression as part of our history, our country has obviously weathered periods of enormous challenge in the past.

But recent developments during the Trump era have chipped away at what has made this a strong, vibrant, and admired democracy. This assault on our system of government should not be taken lightly.

We need to maintain our vigilance and be prepared to reject a future opportunistic seeker of the mantle of authority. Others aiming to emulate President Trump's authoritarian approach have no doubt taken note of how vulnerable our democracy is, and just how effectively discord and mistrust can be marshalled, how easily confusion and disinformation can be sown, and how conspiracy theories and reckless assertions can be successfully used to seize or retain power.

For many of us who have put time and passionate effort into public service and into maintaining the rule of law, the Trump administration's cavalier disregard for the law and its contempt for the brilliant, weighty concepts that created the bold experiment of American democracy are disturbing.

Over the past four years, we have seen our governmental institutional framework challenged on the most fundamental level. We've seen the Department of Justice turned into the private preserve of the president to do his bidding, taking actions to pursue the president's political agenda. We've watched the spectacle of the attorney general of the United States withholding a special counsel's report and then releasing

a distorted summary with massive redactions. The president has imperiled the critically important watchdog role of inspector general in federal agencies by firing those whose actions he felt were against his personal or political interest. Subpoenas issued by Congress have been ignored, threatening the 240-year-old foundation of our democracy—the separation of powers. The president's attacks on judges, their ethnic backgrounds, and their judicial opinions have been a clear attempt to interfere with the historic role of an independent judiciary as a third branch of government.

He attempts to intimidate the press, calling it "corrupt" and labeling it "the enemy of the people." Even in the midst of the greatest public health crisis of our lifetime, he seeks to place doubt in the minds of our citizens about the veracity of stories that are found in print or broadcast on our airwaves. These actions have amounted to an unprecedented attack on another important cornerstone of our society, a free press. He has had Fox News, a one-sided media outlet, as an enabler of his administration, disturbingly reminiscent of authoritarian regimes with their state-controlled media.

The president has cast aspersions on our intelligence agencies that defend our nation's vital interests and our diplomatic corps that presents our principles and policies to the world. His willingness to abandon old allies and to sidle up to dictators around the world has diminished this country's moral authority. The vacuum created jeopardizes a delicate international balance of power. This approach to foreign policy increases the likelihood of conflict in some of the more vulnerable and insecure parts of the globe over which in the past the United States has helped to maintain a stabilizing influence. The country is paying a steep price both in terms of its stature around the world and its security.

Our domestic programs to enforce environmental, civil rights, and consumer protection laws have been threatened, endangering our well-being.

We see a challenge to our bedrock credo that a flow of new immigrants is what our nation is all about and that an infusion of newcomers is good for our economic growth and stability going forward.

A hauntingly disturbing development of the Trump Administration has been the disregard for truth in our public discourse. A democracy cannot survive if truth is abandoned. Without truth, there is no justice, and without justice, there is no freedom or democracy.

It has been painful to see members of the House and Senate motivated by shortsighted political ambition line up behind an administration's threats and talking points, especially when they are an assault on our fundamental values. This unwillingness to voice concerns over ethical lapses or legally questionable behavior or attacks on our cornerstone concepts of democracy is deeply troubling.

Presidents, whether Democrat or Republican, have historically comported themselves in a dignified manner, attempting to lead by example and appealing to our best qualities and to those values that unite us as Americans. That the truculent lack of civility emanating from the White House over the past four years has trickled down to the people is undeniable. It has been the job of presidents past to attempt to address tensions, not to incite them. In times of grave threats and national crisis, we have always had a leader who has attempted to rally and unify our people. Donald Trump, however, has been unwilling or incapable of doing so even in the midst of a pandemic that imperils and terrifies our citizenry.

Especially dangerous is President Trump's unwillingness to accept the results of an election that has been confirmed by Republican as well as Democratic election officials to have been validly administered with the vote count certified. For more than two centuries incumbent presidents of all political persuasions have demonstrated to the world that in the United States there is a transparent, smooth transfer of power from one administration to the next. President Trump with his authoritarian impulses has regrettably stepped away from that tradition.

I wrote this book as an unapologetic progressive Democrat with an abiding respect for the rule of law. But I also have respect for the historical role of the Republican Party and those officeholders who have run under its banner, although Trump has caused the party to veer from its core values.

Sweeping partisan rhetoric, whether denying scientific evidence of climate change or promoting blanket condemnation of regulatory agencies, does a disservice to history and puts all of us at risk. Several cases cited in this book remind me of why regulatory agencies were necessary in the first place and the heavy price paid when federal regulatory agencies have failed to do their job.

During the civil rights era, the federal government had to intercede to guarantee the rights of all Americans. The numerous and significant

collective actions undertaken by state attorneys general during the Reagan administration and continuing through the Trump administration are a reminder of how the states must sometimes step in when the federal government fails to protect its people. We saw similar responsible state leadership by governors during the coronavirus pandemic.

Amidst all of this chaotic uncertainty, I see a path for our nation's future that is bright and that returns us to our progressive vision of a democratic society that protects and provides for its citizens.

In the course of my lifetime, I have found able, honest people working in government to implement the vision of our founders. Republicans and Democrats alike sought to take the good will of the American people and the bounty of this well-endowed nation and manage it in such a way that will benefit all.

I found that in all interactions and decision making, if there was respect shown to others and a listening ear welcoming all points of view, a worthwhile common ground could be achieved. I have also learned that if partisan labels could be minimized and if both sides showed a willingness to understand what the other side was saying, a solution or compromise could emerge. Understanding what the perceived impediments are to reconciliation very often leads to creative new understandings.

But if elected officials or appointed governmental bureaucrats are to be adequately motivated to be sensitive to the will and needs of the people, then the public has to be actively engaged. The electorate has to be constantly applying pressure so that their voices and views are heard. Participation in primary and general elections is key. Visits, letters, emails, and phone calls to government officials really make a difference. Volunteering in a campaign is not only fun and exciting, but it gives the citizen the chance to get to know the elected official personally. Your support for a candidate using social media can be a powerful tool that will be recognized and respected. We are also learning how we must be sophisticated and responsible in using the internet and social media to educate and organize others for the common good.

Every individual can have an impact. It was surprising to me in my campaigns, even in a large state like New York, how a handful of people can have a disproportionate impact. Margaret Mead, the great anthropologist, commented on citizen involvement in the following way: "Never

doubt that a small group of thoughtful, committed citizens can change the world. Indeed, it is the only thing that ever has."

This magical system of democracy functions best when individual citizens get actively involved. It may sound trite but it is true, your voice and vote can make the difference. We have seen in recent years how close election results can be—presidential races, congressional races, gubernatorial races, and contests for local office. Some are decided by a smattering of votes.

Our founders have provided us an extraordinary blueprint. It has enabled the United States, admittedly with significant fault lines along the way—slavery, racial and religious discrimination, sexism, and homophobia—to develop into an admired nation, which has been the envy of the world. The opportunity for the good life has been achieved by so many of our citizens. We have a long way to go to reach the goal of true economic and educational equality. But we have marched a long way and achieved much.

We can do more and be even greater if each of us were to engage in the fight to become a better nation. Each of us should recognize this opportunity. Victories against powerful odds can be achieved. Changes can be made. Let's not abandon the fight and allow other forces to take over and fill the vacuum. Let's carry the banner and do battle for a better tomorrow.

Acknowledgments

THE WRITING OF THIS BOOK WAS a herculean effort. It could never have been accomplished without the devoted and able assistance of Gerald Albarelli, a brilliant oral historian at Columbia University who prodded me in digging deep into my memories for the recollections that are recorded here. He taught me about dialogue and detail. He has been my collaborator and comrade for four years. We have shared the highs and lows of this effort all along the way. His skillful editing, sensitivity, and understanding of the core issues in this book helped shape these pages.

My wife, Diane, was a source of encouragement throughout this project, from its incipient concept through the tough slogging of its research and drafting. When discouragement engulfed my emotions, she provided positive reinforcement. I am deeply indebted to her for keeping me steadily focused on my goal of providing memories and guideposts for my children and grandchildren and, as this project progressed, for the broader public.

I was honored to carry out my responsibilities as attorney general fighting for the things I believed in, but I could not have done that without the tireless and dedicated work of those who were at my side. While I mention a few names in connection with the cases cited in this book, the reality is, I was surrounded by hundreds of lawyers, investigators, paralegals, and support staff who toiled brilliantly on a daily basis without fear or favor to make sure that the people and the State of New York were steadfastly represented. Far from the headlines, that remarkable staff collectively kept the state moving on an honest and legal path by solving problems quietly and in ways that were invisible to those outside government. While I cannot list them all, they are the real heroes of the office I was privileged to lead.

Deeply felt thanks are extended to Blu Greenberg and Marissa Piesman, two distinguished authors who over a period of years prompted me to consider writing a memoir. Blu kept insisting that my many stories

should be recorded, and Marissa felt I should make note of my efforts in the attorney general's office. I will always be indebted to them for their persistence in encouraging me to undertake this enterprise. Once I started to seriously consider writing this book, I met with noted author Joseph Telushkin, who also encouraged me to go forward.

There were innumerable people who generously gave me time and insight in reading drafts of the manuscript, including Blu Greenberg, Marissa Piesman, Timothy Gilles, Jack Schwartz, Joseph Telushkin, Jamie Bernard, Jim Conroy, Ed Perlmutter, and Rene Plessner.

I am grateful to members of my staff at the Attorney General's Office who spent time with me in preparation for the development of the material that appears in this book. My heartfelt thanks are extended to those who generously spent hours recounting the work that they and others were involved in during my fifteen years in that office, including Robert Hermann, Jorge Batista, Richard Rifkin, Ethan Geto, Jack Ryan, Deborah Bachrach, Marcia Cleveland, Jim Sevinsky, R. Scott Greathead, Sandy Mindell, Pamela Mann, Lloyd Constantine, Richard Corenthal, Clive Morrick, Gail Suchman, Ed Saslow, Richard Barr, and Nathan Riley.

Special appreciation and thanks go to Timothy Gilles, my long-term press secretary and director of communications in the Bronx Borough President's Office and the Attorney General's Office. His effectiveness, dedication, and loyalty have been demonstrated in innumerable ways over his long years of service. During the course of documenting and research-ing material for this book, I have benefited enormously from Tim's gener-ous and able assistance, counsel, and sound judgment. I want to publicly acknowledge my gratitude for all he has done on my behalf.

Thanks are extended to Malcolm Hoenlein, Margie Ruth Davis, Zeesy Schnur, and Susan Green for their assistance in documenting my Soviet Jewry activities.

Margaret Provenzano, my long-time secretary at Stroock, provided valuable technical assistance.

David Steinberger and Peter Osnos gave me helpful assistance and good advice in the early days of this effort.

Elsa Solender helped me think about and create my book proposal. She was on target in guiding me to focus on the book's salient messages that would be of interest to the public.

I am grateful to Aaron Priest for providing professional advice and extending efforts on my behalf.

Lynne Ross, former executive director of the National Association of Attorneys General, was very helpful in providing research and source material.

Karen Gantz, my agent, conveyed enthusiasm from the get-go. She energetically pursued a publisher and introduced me to Tony Lyons, president and publisher of Skyhorse Publishing, and many of the talented professional people who back him up at Skyhorse. I am indebted to her for the counsel and advice she provided, particularly for her guidance through all the necessary steps and stages involved in turning a manuscript into a book and ensuring that that book would find its audience.

Thanks go to Tony Lyons who gave the quick green light to allow this project to go forward, enabling it to be made available to readers around the globe. His vote of confidence at a critical juncture made the publication of this book possible. Mark Gompertz, group editorial director at Skyhorse, made critical decisions when COVID-19 struck and created uncertainty about scheduled projects at Skyhorse. His calm, steady hand enabled this book and others to continue ahead.

Brian Peterson, Skyhorse's talented artistic director, executed a creative and attractive cover for which I am grateful.

Rebecca Schoenthal, editor at Skyhorse, provided invaluable guidance in shaping the early drafts of the manuscript.

At a later stage, I was fortunate to have Caroline Russomanno assigned as an editor. The final product has been benefited by her perceptive reading of earlier drafts. Her experienced skillful hand, wise judgment, and sound advice made this a better book. Stories abound about conflicts between editors and authors but in this case the seamless and cordial relationship existed from beginning to end. Once again, good fortune fell into my lap.

Stephen Cardone and Alex Sibirzeff provided tremendous assistance in promoting the book by creating videos that appear on the book's website and on various social media platforms. Their creativity and professionalism injected a big boost to the effort to project the book to a wider audience.

My heartfelt gratitude is extended to all those who helped make this volume possible, including those I have unintentionally neglected to mention.

Index